ADRIAN SHOOTER

ADRIAN SHOOTER
A life in Engineering and Railways

Adrian Shooter

First published in Great Britain in 2018 by
PEN & SWORD TRANSPORT
An imprint of
Pen & Sword Books Ltd
Yorkshire - Philadelphia

Copyright@ Adrian Shooter, 2018

ISBN 978 1 47389 319 1

The right of Adrian Shooter to be identified as Author of this work has been asserted by them in accordance with the Copyright, Designs and Patents Act 1988.

A CIP catalogue record for this book is available from the British Library

All rights reserved. No part of this book may be reproduced or transmitted in any form or by any means, electronic or mechanical including photocopying, recording or by any information storage and retrieval system, without permission from the Publisher in writing.

Typeset in 10/12 pt Palatino
Typeset by Aura Technology and Software Services, India
Printed and bound in India by Replika Press Pvt. Ltd.

Pen & Sword Books Ltd incorporates the Imprints of Aviation, Atlas, Family History, Fiction, Maritime, Military, Discovery, Politics, History, Archaeology, Select, Wharncliffe Local History, Wharncliffe True Crime, Military Classics, Wharncliffe Transport, Leo Cooper, The Praetorian Press, Remember When, Seaforth Publishing and Frontline Publishing.

For a complete list of Pen & Sword titles please contact

PEN & SWORD BOOKS LTD
47 Church Street, Barnsley, South Yorkshire, S70 2AS, England
E-mail: enquiries@pen-and-sword.co.uk
Website: www.pen-and-sword.co.uk

Or
PEN AND SWORD BOOKS
1950 Lawrence Rd, Havertown, PA 19083, USA
E-mail: Uspen-and-sword@casematepublishers.com
Website: www.penandswordbooks.com

Contents

Chapter One	Early years	7
Chapter Two	Apprenticeship	37
Chapter Three	Management training	62
Chapter Four	My first 'command'	97
Chapter Five	Launching HSTs at Heaton	125
Chapter Six	On the border: Carlisle	143
Chapter Seven	Change agent on the Southern	159
Chapter Eight	Learning the passenger business: the 'Bed Pan Line'	181
Chapter Nine	Memphis Tennessee	213
	Index	240

Chapter One

Early years

Both my grannies had the good sense to live in places served by the Great Western Railway. My father's mother lived in Torquay and was, obviously, known as 'Granny at Torquay', while my mother's stepmother lived with Grandpop at Long Ashton, just south of Bristol. Thus it was that my mother would drive me, from the age of seven, from home at Epsom to Paddington Station most Easter and summer holidays.

At Paddington, we came down the narrow twisting taxi road and Mummy would park the car and we would walk to the 'Lawn' which at any other station would be called the concourse. If I were going to Granny at Torquay, I went on the *Torbay Express*, hauled by an immaculate 'Castle' Class. If it was Granny at Long Ashton, there would be an equally smart 'King' Class at the head, not that I would be allowed to see either at this stage. That came later when one of the grannies would take me down to see the engine and say hello to the driver. However, I would get a look at the '9400' pannier tank simmering on the stops of Platform 1 having brought the empty stock in from Old Oak Common.

Mummy would check the buff-coloured seat reservation card and take me to my coach which would be a spotlessly clean chocolate and cream new BR Mk 1 compartment carriage. Having sat me down, she would find the guard in whose charge I was put. Usually I was in the rear coach next to his van so he could keep an eye on me and he did not stray far since this was long before BR's Pay and Efficiency Agreement of 1968, so he did not look at tickets. Instead, there was a ticket collector who did that.

The journey was quite long for a small boy, so sometimes the guard would make it more interesting by inviting me along to his brake van. One day, as we travelled non-stop through Reading, I was shown the periscope and allowed to look into it. I could see the signals we were approaching, which were on a gantry above the train. I remember asking that guard why he wanted to see them since it seemed to me that the driver was the only person who needed to. As a seven-year-old, I found his answer unconvincing. I must say that, 60 years later and after managing several 'driver only' railways, I am still unconvinced. On arrival, whichever granny I was visiting, the first thing to do was to go and admire the engine.

Granny at Torquay was my paternal grandmother. She had married the Reverend Arthur Edwin Shooter, a Methodist minister who served as an Army chaplain in both world wars and died in 1950. He came from a large family who had lived in Yorkshire for many years and it is likely that we are descended from the Vikings who came to rape and pillage.

My Granny, Mabel Kate Pinniger, was the daughter of a successful Exeter draper who lost both his sons in the First World War and, therefore, virtually adopted my father who was born in 1916. He paid for Dad's education at Mill Hill which would have been far beyond the means of a Methodist Minister.

My father went on to train as a doctor at Cambridge and at Barts Hospital, finally qualifying in June 1940 – just as the bombing started. For the next year he was a junior surgeon working as part of a team doing their best for Londoners injured in the Blitz. One night he admitted 120 people after a bomb had gone down the escalator at Bank station just as a train was coming in. In 1943, he joined the Navy as a Surgeon Lieutenant RNVR and was immediately posted to Freetown, Sierra Leone, which was a major Royal Navy ship refuelling and repair station. After an eventful voyage where his ship was bombed and sunk, he arrived safely. Later, in 1946, when assigned to a hospital in Glasgow, he met my mother, who was also a Naval doctor. One Saturday in 1946, the hospital mess invited the female Surgeon Lieutenants from nearby Greenock over for the evening so that the male mess 'could see what their uniform looked like.' Sixty-six years later, my mother's last words to my father were: 'I am so glad you were curious.' My parents were engaged two weeks later and married in Bristol on 5 December 1946.

The first engine I used to see at Paddington was the Pannier Tank that brought the empty stock in from Old Oak Common: 5700 Class No. 9661.

The best man was Dr Martin Wright who later invented the Breathalyser. I was born just under two years later.

My mother was born Jean Wallace in her grandparents' house in Newcastle in August 1918 where her father had also been born in 1891. Unlike his father and elder brother, who were colliery blacksmiths, he had no aptitude for practical work, but fortunately was bright and, with the help of various scholarships, was able to obtain a degree in chemistry at Durham University just before the First World War started. Grandfather had excelled in the Officer Training Corps at university and, as a result, was immediately commissioned as a Second Lieutenant and sent to France in August 1914. The following year he went to Gallipoli where he was awarded the Military Cross for leading a bayonet attack on Turkish trenches. Later he was injured at the Somme in 1916 and was transferred to the Anti gas unit at Woolwich where he researched mustard gas and met a soil chemist whose civilian work was at the National Fruit and Cider Institute's Research Station at Long Ashton near Bristol.

In 1919, when he was demobbed, he accepted an offer of a job there and remained until he retired as Director and Professor of Agricultural Chemistry at Bristol University in 1957. He had become an international expert in plant nutrition and was heavily involved during the Second World War in helping to find ways to improve the efficiency of food production to prevent the nation from starving. He wrote the standard textbook on the subject and, after the war, wrote many scientific papers and travelled extensively throughout the world to advise governments. He was made a CBE for his war work and was elected a Fellow of the Royal Society, among many other honours.

When the Second World War started, Mum was a fourth-year medical student and had had some practical experience which was invaluable when she and her fellow students were needed to help with the many casualties from the bombing of the port of Avonmouth and the aircraft factories in Bristol. She qualified in 1942 and, after a year of general medicine, went to London to help with the injuries from flying bombs. There, like my father in 1940, she got a lot of practical surgical experience. In June 1944, she joined the Royal Navy as a Surgeon Lieutenant.

I was born on 22 November 1948 at the City of London Maternity Hospital which was within the sound of Bow Bells, thus making me officially a Cockney. We lived, then, in a rented house, No. 1 Litchfield Road, Kew, in south-west London. My mother alleged that my interest in railways started with Granny wheeling me up and down the platform

My grandfather, Major Rev'd A.E. Shooter, who was an Army chaplain throughout both World Wars, with Dad, just commissioned as Surgeon Lt R.A. Shooter RNVR, at home in June 1943.

My maternal Grandfather (Grandpop) just commissioned as 2nd Lt Thomas Wallace in August 1914 and about to leave for France with the British Expeditionary Force.

at nearby Kew Gardens Station. Dad had returned to St Bartholomew's Hospital after being demobbed in late 1946 and had decided to specialise as a bacteriologist. In 1950 he won a Rockefeller scholarship which enabled him to go to America to further his studies. Thus the new Shooter family left Southampton aboard the French Liner SS *De Grasse* and arrived in New York on 10 February 1950 en route to Baltimore, where we lived for the next year on the lower floor of a stone house in a quiet street in Baltimore while Dad commuted by streetcar to Johns Hopkins Hospital downtown. My first memories

Grandpop as featured in the fortnightly *Deeds that Thrill the Empire* published after the War. The caption reads: 'In the Gallipoli campaign, on the night of June 10th 1915, 2nd Lt Thomas Wallace volunteered to lead a party to clear the enemy from a trench. Rushing forward at the head of his men, under heavy fire, he bayoneted several Turks and drove back others. He afterwards showed great coolness in leading his men along a communication trench where he remained until the enemy retreated from it. For personal bravery and gallantry in leading his men he was awarded the MC.'

are of that house and the surrounding area. I can clearly recall the tree-lined street and, when I went back there fifty years later, it all seemed familiar. There was even a picture of Dad's streetcar in the local McDonald's. That year away had a huge effect on my mother. We had come from an austere and grey England, surrounded by bomb sites and other evidence of the war, to the land of plenty. No more food rationing. In Baltimore you could have anything you desired and as much as you wanted. Mum bought some of the latest kitchen gadgets which she used for the rest of her life. She also bought rolls of 'color' film for her '8 on 620' Kodak bellows camera. A dozen or so of these came home with us and were used sparingly throughout the 1950s. She sent them back to Eastman Kodak at Rochester, NY, to have them developed and printed. Most people had to wait until 1959 to buy colour film over here. On the way back home in September 1951, by which time I was nearly three, we went up the Empire State Building on 34th St. in New York. I can distinctly remember looking down from the eightieth floor and saying: 'Mummy, why are all those Dinky cars down there?' Perhaps as a result, I have always thought the top of the Empire State Building is one of the most magical places in the world. I have been back many times.

When I was a small boy my Mother never tired of telling me how proud she was to have been one of only twenty-five women commissioned as Naval Officers (as opposed to being Wrens) in the Second World War. She was Surgeon Lt Jean Wallace RN.

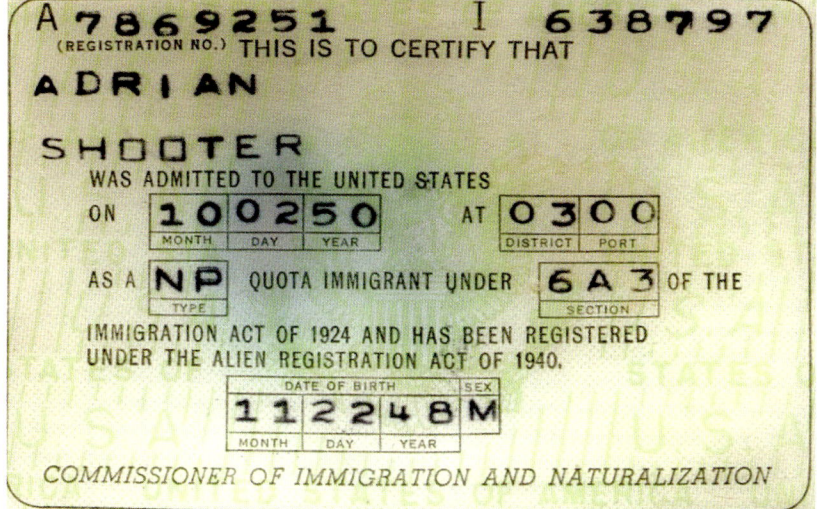

My US Aliens' Card.

I am still excited that we came back on the *Queen Mary*, the biggest ship in the World and, then, still the holder of the Blue Riband for the fastest Atlantic crossing.

We returned on the 81,000 ton *Queen Mary*, the flagship of the Cunard Line, which at the time held the Blue Riband as the fastest transatlantic ship, with a speed of 28 knots. On 11 September 1951, we arrived at the Ocean Liner Terminal at Southampton and transferred to the waiting Boat Train which took us directly to Waterloo Station. Not surprisingly, I had picked up a strong American accent which might have been regarded as cute had I not called Grandpop a 'dirty old trash can'!

I started school in September 1953 at a small private school at the end of our road in Coulsdon, Surrey.

My very first ride in the cab of a steam engine occurred when, at the age of about six or seven, we went to stay for the weekend with one of my mother's friends who was married to the Vicar of Lydney, in Gloucestershire. After breakfast on Saturday morning, I was sent out to play in the garden. I soon exhausted the potential of that and the adjoining churchyard, when I heard the whistle of a steam engine at the bottom of the vicarage garden. The next half an hour were spent watching the ex-GWR '57XX' pannier tank shunting back and forth not 20ft from the fence. Presently, the driver stopped and asked if I would like to come and join him and the fireman. 'Would I?!' He directed me to a gap in the railings and, until I was called for lunch, I was in heaven. The fireman even allowed me to put some coal on the fire!

Me aged two, with Mum, at our house in Baltimore.

Dad often took me to work with him on a Saturday morning. Arriving at Holborn Viaduct Station, a terminus now superseded by City Thameslink, we walked past the Old Bailey, then past the Accident and Emergency department of Bart's Hospital where Dad had worked during

EARLY YEARS • 13

One of my earliest memories is of Mum taking me on a tram along the Embankment in the last week of operation in July 1952. Courtesy of London Transport Museum.

The earliest recorded instance of my travelling by train. With Dad on Exmouth seafront, 1952.

Learning to row with Dad on Swanbourne Lake, Arundel, in 1953.

My first day at school, September 1953, with Mum, Great Aunt and my dog Jason.

the Blitz in 1940. Passing a door with the gruesome label 'morbid anatomy', we went straight to Dad's lab, which was a dark and gloomy place dating from 1780. Soon discovering that a small boy was not as fascinated as he was by looking at 'germs' through a microscope, Dad relented and allowed me to wander about. The hospital is just opposite Smithfield Meat Market which, in those days, was at the height of its activity. While I could not see the freight trains that were hauled on the Circle Line from Paddington by condensing pannier tanks, I certainly had a grandstand view of the Sentinel steam lorries belonging to H.C. Maile Ltd that brought white four-wheel trailers of frozen meat up from London Docks every few minutes. Becoming more adventurous, I made my way to Gamages, a large department store, which had a splendid toy department full of Bassett Lowke live steam and electric models and other exiting proper toys.

One day my mother took me to Lester Bowden, School and Military Tailors, in Epsom High Street. I remember shedding a few tears as we bought my new uniform for my prep school, Kingswood House. I also remember saying sternly to myself: 'You are nearly eight now, much too old to be crying.' Kingswood House was one of the prep schools for Epsom College, where my parents hoped I would go, in due course. It was about three miles from where we lived and was on the other side of Epsom. I started there in September 1956 and from the outset, I walked to school and thoroughly enjoyed the variety of interesting things I saw, including the railway yard where an ex-Southern Railway 'N' or 'U' Class 2-6-0 tender engine could usually be seen shunting coal and other wagons in what was then a very busy goods yard. Sand and gravel came in for Halls of Croydon, builders' merchants, who would deliver it in petrol-engined Bedford 'S' type tippers. Sawn timber came for Longhurst's who ran a timber merchant's from the ex-LBSCR engine shed which had closed in 1929. All sorts of general merchandise came in 12-ton covered rail vans to be transhipped on to trailers which would be hauled by three-wheeled Scammel Mechanical Horses to shops all over the town.

This thing would feel much safer if it had wheels!

Walking along the almost deserted High Street one morning in late 1956, I spotted the prototype Routemaster, 'SLT56' which I knew about from a recent edition of my uncle's 'Eagle'.

Kingswood House School was a large red brick house standing right at the top of West Hill which had been a boys' prep school for many years. We had a selection of interesting teachers including Mr Wharton, our history teacher who, in 1940, had been the same age as us (eight) and, living in Kent, had spent most of the summer with his neck craned back, watching dog fights between Spitfires and ME 109s overhead. His lessons were riotous, with him at the front of the class room, arms outstretched, gyrating as he pretended to be a Spitfire gunning down the Hun, complete with ack-ack and Merlin engine sound effects. There was Miss King, a glamorous young art teacher, who once gave me a lift in her little grey Austin A30, and Mr Somerville, a distinctly shady character, who all the boys therefore liked, and had a 'Maigret'-type Citroën. Our esteem for him only increased when, after quite a short time, he disappeared from the scene permanently and we were convinced that he was something to do with the Secret Service.

One very popular master was the Reverend H.B. Playford, who came as a temporary teacher for a year, having retired, aged 65. He was

Amazingly the actual dust cart, BPL73, that collected our rubbish still exists. It is a 1934 Shelvoke and Drewry Freighter complete with tiller steering. Quite the most unpleasant vehicle to drive!

A view of the railway that I saw every day when walking to school in Epsom. This 1963 picture shows D6534 on the pick up goods from Norwood Jct. Earlier I would have seen an 'N' or 'U' Class 2-6-0 tender engine. On the right is the LB&SCR loco shed, closed in 1929 and then used as a timber shed.

very tall, relaxed and fun. He is also the only teacher from Kingswood House who I have found on the internet, which was because he was an army officer in the First World War, then went to Cambridge and rowed in the winning Boat Race team for three years from 1920. He was then a house master at Stowe for many years. Not surprising that he was relaxed and totally in control of a bunch of eleven-year-olds without even trying – an inspiration.

My father had continued at Bart's and, in 1961 was promoted to the Chair of Bacteriology. As well as his teaching and research duties, he also had picked up a number of other roles. One of his other commissions lasted for several years. In 1946, he had been asked to do some work for the LNER, whose medical officer had become worried that toilets that flushed their contents on to the track might be responsible for an outbreak of polio. He went one morning to King's Cross and took swabs from the outside of a Breakfast Train that had just arrived from Sheffield. As a result of finding contamination on this train, he was asked to design an experiment which was carried out by him and Dr Binning of the LNER. They had a train painted in whitewash and white paper put on the seats. The resulting report, published in 1948, was suppressed. Not surprising, since in 1949 he wrote officially to the Senior Medical Officer of the new BR Eastern Region: 'The present method of disposal of faeces from railway trains is out of date, unaesthetic, and constitutes a potential danger to those living near railways and to railway passengers.'

Over a seven-year period, he also kept asking for permission to publish his findings in a medical journal. I now have the BR file on the matter which was given to me many years later by Dr Mike Andrews, the then BR Chief Medical Officer and who was a friend. There was much consternation and scheming to fob my father off. I have copies of letters written by C.K. Bird, the Chief Regional Officer (GM) of the Eastern Region of British Railways, who objected to 'courting publicity which might exaggerate the dangers.' Even John Ratter, who was a member of the British Transport Commission, got involved and in 1956 he suggested that a good way of silencing my father would be to invite him and Dr Binning to join a committee to study the problem and to look at what other railways abroad had done. Another member was Albert Smith, head of the BR Area Chemical Laboratory at Swindon, who, by an amazing coincidence, was the father of a friend and near neighbour of mine as I write this. I have a copy of the report, dated May 1957, which is as detailed a description of train lavatories worldwide as you will find. Sadly, they did not find any magic solution and Dad was fobbed off again until BR started taking the subject seriously in the 1980s when lavatories with storage tanks on the train began to be fitted in any number.

Father remained at Bart's until he retired in 1981 at the age of sixty-six, having completed two five-year terms as Dean of the Medical

Until the late '50s I was issued with one of these Bell Punch tickets slipped out from under the clip on the conductor's wooden ticket rack. It was punched to show how far I could go for my penny halfpenny.

School. He continued to be Professor of Bacteriology and, in that role just before retiring, was asked by the government to investigate the death of a lab technician who contracted and died of smallpox at a hospital in Birmingham. He was made a CBE for services to medicine and died, aged ninety-seven, on Christmas Eve 2013.

Having passed my Common Entrance exam, I started at Epsom College in January 1962. Clearly the College was struggling to come to terms with the rapid changes that were taking place all around it. The underlying objective of our education seemed to be to equip us to go forth and run the Empire. One had the impression that the school hadn't quite grasped that this Empire was rapidly disappearing. For all that, Epsom College was very good at instilling the confidence that you really could go and tackle anything that was thrown in your direction. I thoroughly enjoyed my time at the school and very much appreciated the considerable sacrifice my parents had made to pay my fees.

The masters (there were no mistresses) were a rather mixed lot. Most were Oxbridge graduates; many were bachelors and most spent their entire career in the somewhat sheltered and highly organised environment of a public school. (For the benefit of any Americans reading this, that means private. OK?) There were, undoubtedly, several brilliant all-rounders as well. When I was there, many masters took a lead from the austere Headmaster, the Rev H.W.F. Franklin (known behind his back as 'Henry' to all and sundry), who had been in that post since 1939. Henry was always immaculate in his academic gown and mortarboard whereas some of the under-masters, particularly the unmarried ones, were decidedly scruffy; indeed, at least one used his gown as a blackboard duster and hence was always to be seen in a cloud of chalk dust wherever he went.

The fact that I have some passing familiarity with French, although not a natural linguist, is undoubtedly the result of two years in 'Nifty' Collier's class. He was an urbane individual in his fifties who had the bearing and appearance of a Spanish aristocrat. He insisted, when in his classroom, that he only knew French and he engaged us in continuous conversation in that language. One result was that twenty or so years later I was able to make a presentation to the Board of SNCF in French. They did not buy my proposition (which was about our parcels businesses working together), but they did give me an excellent lunch!

Boys at Epsom were all allocated to a school house. If you were a boarder, which most of the pupils were, that was a big deal because most of your life apart from chapel and lessons was arranged by the house. As a day boy, the house was not much more than a place where you reported in the morning, kept your things and played sport. While I was there, fagging was alive and well. Despite a bad press, all I observed was the most junior boys being made to clean up the prefects' study, make toast for them and, sometimes, clean their Combined Cadet Force (CCF) boots. It did not seem to do them much harm. I was never asked to do any of this. One afternoon a week was devoted to the CCF which was the postwar version of the Officers' Training Corps that my grandfather and father had been in. The officers were all masters, many of whom had been officers during the war. Even the youngest ones had done National Service, which had only just finished, hence they all knew what they were doing. The school had an armoury presided over by a fulltime Company Quartermaster Sergeant, one Raker H. Each Wednesday he dished out our First World War Lee Enfield .303 rifles with which we drilled in our hairy serge uniforms. We each had our own rifle which we had to keep well cleaned and oiled in our own time.

I rose to the dizzy height of Corporal and thus was able to shout out commands to the assembled company on occasion. The process of being assessed for suitability for promotion was a little traumatic in that a couple of regular army Company Sergeant Majors would come from Aldershot and drill you all afternoon. They had a particularly charming habit of standing with their mouth about two inches from your ear and shouting instructions at the top of their (very loud) voices. However, this temporary inconvenience was more than compensated by the splendid range of vehicles they would turn up in. Most were left over from the war and included Bedford OY three-ton general service trucks, Bedford QL 4x4 trucks and Austin field ambulances as seen in the film *Ice Cold in Alex*. We also saw Austin Champs, which were an excellent example of a camel being a horse designed by a committee. Champs were an attempt to create a British vehicle to replace the American Jeep used in the war and to improve on its capability. For example you could drive one at 70mph in reverse, if you were brave/silly enough. The result was over-complicated and cost twice as much as contemporary Land Rovers which were also bought by the Ministry of Defence. Some 13,000 Champs were built in the early 1950s, but all had been sold by 1968.

There were quite a number of school clubs, called societies, but few were appealing. It seemed to me that there might be interest in one for boys interested in cars, lorries, buses and other things that moved. A little research among some of my friends confirmed that I was correct so, after finding a master to sponsor it, I announced that the inaugural meeting of the nattily named 'Road Transport and Motor Racing Society' (RTMRS) would be held in the chemistry lecture room one evening in January 1963. I was very gratified that more than eighty turned up on that first occasion although I do remember, as a fourteen-year-old, feeling a little daunted at the number of sixteen and seventeen-year olds looking down at me from the rows of tiered seating. The prospectus that I set before them was a programme which would include talks by rally and racing drivers, films about cars and

From an early age, I was fascinated by cross-London railway lines. Just after Christmas 1964 I obtained permission to ride in the brake van of 8T53 12.10 Willesden to Norwood Yard unfitted freight, which was hauled by Stanier 8F 48314. More accessible was the *Kenny Belle,* which for very many years ran twice in the morning and twice in the evening in order to get Post Office workers from Clapham Jct to Kensington Olympia. It was not in the public timetable but it was permissible for ordinary passengers to travel and you could buy a ticket at each end. Here 80144 prepares to take the postmen home in December 1964.

trucks including technical subjects and race reports together with visits to motoring places of interest. The first meeting comprised a debate about whether the newly introduced Lotus Cortina or the traditional Morgan was the more desirable. A short presentation by a proponent of each was followed by an extremely lively session with very strongly held views being aired. I must admit to coming down on the side of the Lotus Cortina. The society was very successful and, in the time when I ran it, it had more than twice as many members as any other in the school.

The other organisation that I joined was, not surprisingly, the Railway Society, which was not very active at the time. A number of us decided to change that. They included Graham Miller, who, after Cambridge, joined BR and became Personal Assistant to Chairman Peter Parker before leaving to join his family business. Andrew Turk was absolutely mad keen on steam engines, so much so that when he left school he went to South Africa and, later to Rhodesia to work as a steam loco fireman on the main line. He wrote several times to describe

One of the coaches that was used in this train for a few years in the mid '60s was S1000S, which represents a huge missed opportunity. It was built at Eastleigh in 1962 on the frames of a coach which had been written off in the terrible Lewisham crash of 1957. The body was made of reinforced fibreglass although it looked very similar to conventional steel examples. It remained unique because it was said to have cost too much to make. That calculation failed to take account of the huge savings in overhaul costs that the design would have achieved. As it was, it was sold in 1973 to the East Somerset Railway where it has required very little work on the body in over 40 years of use.

There was a steady flow of freight trains over the West London Railway. Here D6327, a Western Region Diesel Hydraulic loco, later to be Class 22, heads a freight from the Southern through Kensington Olympia. These had all gone by the end of the '60s because BR had ordered far too many small diesels and the maker, North British, had gone bust thus making spares difficult.

I was constantly surprised how helpful BR could be. I wrote several times and asked to be allowed to visit unusual places. This early 1965 picture shows BR Southeast Division Inspector Andrews who took me on a personal tour of the cross London link from Farringdon to Blackfriars. Here we are being led by an LT Inspector towards the tunnel leading to Holborn Viaduct low level station, which was closed to passengers in 1916. There had been no scheduled passenger trains since then, although there were many freight trains. The old station, roughly on the site of today's City Thameslink, was still there as was Snow Hill signal box, fully operational and totally in the tunnel. The tracks to the left go to Moorgate.

his experiences which he thoroughly enjoyed. Unfortunately he died of leukaemia in his late twenties. Malcolm Dobell was sponsored through university by London Underground and trained as a rolling stock engineer. His career and mine have brought us together many times, including as I write this. We put together a very busy programme of meetings and visits, some of which are shown.

The Beeching Report was published in 1963. Dr Richard Beeching, a director of ICI, then one of the largest blue-chip companies in the UK, had been appointed as Chairman of British Rail. He had a remit to propose changes which would restore it to profitability. There has been a tendency to forget that he encouraged many positive, revenue generating activities such as 'merry go round' trains connecting colliery and power station, Freightliner container trains and the

This picture, taken a few minutes before the previous one, shows a Class 24 hauled freight on the City Widened Lines approaching Farringdon. It has come from Ferme Park on the Eastern Region and is bound for Hither Green yard on the Southern. It will stop when the loco is just outside the tunnel in order that a Class 08 shunter can come on and bank it up the 1 in 31 necessary to get over Blackfriars bridge. It was this gradient that caused the route to be closed in 1971. Modern electric trains have no problem with the even steeper 1 in 22 today.

In my last couple of years at school, 'Beeching' closures became common. Members of the Railway Society bunked off early on Saturday 12 June 1965 to ride on the last scheduled train from Guildford to Christ's Hospital. No. 41287 is probably not long for this world. There have since been several attempts at re-opening this line, including in recent years.

The previous year, 41299 was looking a bit more cared for at Guildford shed.

The Isle of Wight still had quite an extensive steam hauled service right until the end, although some other lines had been closed in the '50s. Class O2 No. 35 is running around its train at Ventnor. All the coaches on the Island were pre grouping and were kept in superb condition. Fortunately, a few survive on the preserved part of the network.

I was a frequent visitor to Nine Elms shed in the mid '60s. The driver going home, fag in mouth, is Brian Aynsley who had recently transferred from Guildford in order to get promotion to driver. When Nine Elms closed in 1967, he went as a driver to Waterloo, later became an operations manager and eventually retired from Network Rail. He still attends Nine Elms re-unions. The engine, Bulleid rebuilt Battle of Britain Class 34056, *Croydon*, lasted another three years after I took this 1964 picture.

Much less common were Maunsell 'Q'Class engines. No. 30530 has just returned from Eastleigh Works. Note the steam operated reverser mounted on the running board. This would be especially appreciated by drivers when shunting.

'InterCity' concept. He is chiefly remembered for closing a great many rural branch lines about which there were many vociferous rows.

Four of us, Graham, Andrew, Randall Cape and I, decided that we would like to travel on as many lines in the South West as we could before they closed. Having each bought a Rover ticket valid for all of Somerset, Devon and Cornwall plus connecting lines from Bristol and Salisbury from 5 to 11 August 1964 for £4 15s, we met at Bristol Temple Meads on the first day. Our plan, which we achieved, was to travel on every line in the area before the closures started. We took with us my grandfather's Great War army ridge tent which was very heavy but slept all four of us easily. What did the weight matter? When you are fit fifteen-year-olds, you can easily share the loads and carry them the mile or two between the station and the campground.

After touring the Bristol area, including the loco sheds at Bath Road and Lawrence Hill, we set off for Taunton and boarded a short train headed by a GWR 'Mogul' (2-6-0) tender engine for the journey to Watchet on the Minehead branch, now the West Somerset preserved railway. Our pre-booked campsite overlooked both the railway and the sea, and was ideal. The following morning we continued to Minehead before exploring more soon-to-be-closed lines in North Devon. We went to the terminus at Ilfracombe before taking a single-coach train on the BR-operated light railway from Torrington to Halwill Junction. This line, opened as recently as 1925, was constructed very cheaply and had many permanent speed restrictions of 5mph, which I observed by hanging my head out of the window despite torrential rain. After

In August 1964, four of us set out to travel on every line in Somerset, Devon, Dorset and Cornwall. Here we are on our first night, tent pitched near Watchet on what is now the West Somerset Railway.

Randall Cape admiring ex-LB&SCR 'Terrier' No. 32678, which had just arrived from Eastleigh ready to be taken to the nearby Butlins Holiday Camp. We had seen it the previous week at Eastleigh being painted. It is today in full working order on the Kent and East Sussex Railway.

a night in Bude, we set off via Launceston to Padstow. In so doing, we passed over the trackbed of the present day 2ft gauge Launceston Steam Railway owned by my friends Nigel and Kay Bowman. They allowed me, in 2009, to drive my Darjeeling Himalayan engine over this same route. At nearby Bodmin Road we joined the first diesel train for a couple of days and set off for Truro, the Falmouth branch and ended up in St Ives. The following day, a Saturday, the trains were a little busier, but it was very easy to see why most of these lines were being proposed for closure. Most of the trains we went on were almost empty, even in August.

That evening we had a few minutes between trains in Plymouth and, since it was a warm evening, thought that a beer would be good. We were halfway through being served in the station bar when the barman asked Turk, who was actually the oldest of us: 'How old are you?' 'I'm sixteen!' he replied indignantly. Minutes later our train arrived and we had to leave with thirst unslaked. At the inevitable inquest in the train, Turk said he thought that the legal age was 16. It was 18!

On Monday, 10 August, we visited Exmouth Junction loco shed which was the Southern shed in Exeter, although all the Southern lines west of Salisbury had recently been transferred to the Western Region. This had meant an immediate influx of GWR engines, particularly pannier tanks, to places they had never been before. It also meant that the Lyme Regis and Seaton branches had very recently lost their steam service in favour of new single car DMUs, so we were sorry to have missed the Adams 'Radial Tank' on the Lyme Regis branch. Much of the Seaton branch is still open as the Seaton Tramway, where you can ride in narrow gauge electric trams alongside the River Axe.

Later that week we found another engine that has since been preserved: 34023 *Blackmore Vale* was being prepared early in the morning at Exmouth Jct shed. It was eventually bought by a group of BR drivers and has been at the Bluebell Railway since 1971.

From time to time, lectures were arranged for the whole school. The most memorable one was by Barnes Wallis who was a member of the Governing Council for the school. He is chiefly remembered for designing the 'bouncing bombs' featured in the film *The Dambusters* but his contribution to aerospace extended from designing the R100 Airship in 1930 through to early preparatory work that led to the Harrier Jump Jet. He had the ability to light up a subject and inspire people. Another, less memorable event was just ending when the Headmaster announced the result of the May 1964 General Election, which was that Harold Wilson's Labour Party had won. A resounding 'Boo!' almost lifted the roof off.

My favourite subjects were physics and chemistry and I chose to go into the Science Sixth where we were prepared for those A levels plus maths. Uncle Bill, or William Ashhurst BSc, MSc, was Head of Physics and was the author of the physics textbook used by generations of students.

He had a much older lab technician, Mr Mears, who was tall, wore a brown smock and shuffled along because of his arthritis. Most of the boys thought him a silly old fool and ignored him but I found that if you got to know him, he was a mine of information. He had been born in 1880 and so was about eighty-five when I knew him. I often spent break time and lunchtime in his workshop where he taught me how to use a lathe and other tools. He would tell me about the exciting life he had had before and during the First World War. After he finished his apprenticeship in 1902, he had joined the then brand-new aeroplane industry in South London. Remarkably, that was before the Wright brothers' first powered flight. He described his involvement with a whole series of different designs of aircraft, at first very primitive, but gradually evolving into the fighter planes used in the war. He stayed in the industry until the early 1920s. His influence absolutely confirmed my long-held ambition to be an engineer. His ability to convey the sheer excitement of being at the forefront of ideas was infectious.

There were various opportunities to visit companies with a view to seeing if you might like to work there. They would arrange for suitable sixth formers to spend several days with them, which was really useful in understanding what industry was like. I went to Richard Thomas and Baldwins' steel works in Ebbw Vale (No), Vickers Shipbuilders in Barrow (No) and British Railways, Southern Region (Possibly). By a very strange quirk of fate, some fifteen years later, I became the boss of

One bright January day in 1966 I had to go for an interview in Leamington Spa and I arranged to call in on Banbury shed which had been taken over by the LM Region a couple of years before. As a result, all the ex GWR locos had been banished and replaced by 8Fs, 9Fs and Black 5s, like this immaculate 44871, fresh out of Crewe Works. This loco is also still operational and has been mainline registered for many years.

No. 6921 *Borwick Hall*, however, was well on the way to that great engine shed in the sky, as a scrap man had been brought in to despatch locos at the back of the shed. The asbestos, which went all over the place, is being dealt with in 2017 because Chiltern Railways are building a small DMU servicing shed on the site.

the BR chap who had shown a dozen of us around the railway works and depots on the Southern Region. Unfortunately, almost my first task was to dismiss him for some misdemeanour he had recently committed.

One of my classmates, Nick, was the son of George Curry, Director General of the Locomotive and Allied Manufacturers' Association (LAMA), the predecessor of today's Railway Industry Association, and he was able to get us the latest promotional films which LAMA produced. As I recall, they were mostly about big steam engines in East Africa. Quite why such things were being promoted in the early 1960s is a puzzle, but perhaps has something to do with the sad demise of the British locomotive building industry which had been very sizeable.

Having already arranged numerous outings for members of the Railway Society, Graham Miller and I decided that we would be a bit more ambitious. Our plan was to charter a train from BR and sell tickets to the public with a view to making a profit. Our chosen route was from St Pancras to Derby, with a visit to the locomotive works, then continuing to Crewe Works and, finally returning to Paddington.

First step was to go and see a very helpful chap called Stewart who was the head of the Charter Train section in the Midland Line Division of BR London Midland Region. His office was in St Pancras Chambers which was the name for the old Midland Railway Grand Hotel, closed and converted into offices by the LMS in 1935. As we outlined our plan to him, we took in the interesting bird's-eye view of the station out of his window. In retrospect, it seems rather surprising that he should have taken two schoolboys seriously, but he did. We asked for, and got, our chosen diesel loco, D100, named *Sherwood Forrester*, which would haul the train from St Pancras to Derby and then right on into Crewe Works. After bringing the train back to

Crewe Station, it would be relieved by a 'Britannia' steam loco for the return via Shrewsbury and Birmingham Snow Hill to Banbury. It would have to be replaced by a Class '47' there as the Western Region had eliminated steam the previous year and would not countenance the dirty smelly things sullying its railway.

We fixed the fare at a very reasonable 49s.6d and distributed more than 4,000 leaflets. Advertisements appeared in several magazines during February and March, and a small one even crept into the personal column of *The Times*. One of the conditions that BR, not unreasonably, imposed was that the charter fee had to be guaranteed by someone who was not a minor. Both Graham and I sounded out our fathers, with the same predictable result so it fell to me to approach the rather fierce Headmaster to invite him to help out. It was a short conversation, but when I put the form that needed signing under his nose, to my surprise, he signed it, saying as he did so that he would not pay up in the event that the guarantee was called. I remember thinking that he was naive in that he had not even questioned me to understand how we were going to mitigate his risk! Great for us, all the upside and none of the downside.

Bookings were coming in well and everything seemed set fair when, about a week before the train was due to run, we got the news that the promised buffet car would not be available. This was unfortunate since it was a long day and we had advertised the facility. However, a moment's thought revealed this as a further profit opportunity. We said that we would accept the lack of a buffet if we could have a brake vehicle in its place. On the day before the charter, I got my father to drive me to a supermarket where I bought the ingredients for several hundred sandwiches and a large quantity of cans of soft drinks. Several members of the Railway Society were roped in to man the impressive sandwich production line which we set up in the physics labs at school. Later, Dad drove a couple of us to Cricklewood Carriage Sidings in North London where we transferred the food to the brake van. We had also secured permission to stay overnight on the train to guard the food from humans and rats and then to stay on the empty stock as it was taken into St Pancras. It all went exactly to plan and everyone we came across was extremely helpful.

On the day more than 300 passengers joined us for the 08.40 departure from St Pancras headed by D100 as planned. We were booked via Nottingham because of engineering works and arrived twelve minutes late in Derby because of delays associated with them. As a sign of how differently things were done in those days, we experienced single line working six times between St Pancras and Crewe. However, at least the railway was almost always kept open in those days and the use of buses was minimal.

The impromptu buffet car was profitable and worked very well. Our tariff card demonstrated, by comparing prices, that we were much better value than BR and that we had a more enterprising range of fare, including such delicacies as veal and ham pie (a shilling a portion) and jam tarts (3d each).

In a rather rushed tour of Derby Loco Works, we walked through several of the shops, all of which were devoted to repairing diesel locos as, by 1966, Derby had repaired its last steam engine. We also saw, ex-LMS main line diesel 10000 and the Southern diesels 10201/2/3, all of which had been withdrawn. Leaving Derby at 12.45, we arrived at Crewe station at 14.17, as booked, where we spotted several people climbing aboard the train for the works visit. It turned out that they planned to ride back to London without tickets. We caught up with them later and relieved them of the full 49s/6d after a little persuasion. We took on yet another pilotman to conduct us past the Works General Offices on the Old Chester Line to our destination, which was the platform at Stonebank inside Crewe Works. Unlike at Derby, the guides here were organised with military precision and took us in parties of fifty around most parts of the works.

When, a week before our charter train, we were told we could not have a buffet car, we asked for a brake van to be placed in the middle of the train. Here, I am loading our home made sandwiches and supermarket cakes into the van with the help of the Cricklewood Carriage sidings inspector. He allowed me to sleep in the coach that night to guard the loot!

After visiting Derby Loco Works, we were able to take the train past the General Offices to the platform at Stonebank yard right inside Crewe Works.

A few yards away, outside the paint shop, was experimental Pacific 71000 *Duke of Gloucester* looking rather sorry for itself having been out of service for 4 years. We were, wrongly, told that it was on its way to the British Transport Museum at Clapham. In fact, it was sent to be scrapped at Barry after one set of its unusual Caprotti valve gear had been removed for display in the Science Museum. However, it cheated death and has been running since 1986.

After the paint shop, we were led past the reception sidings where engines scheduled for works attention were delivered. Little did I know that seven years later I would walk past this spot on my way to work each morning. By then, of course, the steam engines had given way to Class 40s, 47s, 50s and various types of electric loco.

Crewe in those days was a very interesting and varied place. On the one hand, steam locos, mostly 'Black Fives' and '8Fs' plus a couple of 'Britannias', were still having heavy repairs in the huge 1926 Erecting Shop, while new Class '47' locos were being built in the next bay alongside Class '40s' and '47s' and electric locos in for overhaul. We also saw 71000 *Duke of Gloucester*, about to be restored for display in Clapham Museum, we were (inaccurately) told, together with 46235 *City of Birmingham* newly painted and ready to be displayed in that city.

In 1966 a few steam engines were still being overhauled at Crewe. No. 76040 would have been one of the last.

All too soon it was time to rejoin the train, still headed by D100, which had run round for the short journey back to Crewe station where it was replaced by 70012 *John of Gaunt*. This 'Britannia' class steam loco had been cleaned to a very high standard and was in the charge of Driver Robertson of Crewe South shed who promised us a fast run. We certainly got that with 85mph before Shrewsbury before suffering several more sections of single line working. We were routed on the ex-GWR route via Wolverhampton Low Level on what is now the Midland Metro to a deserted Birmingham Snow Hill. More engineering work and more spirited running brought us to Banbury twelve minutes late. Here 70012 was replaced by Western Region Class '47' D1701 which left Banbury twenty minutes late and arrived at

D100 ran around its train inside Crewe Works and took our charter train back to Crewe Station, where Britannia Class 70012 *John of Gaunt* took over for a fast run to Banbury via Shrewsbury and Birmingham.

Paddington at 21.18, only three minutes down, having touched 100mph through Denham. The trip was a great success in that everyone seemed to enjoy themselves and we made about £75 for the Railway Society.

At the start of the autumn term in 1965, choices had to be made about which universities I should nominate on my application form. Since I had decided that I wanted to read mechanical engineering, I required somewhere that had a good reputation in that field. Loughborough was one that I investigated and I very clearly remember walking on a dark foggy evening to the grim, dimly lit, GC station at Loughborough, standing on the deserted platform and seeing the front of my train emerge out of the gloom. The number 70013, indicating BR 'Britannia' *Oliver Cromwell*, still sticks in my memory. Of course, I did not know then that this very engine was to play a major part in the last official day of steam operation or that the engine would be preserved and still operational fifty years later. The run, in the almost empty train, was quite spirited and I distinctly remember passing through Aylesbury station at what seemed like about 70mph.

Another university that I chose to visit was Newcastle. I was looking forward to this visit for another reason, which was that my mother's side of the family came from the area and my mother had been born there. The journey from King's Cross, hauled by one of the new 100mph 'Deltics' in a Mk 1 coach, was exciting because of the lively ride and tremendous wind noise from windows only slightly ajar. On arrival at Newcastle, I transferred to one of the ex-LNER articulated two-car third rail electric multiple units which took me to Jesmond, a station now served by the Tyne and Wear Metro. I was going to stay with my mother's Aunty Nora and her husband Wilfred Carter. They were in their eighties and had lived for the past forty years in a small 1920s semi in a genteel suburban road.

After dinner, Uncle Wilfred and I retired to the sitting room. As it was a cold evening and, of course, the house did not have central heating, we sat, facing each other, in two armchairs close to a large open coal fire. We each lit up an enormous cigar which lasted for about three hours during which my great uncle described what it had been like to be an officer in the trenches in the First World War. While I can very clearly remember the scene and can visualise him sitting opposite me by the fire, to my great regret, I cannot remember much of what he actually said. I do, however, recall that it was pretty detailed and at times gruesome. It has, more recently, occurred to me that he may never have given this account to anyone else, including his wife. Maybe, as he approached the end of his life, he felt the need to unburden himself. In any event, I feel very privileged to have been confided in. After I finished my cigar, I said that I had thoroughly enjoyed it, but that I knew that smoking was unhealthy and that I would never smoke again. And I have not.

In the event I decided, on balance, to apply to go to Leeds and accepted an offer from BR to sponsor me, subject to my gaining entry.

CHAPTER TWO

Apprenticeship

July 1966 was a very exciting time because, at long last, nine months after my seventeenth birthday, I was allowed to start driving lessons and I passed my test a few weeks later. The reason that my mother (she made all the rules) had forbidden any question of learning to drive before sitting my A levels was to ensure that I concentrated on them without distraction. Clearly, this was a good plan. Unfortunately I miscalculated the amount of revision I needed to do to pass my maths A level. I probably would not have had to do much, but I did successfully demonstrate that doing none at all was not a winning strategy.

Hence, I found myself in August with no place at Leeds University, no job with British Railways and no plan 'B'. I had passed the two subjects I really enjoyed, physics and chemistry, so I set about seeing where I might go to study mechanical engineering with two A levels. Rather more by luck than judgement, I discovered that Bamfords Ltd, a firm of agricultural engineers, might be able to take me on their training scheme and I was interviewed at their office in Uttoxeter by a young

My journey to Uttoxeter to visit Bamfords included a fast and noisy ride on one of Derby Etches Park's six Birmingham Rail Carriage and Wagon DMUs. Later I got to know these intimately. Here, one lurks in the, by then, truncated stump of the former Ashbourne branch at Uttoxeter.

man called Anthony Squire who was smartly dressed in tweeds. I learnt later that he was the Chairman's step son. His father was Adrian Squire, who at the age of twenty-one in 1932 had set up a company and made a small number of high performance Squire sports cars which, with their very stiff chassis and 100 bhp Anzani engines, had sensational performance. Adrian Squire had been killed by a bomb in 1940, leaving six-year-old Anthony and his mother. Later, she married her late husband's school friend Vincent Bamford, who paid to educate her son.

Anthony and I hit it off immediately and I was offered a job in the first few minutes of the interview and asked how soon I could start as a student apprentice.

Bamfords had been founded by Henry Bamford in 1845 and had grown to be quite a sizeable business. When I started with them, they had about 950 employees. In the nineteenth century they had manufactured a huge range of machines, all of which were designed to increase the productivity of the agricultural industry, which had not changed much for the previous 1,000 years but which was then required to feed a growing population of workers who were participating in the Industrial Revolution. They made things like mowers, reapers, hay rakes, potato diggers, corn mills and even cheese presses. Very many of these were still in use either at home or in the Empire and spares could be, and were, provided in quite large quantities, sometimes for machines that had been supplied 100 years previously.

I had yet to discover all this when, at about 14.00 on my first Sunday, I knocked, with some trepidation, at the front door of the Bamfords Apprentice Hostel which was opened by one of the youngest, Peter Proudlove. He took me through to the kitchen which was long and thin and smelt of chip fat and cabbage. At the far end was a large old-fashioned gas cooker while just inside the door was Terry Bromley, formerly Chief Petty Officer Bromley, RN. He was a wiry chap in his late forties, about 5ft 6in tall, with receding curly brown hair. As was common then, he and his wife both smoked incessantly, including when cooking their deep-fried creations. Terry, not surprisingly, ran the hostel a bit like a small ship, in that everything had a place and everything was in its place. There were rules but fortunately they were quite few in number. However, it was not advisable to get caught breaking those that did exist. Having had the discipline of public school, I found all this very easy to deal with but some of the other boys found it really difficult. In truth, I was probably also more practised at not getting caught than they were.

I was taken to my bedroom which was quite large and, like the rest of the place, shabby but functional. I was to share with two Geordie lads, both of whose fathers were coal miners in Ashington, Northumberland. Malcolm was an apprentice in the Machine Shop and did not seem to have any ambition. He was exceptionally laid back. Archie was a technician apprentice and was interested in all sorts of things. I suspect that, given different circumstances, he would have gone to university and been very successful. I imagine such a possibility was not even considered in Ashington in those days. Both lads were very friendly and regarded my various antics with a kind of amused incredulity. My education from them in 'Geordie' was to prove invaluable years later when I worked in Newcastle.

The following day, Monday, 19 September 1966, I was told to present myself to Mr Edwards, the Personnel Manager, who was a tall, exceedingly thin, man who seemed to tangle himself around the furniture like a python. He was very friendly and helpful in his own way, but like many personnel people I have come across, he did not have a clue about education or training. Edwards took me into the factory to where I had to clock in and out using my new clock number, 702. If you clocked in even one minute late, you were 'quartered' – had fifteen minutes deducted from your pay. If you were more than fifteen minutes late, the timekeeper would withdraw your card and you had to go to your foreman and await your fate. Many years later, when each week I saw a queue of miscreants who could not get up on time, I could place myself in their position, except that I took good care never even to be quartered.

I was taken into the Toolroom, whose purpose was to produce the jigs and special tools and fittings that were needed for the production departments.

Here were some of the most skilled men in the factory, led by the foreman, Sam Salt, a nervous man always darting about, never still. He had a pinched, foxy look and spoke very quickly and a bit indistinctly. He was very welcoming and gave me the impression he was genuinely pleased that I had come to join his team. He was always very friendly and nothing was too much trouble if I asked for help. He was a highly skilled toolmaker and was very knowledgeable. A bachelor, he lived with his mother in a 'chocolate box' cottage with roses around the front door. After he heard that I was interested in railways, he invited me to come and visit him one Saturday. In the little cottage garden was a small garden shed fitted out immaculately as a model maker's workshop. Sam made the most exquisite 7.5in gauge live steam models.

Sam took me over to see the man who, for the next six months, was going to impart his knowledge to me. His name was Graham Darby and he was about thirty; an energetic, active man with close-cropped dark curly hair who was also the Shop Steward for the Amalgamated Engineering Union (AEU) for the whole Machine Shop, including the Toolroom. I was very fortunate to have been put with Graham because he was very skilled, was an excellent teacher and was incentivised to get me quickly up to speed so that he could leave me to do the job while he went about his union and football pool business. He was a classic case of someone who was ripe for development and whose talents were wasted.

In an office above Sam's was a youngish draughtsman called John Buxton. He took drawings from the main Drawing Office where

My mentor for the first six months of my apprenticeship, Graham Darby, is showing me how to use an Archdale vertical milling machine. The one I was using when Fred Harley accused me of trying to kill him.

machines were designed, and worked out what tooling was required. In recognition of his salaried status, he always wore a suit, white shirt and tie at work.

A typical press tool that Graham and I would make would be required to crop and pierce a mild steel strip, say, 12in wide and 10swg – that is, one-eighth of an inch thick. The strip would have been made by putting an 8ft x 4ft sheet into a press brake, a large power-operated version of the guillotine that you might cut paper with. Our press tool would allow the strip to be poked in as far as a

Some of my fellow apprentice hostel dwellers at our Christmas party in 1966.

September 1966 was the last month of steam at Uttoxeter. No. 75035 is shunting the yard which British Railways later tried to sell to Bamfords, whose factory is in the background.

stop and then, as the press came down, with the operator's fingers well out of the way, it would chop off the requisite length plus any other shapes called for, and possibly pierce some holes. This process would take a couple of seconds so the rate of production could be quite high. The resultant piece of steel might then be incorporated in a welded assembly or it might go straight to the production line to be built into a baler or other machine.

Sam would start us off by bringing us an engineering drawing that John Buxton the draughtsman had done and, perhaps, emphasise some critical feature. We would take some time to make sure we understood how it was supposed to work. This meant visualising in 3-D what had been drawn in 2-D. Nowadays computer generated images will show you the 3-D image and make the whole process much easier and quicker. The same software will also control the machine tools, thus mechanising much of what we did manually. In the days before computer graphics, the process took much longer and there was much more scope for misinterpretation. Also, it was not unknown for draughtsmen to draw things that could not be made.

One of Bamford's best sellers.

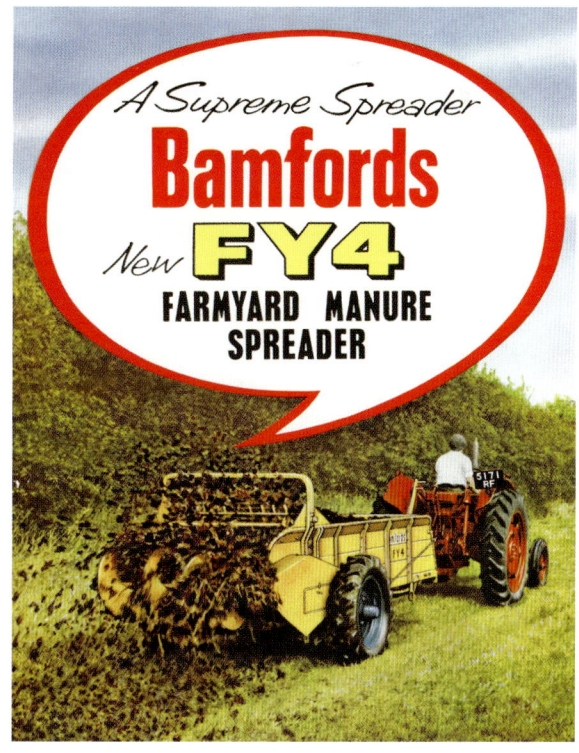

Part of the product offering in the 1920's. Slightly updated versions of most of these machines were still in production in my time and we certainly supplied spares for all of them, and for much older machines.

Having got our minds around what John intended and perhaps with a little help from him, the next job was to get out a list of all the steel and proprietary parts that we needed to collect for the job. This entailed selecting suitable sized pieces of the correct grade of steel from the stores and then taking them around to the Maintenance Shop a couple of hundred yards away to cut them roughly to size.

'Come, my man,' would be Graham's cry when he took me for the first time to any new place. He would show me how to use a whole range of machine tools either in the Toolroom or other parts of the factory. Once I had been shown, Graham was off on one of his many extracurricular activities.

The Toolroom contained several 'characters'. Among them was Vernon, who did some of the simpler jobs. Not long after I started, he stopped me as I walked past his machine on the way to the stores and, checking no one was watching, pushed a large round tin containing Rich Tea biscuits in my direction. 'I know what it's like being an apprentice,' he said. 'I was always hungry.' Thereafter, I always got a biscuit to go with the tea that came around on a trolley mid-morning.

Next to Vernon was Jim Andrews, who was also a machinist, in his case a turner, which meant that he operated a lathe, usually making parts for one of the toolmakers. Jim was a squat man with a pockmarked foxy face invariably topped by a greasy flat cap of indeterminate colour. I was to see more of Jim later because after Bamfords closed in 1971, he got a job as a turner in the Railcar Engine Shop at Derby Loco Works and travelled with me on the train to Derby for a while. Another turner was old Clem who had been an apprentice during the First World War with Fred Harley, the Chief Foreman in the Machine Shop and the boss of Sam, our Foreman. Every day, without fail, Fred would waddle his arthritic way towards Clem's workplace. Fred always wore a plain and slightly shabby black suit and a bowler hat. His mission was to sidle up to the small tool cupboard that Clem had beside his lathe. Inside would be the day's Daily Mirror. When Fred thought no one was looking, he would surreptitiously slip his hand into the cupboard, feel for the newspaper and put it under his jacket. He then set off for the gents' which had been thoughtfully provided high up in the roof, up two flights of stairs so that the foremen could see anyone going in. This enabled them to easily check that shop floor staff were not spending more than the permitted five minutes away from their machines. Fred was not aware that, once a week, my mentor Graham Darby ran a sweepstake for everyone in the shop based on the time Fred took in the lavatory reading Clem's Mirror.

It was on one of these journeys towards Clem's cupboard that Fred uttered his only words to me. I was operating a new and powerful milling machine which had a type of cutter that was then new. It had replaceable ceramic tips which enabled you to take a substantial cut even out of tool steel, which is very tough. I had a piece of such steel about the size of a brick secured in the machine's vice while the hi-tech cutter was taking off about a quarter of an inch and sending out a very satisfactory stream of sparks. I had set the machine to operate automatically and was admiring the results of my handiwork as I noticed Fred shuffling towards me on his way to Clem's cupboard. He had to pass right by me. When he was about 2ft away, there was the most almighty bang caused by my piece of steel flying across his path and hitting a steel locker. 'Are you trying to kill me, lad?' were the only words Fred ever spoke to me.

Soon after arriving in the Apprentice Hostel, I became aware that it was a tradition that every new apprentice had to be subjected to an initiation ceremony. This invariably comprised throwing him fully clothed into a bath full of cold water. After a couple of weeks, my turn came. One evening, after supper, I was descended on by four lads as I lay on my bed reading. I had already concluded that there was no way of avoiding my fate, but I had decided that I was not going down without a bloody good fight. I was very strong in those days, much stronger than most of the others. The four managed to drag me to the door, but I wedged myself into the frame and they were quite unable to move me. I was quite proud of the fact that it eventually took eight of them, two on each limb, to chuck me in.

In my first six months I was paid £6.10s for a forty-five hour week, which included one hour's compulsory overtime each day. From this was deducted £2.10s for board and lodging. In addition to this, my father gave me £10 a month. Meagre as these amounts now seem, I was able to survive quite happily; indeed, farm workers were bringing up families for not much more at the time.

I could afford to get the train home from time to time although I soon felt the need to have my own car. Asking around, I discovered that an older ex-apprentice called Archie had a 1954 Ford Popular (always known as a Ford Pop) for sale. After a bit of haggling, I got OXM 843 for the sum of £5. Insurance, payable in instalments, was £13.10s a year and tax was £17.10s, and you could pay for three months at a time. Now, I am not going to pretend that it was the best car in the world, but it was just about roadworthy. It went as well as could be expected given its 1172cc side valve engine and stopped reasonably well with its cable brakes.

At the beginning of February, after a most enjoyable six months, I started at the College of Advanced Technology in Stafford, which was a very congenial place. Until a couple of years before, it had been owned and run by the English Electric Company, which in those days was Stafford's biggest employer. While I was there it became a polytechnic and is now called a university, having combined with another establishment in Stoke on Trent. In 1967 there were just over 100 boys (and with one exception they were all boys) in each year. The subjects taught were mechanical engineering, electrical engineering and computing. I enrolled on a three-year 'thin sandwich course' with a view to obtaining a Higher National Diploma (HND) in Mechanical Engineering. I was to attend the college from February to July for each of 1967, 1968 and 1969. In between, I would work at Bamfords. There were twenty-seven in my class, most employed by English Electric, together with a couple each from the CEGB and the Coal Board. All, including me, were paid while we were at college and there were no fees in those days.

The English Electric boys were paid substantially more than the rest of us, but we all took pity on a lad called Mahendran from Ceylon. At twenty-two, he was older than the rest of us and was very quiet, only ever speaking when spoken to. If you did engage him in conversation, however, he was very interesting. He had lived with his uneducated parents in a small village in the jungle. As a small boy, he had been taken by some American missionaries to a school they had set up. When he was fifteen, he was sent by his government to England to be trained as an engineer. The Ceylon Embassy enrolled him, initially, on an Ordinary National Certificate (ONC) course followed by an HNC. These were qualifications for skilled tradesmen. Having passed them, he was enrolled on our course, which was for engineering technicians and managers. His government was extremely tight on money, with the result that he had to live in really cheap digs and had no spare money for the weekend. Also, he had not been able to go home for seven years. Like most of the rest of us, he did pass his exams, after which he went back to Ceylon (which became Sri Lanka in 1972). About twenty years later I tracked him down, by then in a senior government job in Sri Lanka.

The teaching at Stafford was much more like a school sixth form than a university lecture system. There were no tutorials, although there was ample opportunity to talk to the lecturer to make sure you understood the subject being taught. The atmosphere was very businesslike and professional. You had to be there from 09.00 until 17.00 Monday to Friday and there was homework set and marked. Most of the lecturers had worked in industry and, whatever the subject, there were always anecdotes to illustrate how you might use today's teaching.

My favourite lecturer was Dennis Smith, who came from the nearby Black Country where he had been a Shop Superintendent in a small steel rolling mill in Darlaston during the war. He taught us a variety of subjects over the three years and he was equally interesting on 'Theory of Machines' (which was about machine tools) or 'Industrial Organisation' which was about systems of management and trade unions and how to deal with them. Every lecture would be illustrated by little cameos describing individuals he had had a run-in with, or who had gone the extra mile in very difficult circumstances: for example, when the roof of the rolling mill was ablaze from multiple incendiary bombs and his chaps carried on melting steel and rolling it as if nothing had happened. Dennis was also a very keen and highly competent model maker. His passion was for O Gauge , modelled, obviously for someone brought up in the Black Country, on Great Western practice. I was invited to supper at his house many times to help work the amazing layout he had in his loft. He had full length trains of Churchward and Collett coaches hauled by just about any twentieth century Great Western engine you could name, from an 'Atbara' to a 'County' Class. I can still remember the 'clickety clack' as a 'Castle' pulled twelve coaches around his loft at a scale 70mph! Everything was produced to the highest of standards. He also modelled diesels and I remember admiring his 'Hymek', a class I liked in the flesh. The next challenge after that was a Class '47' as they had recently started appearing at Paddington. When he was nearing the time to paint it, he called upon his twin daughters to assist. They were about my age and were both reading mechanical engineering at Brunel University, in West London. They were requested to go to Paddington and, while one acted as lookout, the other was to scrape a sample of the green paint off the new loco for father to match.

Apart from wanting to share his enthusiasm for his hobby, it soon became clear that Dennis had another motive. For some reason, he had formed the view that I would be a suitable candidate for the role of son-in-law. I did go on a couple of dates with one of his daughters, Elaine, but it was clear that we were not destined for each other.

One of the English Electric boys, John Dulcamara, and I, soon found that, although quite different in temperament, we got on very well. He was the grandson of an archetypical Italian ice cream seller. He was very arty and expressive in a way that I certainly was not. For the whole of our time at college, we would spend most lunch hours together, usually going in my car the two miles to Stafford town centre. One day we might go to the market where I would buy my supper, sometimes pigeon, 9d with feathers or, if I was really flush, 1/6 ready plucked. Another day we would sit in the public gallery of the County Court, surreptitiously eating an utterly delicious meat pie bought from the Roebuck pub opposite and trying not to make too much noise as we observed one of the barristers questioning a witness or the judge summing up in a murder case.

The style of teaching at Stafford really suited me and, because of the very practical and, usually, lively teaching style, I had no difficulty achieving the necessary grades. In particular, I was sufficiently competent in maths, which I had failed at A level. We were the last year to be taught entirely in the Imperial system of measurements and were, in a sense, witnessing the end of an era. Not for us insidious French measurements like hectares, Newton-metres and kilograms. We used such noble concepts as British Thermal Units, chains and foot/pounds that had made the Empire great! As a result, I am still more comfortable with inches, miles, pounds, stones and Fahrenheit, although millimetres and centimetres are familiar, as rulers, even at my prep school, had inches on one side and centimetres on the other.

In my first session at Stafford, I met Ted Talbot, who lived just down the road from the college. He was then, and is even more so now, a real expert on the London & North Western Railway. He has written many very readable books on his lifelong passion and I am pleased to say that I have had many opportunities to hear from him about it.

My first semester at Stafford finished at the end of July with internal exams, which we all passed. After a brief break, corresponding to the works fortnight, I reported back for duty at the factory. I had continued living in the hostel whilst driving every day the fourteen miles to college. With petrol at 4/9 (24p) per gallon, that was just about affordable. However, I had supplemented my income very substantially by promoting a railtour on the same basis as the one I had promoted with Graham Miller the previous year.

1X75 ran on Sunday, 16 April 1967 from Euston to King's Cross. I had figured that the electrification of the West Coast Main Line was sufficiently new to attract a significant number of passengers if you combined it with some main line steam interest. To set it in context, in April 1967, the only BR steam left operating was the Waterloo to Weymouth route of the Southern Region, to be replaced by electric trains that summer, and in parts of North West England on the London Midland Region. This latter was to end in August of the following year.

My tour left Euston with nine packed coaches hauled by a new Class '86' electric loco, which was then, at 4,040hp, the most powerful locomotive ever in the UK. After a 100mph run to Stockport (always exciting in a Mk 1 coach with the windows open), we ran past Edgeley steam shed as we pulled into Stockport Station. There, E3103 was detached, and the green loco that could be seen standing on the viaduct backed down to take its place. Some months previously I had approached Lord Garnock, owner of LNER 'K4' 2-6-0 *The Great Marquess,*and, sportingly, he had no hesitation in agreeing to hire the loco to a seventeen-year-old for £75. Part of the deal was that I got to ride on the footplate so, after 3442 was coupled on, I joined the crew and a Loco Inspector for the journey around the suburbs via Manchester Victoria before halting at Bolton to have an assisting loco attached. This materialised in the form of 'Black Five' 45377, which, like most steam engines then working in the North West, was filthy. The assistance was needed because of the steep gradients between Bolton and Hellifield, where the 'Black Five' was removed. After a spirited run, we arrived at Keighley on time at 14.44.

Lord Garnock had told me that the banking engine would not be required. He cited as evidence the testimony of T.C.B. Miller, then

No. 3442 *The Great Marquis* near Skipton with my Euston to Kings Cross charter special on 16 April 1967.

We entered Leeds Central on its last day of operation with 3442 and came out headed by 4472 *Flying Scotsman*, which took us all the way to Kings Cross.

CM&EE of British Railways and the man behind the HST and the Mk 3 coach, which were both being designed then. Miller had been Loco Shedmaster at Glasgow Eastfield before the war and he vouched for the prodigious pulling power of these engines. However, the LM operating department was having none of it: 'You can't trust these foreign engines.'

At Keighley we were met by a fleet of buses which were necessary because the Light Railway Order had not yet come through. We were, however, well entertained at Haworth and then rejoined the train at Keighley Station for the short run to Leeds Central Station. This was the last day that this station was used as, on the following day, all its former services that remained were operated from Leeds City Station. As we ran into the terminus, our next loco was waiting in a neck at the station entrance. I had broached the question of hiring *Flying Scotsman* with Alan Pegler, its owner, when I met him in the cab while it was standing on Basingstoke shed the previous August, after working a Gainsborough Model Railway Society charter to Farnborough. I had not previously intended running 1X75 but, when I saw Alan Pegler in the cab, I decided on the spur of the moment to ask if I could hire his engine. His response was so immediate and positive that I spent the next few weeks making a plan.

The charter team in the BR Euston office turned out to be the same people I had dealt with the previous year at St Pancras, the St Pancras Division having been abolished. I did, however, think that their price was a bit high and I managed to negotiate them down a bit when I pointed out that I would be paying a huge amount to hire locos for more that half the route. As I recall, I got a lot more off than the £75 which I paid for *The Great Marquess* and the £250 that Alan Pegler wanted. I ended up paying BR £1,500 – quite a lot for an apprentice earning about £8 per week.

Flying Scotsman backed down on to the coaches and soon left for King's Cross. I was on the footplate as far as Doncaster and was able to experience speeds of up to 80mph, which was very exciting after the steady 35 to 40mph of the previous engine. The whole day went very well. Nothing of any consequence went wrong and all trains ran on time. I think the passengers enjoyed themselves. After all expenses, I cleared about £150 profit, which was very useful.

My second six months in the factory started in August 1967. Previously I had learnt a lot about that wonder material, steel. I had discovered that there are a great many grades, each with their own properties, and that it is almost endlessly versatile in that it can be put to hugely diverse uses and can be machined, formed and shaped in multiple ways. Truly a wonder material which has made a contribution to society greater than almost anything except the wheel. Now, I was to learn about another fascinating and much underrated material: cast iron.

Bamfords had invested in a very modern iron foundry, which had been opened in 1961, replacing a much older plant. Cast iron was used in all of its products, ranging from simple cattle drinking bowls through gearboxes for balers to cylinder blocks for diesel engines. Like steel, cast iron comes in a great many grades whose chemical composition is very similar but whose properties can vary markedly. Bamfords' requirement was for so called 'Grey Iron' which was a general grade that could be used for a whole variety of medium strength applications. It was comparatively soft so that it could be machined easily and quickly, had good compressive strength, although was less good in tension, was good at damping vibration (important, for example in an engine crankcase), and fairly corrosion-resistant.

In order to achieve these and other properties, a team effort was called for between the designer, the pattern maker, the metallurgist and the moulder. The designer could, for example, call for sections that were too thin and which would cool too quickly after the molten iron was poured, leading to brittleness. The pattern maker, a very highly skilled job, had to allow for shrinkage when the molten metal cooled. This was quite difficult to accurately predict for a complex shape. Beware if you are ever given a 'pattern maker's rule' as it will read

Later that summer, a group of us who had chartered 4472 hosted a dinner at the Savoy. I was asked to make a speech thanking Alan Pegler, the engine's then owner, for having saved it for the Nation. To an eighteen-year-old this was preferable to the alternative of paying my share of the dinner! School friend Paul Thompson and college friend John Dulcamara joined me.

high to allow for this contraction. The metallurgist has to ensure that the iron and steel being melted is of the correct composition, that the appropriate chemicals are added and that the 'pour', as it is called, is at exactly the right temperature. The moulder must make sure that, using the pattern, he creates the correct inverse shape in the sandbox so that, when filled with molten iron, the desired finished casting materialises. You could imagine that when hot and heavy molten iron is poured into a sand mould, there is a tendency for the mould to collapse or distort. If that happens, a misshaped casting will result. All of them must work together to make sure that when the iron is poured, no air is trapped. I had learnt about this at college and in late August 1967, I reported to Derek Jones, the Foundry Manager to see it in practice.

You could not find a more different person from my previous manager in the Machine Shop, Fred Harley, he of the bowler hat and Daily Mirror. Derek had been the proudest man on earth when selected to manage the new foundry in 1961 and he still displayed that enthusiasm. I already knew him socially through our membership of the Uttoxeter Camera Club. He arranged a programme that took me to all parts of his empire. I started in the Pattern Shop with another member of the Camera Club, Peter Rock, who as well as being a very skilled craftsman was a very kind and gentle individual. Going from the mayhem, noise and smell of the Foundry into the Pattern Shop was to enter another world. Here, all was calm and harmonious. There was the sweet smell of wood and vegetable glue as most of the patterns were made of hardwood which was machined to size (allowing for shrinkage) and often laminated by building up layers which were glued and pinned together. Next, I spent a couple of days with the metallurgist, where I checked on the composition of the scrap iron and steel that was bought in and mixed with pig iron to make up the correct mix. I also did various tests on the actual iron that we made. This took me within a few feet of the electric arc furnaces that melted the scrap and which fed the pouring ladle that held a ton of liquid iron. After that, for a couple of weeks of moulding, apprentices were put in the charge of Arthur, a wild-looking, scruffy man who did most of the one-off and short run work. He never seemed to wash the foundry black sand out of what remained of his hair and his clothes, and if you saw him in the town, you could easily mistake him for a tramp. He was also what we youngsters called, in those days, a Dirty Old Man. I had been warned about him by other apprentices. A few short, sharp Anglo-Saxon words from me were sufficient to make it clear to him how things were. We got on fine after that. He was a very good teacher: that is, if you could understand what he was saying.

My next stop, the Fabrication Shop, comprised three main elements: the Press Shop which I was quite familiar with having been servicing it in my Toolroom role at the start of my apprenticeship, the Blacksmiths and the Welding Department. There were several blacksmiths and their assistants called 'strikers'. This was nothing to do with industrial action but was the name given to an unskilled man whose job was originally to wield a large hammer for the skilled man. This did still happen to a small extent in that there was some 'fire welding' carried out. The technique, which has been practised since before Roman times, involves heating two pieces of metal in a fire until they are red-hot, then placing one on top of the other, in the desired position, and striking a series of blows with a hammer until they are fused together. The 'brain' is in judging the correct temperature and when they are properly fused. The 'brawn' is the hitting.

I was set to work in the Welding Shop where various assemblies ranging from small brackets up to parts of baling machines several feet long were welded together, often from many parts. Sometimes, perhaps in haste to earn more money, mistakes were made and the Inspection Department would reject the items. In that case, the welder concerned did not get paid and, usually, the defective assembly would be scrapped. However, when there was an apprentice to hand, he could be taught to weld and could then practise by rectifying these mistakes to save some money. In my experience, welding is a bit like riding a bike in that before you learn how to do it, it seems impossible, but once you have learnt you never forget.

There are various forms, but the most common is electric arc in which an electrode is held just close enough to the material, usually steel, to be welded ('the job') to draw an arc. This melts the steel close to it and, if positioned correctly, can cause two pieces to fuse together just as effectively as if they had been made as one. When you start, you are given protective wear so you do not get burnt by flying pieces of molten steel, and an eye mask to look through so that you are not blinded by the intense light of the arc. Starting with a test piece which has been earthed to one side of the welding power supply, you hold a gun which grips a piece of coated steel wire, known as a welding rod, and attempt to draw an arc by touching it lightly on exactly the right spot, then lifting it off fractionally.

The first problem is that the eye shield is so nearly opaque that, without an arc going, you cannot see anything. This means that you cannot see where to touch. When you pluck up courage and prod the job somewhere, you are rewarded by the rod sticking fast to it. This causes a current of several hundred amps to pass through the rod which very soon starts to glow red-hot. That is the point at which you find out why the welding gun has a quick release feature to let go of the rod. At this stage welding seems impossible. However, you persevere and after a while you wonder what on earth your problem was. Nowadays you can get clever masks which allow you to see what you are doing before the arc strikes up, then instantly become almost opaque so as to protect your eyes when it does.

I got to quite enjoy taking some of the larger failed assemblies out of the scrap bin and recovering them for use on the assembly line.

After that, I was introduced to other welding techniques including welding with a gas flame using oxygen and acetylene.

I had quite a lot of cars as an apprentice. The £5 Ford Pop lasted a few weeks until I tired of its slowness. It was moved on for £20 to a local lad without my having done anything to it other than put in petrol and lots of oil. It was followed by a 1960 Ford Thames 15cwt van which was a bit rough but was very fast and had the advantage of plenty of space for sleeping in. It caused rather a stir when I handed the keys over for valet parking at the Savoy in London when I went to a dinner there. It was swapped for a 1961 Ford Anglia (the one with the backward sloping rear window). That lasted less than a week as I did not like driving it.

Then I spotted a fine car in the local Ford dealer's showroom. It had been taken in part exchange from a local farmer and was a beautiful 1959 Ford Consul, white with a green roof. It was a deluxe model with a chrome horn ring and a lovely green leather bench seat in the front. A deal was done and I was the proudest car owner in miles. It was a lovely car for long journeys such as going back home to Epsom but, sadly, its big end gave up and I made the mistake of getting the local garage to fix it. They simply fitted a genuine Ford re-con engine which was fine except that I could not afford to pay for it. It was suggested that I borrow to cover the cost but I have always believed that you should earn money before you spend it. I have never, before or since, ever borrowed money other than through a mortgage for house purchase. Consequently, my pride and joy had to go. It was replaced by YLB 627, a 1960 ex-Post Office Morris Minor van which I bought from Stevensons. Despite its simplicity and noisiness, I grew to like it. So much so that I have rarely been without a Morris Minor of some sort over the ensuing fifty years.

Bamfords had an Apprentice Association which was encouraged by the company but run by the apprentices. The idea was that we visit other companies to broaden our engineering knowledge. It was, in retrospect, an amazing tour of British industry, much of it not in the best of health. I well remember going to the Pirelli tyre plant in Burton on Trent, with a sickening smell of hot rubber; to Rubery Owen in Darlaston which made components for the car industry, where there was of a forest of belts taking the drive from old-fashioned overhead line shafting down to hundreds of pre-First World War lathes. To Brush at Loughborough where we saw Class '47' locos being built, little knowing that forty-six years later I would become a director of the company. To Ferodo at Chapel-en-Le Frith where we saw brake linings being pressed out and machined, with asbestos all over the place. To Sheffield to see fifty-ton steel forgings being squeezed into shape by a steam hammer to become shafts for ships or steam turbines, something you have to go to China or Korea to see today.

Just before Christmas 1967, a poster caught my attention on the notice board on the front of the police station which was next to the club and right opposite the hostel. It was about a new automatic level crossing that had been installed at Hixon, not far away. It was positioned such that anyone entering the building could not really miss it. It clearly said: 'Drivers with exceptional or heavy loads should phone the signalman before crossing.'

Just after Christmas, in fact on Saturday, 6 January 1968, I drove with Tony Appleton to his parents' house in Wolverhampton. This was because he had invited me to go with him to see his team, Wolves, who were playing at home. This was my first FA match. As we drove up Weston Bank on the way to Stafford, we were passed by dozens of ambulances, fire engines and police cars. It was not until the television was switched on, to see the news at the Appleton house after the match, that we discovered a passenger train had run into a massive transformer that was stationary on the level crossing at Hixon, killing eleven people.

As details of what happened emerged, I realised the relevance of that poster. It was reported that an oversize load in the form of the transformer from the English Electric works at Stafford had bottomed and got stuck on the level crossing with the result that a train ran into it at 80mph. What caught my eye was the report that two policemen had been escorting the load. Now it seemed to me that if that was the case, anyone would assume they would be in charge of the movement and that, therefore, they would obviously ensure that the lorry would stop before the crossing. Indeed, there were signs specifically instructing this. My suspicions were alerted when, on the following Monday, two days after the accident, the poster was removed from Uttoxeter Police Station notice board. I decided to write to Her Majesty's Chief Inspecting Officer of Railways to report this. I was not satisfied with the outcome of the eventual report which cleared the police of any culpability.

My second semester at Stafford started in February 1968. By that time, still smarting from the loss of my wonderful Ford Consul, I had another plan for supplementing my income. When one of the lads in my class came in on a Monday morning with a very long face, I soon found out that he had been driving his 1956 Ford 100E side-valve car flat out for several hours on the newly opened M6 motorway. It had 'put a leg out of bed' – a big end came apart and the con rod smashed through the cast iron crankcase. End of engine. This happened a lot when the motorways were first opened because an old engine that used a lot of oil, and was happy pottering about on local journeys at 40mph, soon ran out of oil if run at high speed for any length of time. This is what had happened here. Obviously, as an aspiring engineer, the owner should have anticipated it. I commiserated very convincingly, I thought, and offered at great personal sacrifice, to take the car off him for £5. We settled on £6.10s. I knew that the local scrapyard would provide a replacement engine for £10 and that if it did not work I could take it back and exchange it for another one. I collected an engine from the scrapyard in Stafford one lunchtime and swapped it over the same evening and had the car running before dark. I sold it on for £35 in a couple of days. This was money for old rope.

Thereafter, I was a frequent visitor to the motor auction at Checkley not far from where I was now living. My objective was to buy something that either had an MOT, or on careful inspection (which was permitted) seemed capable of getting one, but to which some mechanical misfortune had happened. Best if it had to be pushed into the selling arena by the Mercury tractor with an old truck tyre on the front which the auctioneer had for just this eventuality. This always caused most of the shady dealers I was bidding against to look at their feet. Quite a number of cars passed through my hands in this way. I found that if I could buy one which I could sell on for no more than about £60, then I could sell almost anything within a day or two provided that it had a fairly long MOT. My best bargain was a beautiful 1959 Morris Oxford, green and cream like my Ford Consul and with leather seats. Fiddling about with it before the auction, I found that the gear lever could be lifted right out because the circlip that should have prevented this was missing. Now I felt it was my duty to alert other potential buyers to the absence of this vital part. So I left the gear lever on the floor. When the porter came to drive it in, he could not get a gear, so the Mercury tractor had to be summoned. I was happy with £10!

The place where I got most of the spares to fix up my auction cars was run by Bill Barlow, a lovely man in his late thirties who lived, with his mother and father, in a pair of old railway carriages which, although tarred on the outside, were immaculate inside and replete with original brass fittings, all highly polished. They relied on a couple of oily old diesel engines for electricity, which was used very sparingly. To a young engineer, the yard was full of treasure trove: cars and lorries of all ages plus every kind of old machinery. Bill was always very friendly and gave freely of his help and advice for many of my old car projects. Many years later, having visited him a few times over the years, I was truly shocked to hear on the radio one morning that he had been cruelly beaten to death at the age of seventy-nine by his nephew over a disputed piece of land.

When I returned from college I was moved to a really interesting place. I needed to get some practical experience of engineering design, having been taught the principles at college. I had assumed that I would be put in the Drawing Office which was presided over by a brilliant designer called Ivan Smith who had taken the lead, with the Experimental Department, in designing and developing several innovative products which had considerably improved Bamfords' rather old-fashioned and stolid reputation. I knew a bit about this because his assistant, Cyril Freer, came on many of the Apprentice Association visits. Cyril was a rather intense young man who was a Christadelphian and was also a railway enthusiast. He and I got on very well, although he left Bamfords before I did to fulfil his ambition of designing trains. He achieved this in that he found himself on the team that designed the amazingly good Mk 3 coach. When, later, I commuted to Derby in the train, Cyril would often update me on progress with the HST, as it became known.

However, it was decided that I would go to the Plant Drawing Office to get my design experience, tutored by Steve, the Plant Draughtsman. That was fine, except that Steve gave his notice and left after three weeks. The Plant Department was managed by a delightful, 'mad professor' type of man, with extra-bushy eyebrows, called Ray Whitney, who had joined the company after he lost his job when Prime Minister Harold Wilson cancelled the TSR 2 supersonic bomber in 1965. A small team from the same project formed the nucleus of the Advanced Passenger Train team at British Rail's Derby Research Department at the same time. Ray was a good engineer, but was totally unfitted to run the Plant Department, whose role was to provide the production departments with the buildings, services, machine tools and transport that they needed. Fortunately, he had an excellent man in my friend Roy Lynch, an ex-apprentice, to employ all the workman and actually make things happen. The other parts of Ray's job included things to do with developing the business, such a laying out new production lines, buying new machine tools or managing transport, none of which he had much idea about.

While this might not sound much of an environment for an apprentice to learn in, that would be quite wrong. The range of things I was asked to turn my hand to was extensive. It was a really good opportunity to put into practice lots of stuff I had learnt about at college. Over the next few months I found myself doing a great variety of interesting things including:

Designing and having made an automatic welding machine to speed up production.

Making a planning application for a factory extension.

Designing a new assembly line for a new type of mowing machine.

Designing an electrical installation compliant with the current IEE Regs, despite having no real understanding of the subject.

Specifying a new fleet of fork lift trucks.

Investigating a sale and leaseback deal for some other trucks. Then writing a paper explaining how it would release much needed cash.

Negotiating with British Railways who insisted that, if we wanted to continue shipping by rail to the docks, we would have to buy the Railway Goods Yard at Uttoxeter.

This last item was a piece of absolute nonsense. Bamfords sent to Immingham Docks, for much of the year, complete trains of carflats loaded with balers for export. They were loaded in the railway yard, which was immediately adjacent to where they were made. The BR people at Stoke Division asked if they could come and see someone at Bamfords about all this. The job fell to Ray who immediately passed it to me, claiming that he did not know anything about trains! After I had listened to them, I said that we would have to think about it and please come back next week. In the meantime, I got out all the costs we were put to and added in the cost of buying the yard which we did not need. I then compared it with increasing the size of our fleet of lorries and running the extra mileage.

At the time there were six Commer tractors which hauled articulated trailers. They had the wonderful three-cylinder Commer TS 3 two-stroke diesel engine which made a kind of ripping sound when accelerating – very exciting. The Transport Foreman said he could only get four balers on a trailer. I designed him a rack which would hold six and still be within the weight and height limits. I then calculated that if we bought three more lorries, and they worked six days a week, we could more than move the volume that went on the once weekly train.

When the BR chaps came back, I told them that their daft idea of trying to force us to buy their yard was now going to lose them all our rail business, provided our board supported the paper I was about to write. I asked them why, when their Chairman was making great play of wanting more trainload business exactly like ours, they were not prepared to be flexible. (I read my Modern Railways every month.) The answer came that they had their instructions and they dare not question them. My paper was approved by the board, we bought three more wonderful Commers and gave notice to BR and saved a considerable sum. The railway yard remained unsold for years.

There is an unusual postscript to this story in that, some nineteen years later, this same pair of BR people became my employees when I was Managing Director of Red Star Parcels. Talking to them, it was clear that what happened, which they could see made no sense, was the result of an edict that surplus land must be sold at once. OK, but senior people who make such edicts (I suspect Bobby Lawrence, Deputy Chairman of BR, in this case) should realise that unintended consequences often arise if they do not explain properly what the real objectives are. I have seen similar stupidities perpetrated by Railtrack and Network Rail more recently.

In the Plant Department, you never knew what was coming next. One morning, a call came in from the United Dairies (UD) milk bottling plant on the other side of town, next to the railway station. Until recently, it had sent daily rail tankers of milk to the UD plant at Cricklewood, North London.

'You have a problem with diesel spillage into the Pinfold Brook and we're going to report you.'

'Hold on a bit,' I said. 'I'll meet you by the brook next to your place in half an hour.'

I went, first, to have a look at the Pinfold Brook which passed right by our factory. There was, indeed, a small amount of diesel there which you could tell because there was a faint rainbow film on the surface. Downstream of the United Dairies plant, however, the water looked like stewed rhubarb with curdled milk. It was quite a pretty pink, really. I pointed out that it might not be such a good idea to shop us to the Enforcing Authority since they were obviously, and illegally, putting milk into the brook. It turned out that they had been doing so for years whenever they cleaned out a milk storage vessel, but that they had got away with it because they usually did it at night and, anyway, the milk got diluted fairly quickly. I do not know whether they changed their habits, but I got our very small diesel leak rectified straightaway.

Another time, I needed a piece of plant that I had ordered from a company in Worcester. So I asked the Transport Foreman if he could have it collected. The answer was: 'No, but you can take one of the pickups and collect it yourself.' I most certainly did not need asking twice as the pickups concerned were rather special. They were an almost new Bedford 15cwt type based on the then current American Chevrolet version. They had a three-litre, six-cylinder petrol engine and a lorry cab, so were quite big. Contemporary Bedford brochures described them as a 'bosses' truck'. My route took me through Birmingham and then on to the newly opened M5, which was practically deserted. At this time, there were no speed limits on motorways so, obviously, I set out to find just how fast this rather fine truck was. I got it up to just over 85mph which, at the time, was the fastest I had driven any vehicle.

At the end of my third semester at Stafford, in July 1969, I had a Higher National Diploma in Mechanical Engineering. When I had embarked on the course, three years earlier, it would have given me the academic qualification I needed to become a full Member of the Institution of Mechanical Engineers and hence a Chartered Engineer. However, a debate had been raging over whether Chartered Engineers needed to be graduates or not. It had come down on the side of graduates. Recognising that this put a lot of students, like me, in a difficult position not necessarily of their own making, a solution was devised which entailed us doing a 'top up' course that was recognised by the Institution as taking us to graduate level. I and most of my class opted for this. I was concerned that Bamfords might say they would not pay me for the ten extra months. However, I just told them that I was going to do the extra course and they carried on paying me. Incredibly, no one asked what it was for or why I wanted to do it.

I must finish my account of my time at college by describing a fantastic scam that John and I pulled off. One afternoon, in early 1970, one member of our class, Todd, got very excited because he was thinking of joining the Royal Navy as an Engineer Officer and he had discovered that a team from the RN was coming to the college to sell the idea. He asked John and me if we fancied coming along. We both thought we had better things to do. However, we asked him the following day how it had been. When he said that the Navy were inviting interested students to spend a week with them, we, who were both a bit tight on cash at the time and spotting the opportunity for a free holiday, suddenly became very enthusiastic about the Senior Service. Problem was that Todd only had one blank application form and he had been told that application must be made on the official form. Up to that time, copiers were messy, smudgy things and there is no possibility that one of them would suit our purpose. So, much against Todd's better judgement, I persuaded him to lend me his clean form which I took into the Goods Receiving office at Bamfords, which I happened to know had just been issued with a new Xerox copier at goodness knows what cost. It produced two flawless facsimiles and we were in business.

The week was during the short Easter vacation and started at RN *Manadon* in Plymouth. This establishment, long ago the victim of defence cuts, was the Navy's engineering university and also housed the training establishment for RN stewards and chefs. Now these latter needed victims to practise on and this was the lot of the hapless engineering students. We were happy to step into the breach and afford them some relief. You could soon get used to silver service at every meal, ten different types of marmalade for breakfast (full English, of course) and no fewer than eighteen different types of cheese offered at the end of dinner, along with the third type of wine since you started the meal. This was every day.

The thing that really shocked us, however, was the matter of mess bills. We were invited to dine on board ship with the officers of an RN vessel moored in Devonport Dockyard. Chatting to them over the obligatory drinks before lunch, we found that the Navy charged its officers 3d, or less than one and a half pence, per measure of spirits. Despite this, the average mess bill, we were told, was about £40 per month for booze and tobacco alone. We were just left wondering how on earth naval officers could afford to sustain their habit after they retired. As well as seeing massive amounts of waste, we did have huge fun that week. This included a ride in a Sea King helicopter, standing inside a 14in gun turret when the gun was fired, and driving a 42ft launch down the River Dart and out to sea. All in all, it was the best week's holiday that I had for years.

I did not have much contact with the factory during this last year at Stafford and had plenty of opportunity to think about what I wanted to do next. I decided to see what Bamfords had to offer, but to investigate other options as well. Returning to Bamfords after ten months with very little contact, it was immediately obvious that the company was in trouble. The Works Director, Rayden, had left and been replaced by a rather belligerent individual called Keeling who had come from the English Electric washing machine factory in Liverpool. I sought him out and introduced myself to him. He quite clearly had no idea that I even existed or what qualifications I now had. At no point had anyone at Bamfords, including Edwards, the pythonesque Personnel Manager, taken the slightest interest in what course I was doing at college or how I was getting on. This did not particularly bother me as I knew what I wanted to do and I was determined to do it. It did, however, strike me as strange that they continued to pay me with no objective in sight.

The new man did ask about me and then asked what I was being paid. I told him £850 a year, which was not enough, to which he replied that no one knew anything about me.

'Correction,' I said. 'You don't, but others know a lot about me.'

'Well,' he said. 'What do you want?'

I said that the English Electric lads in my class were getting £1,200 now that they had qualified. That is what I wanted. I was dismissed with a grunt, but a couple of days later, Edwards called me in to say that I would get £1,200.

It was clear that Keeling had been brought in to make substantial (and rather late in the day) changes which were urgently needed. The impatience of youth did not allow me to appreciate that, had I stuck around, he wanted me on his team. In the meantime, I was told to help out the Chief Progress Chaser, Norman Castle-Clark, which was pretty mundane. I had got to know him reasonably well and, after a few days, he said: 'This is a waste of your time. You ought to look for something more challenging if this lot can't see your potential.'

I had already come to the same conclusion and had worked out that there was only really one job that I would want in Bamfords and that was the one my friend Roy Lynch, the Maintenance Manager, had. He had no plans to move and, even if he had, I could not see a career progression that I wanted to follow. I, therefore, started to scan job advertisements as well as writing to companies that I thought I would like to work for. Included in those was British Railways and I wrote to the Chief Mechanical and Electrical Engineer, London Midland Region, at Derby. One or two companies replied. Most did not and I was not called for interview anywhere. At that time, I saw myself as a production engineer: someone who worked out how to make things. Indeed, I was a Student Member of the Institution of Production Engineers. Accordingly, I applied to Birmingham University, which had a very strong reputation in this field, to do a one year Master's in Production Engineering. I was accepted but by then another opportunity had arisen.

At the end of July, I was manning a Festiniog Railway Society stand at a traction engine rally on the Staffordshire County Showground. Part way through the afternoon, my friend Gordon Rushton, who I had first met on the Festiniog Railway five years before, appeared at the stand along with a rather portly chap of about the same age with a mop of pale ginger hair. Gordon, who by then had finished his BR management training, asked what I was doing. I told him and also said that one option I was quite keen on was joining BR. I went on to add that I had written to Derby but was a bit disappointed not to have had a reply. At this, the portly gentleman, burst into life with: 'You don't want to waste your time with those sort of people. You should write to the Chairman.'

This was said in an extremely robust way that brooked no argument. Nevertheless, it seemed like a stupid suggestion to me. How could I write to the Chairman? This was my first introduction to David Sumner. Later, I thought about it and concluded that it could not do any harm and just might work. The following Monday, one of the women in the Production Office at Bamfords typed yet another letter for me, this time to Sir Henry Johnson, Chairman of British Rail. Only a week or so later, I got a reply from a man called Cedric Rose calling me to an interview on 13 August at his office at Melbury Terrace, next to Marylebone Station in London.

Cedric, who had been Assistant Works Manager at Doncaster, now had the job of planning the careers of Chartered Mechanical and Electrical Engineers within BR so that the company got the best out of them. I did not find out until much later that my letter to the Chairman arrived on his desk the same morning that he had one from a graduate who had been offered a place on the Engineering Management Training Scheme but had turned it down in favour of another company. I saw him alone and the interview went OK until I mentioned that I had seen A.E. Robson, the then CM&EE of the London Midland Region, in 1966 and that I had been offered a place on the graduate trainee scheme which I lost because I failed my maths A level. I had not previously mentioned this because I thought it might count against me in some way. How wrong could I be? On hearing this, he got up, went to a filing cabinet and withdrew my 1966 file. I was impressed. After a couple of minutes looking through it, he offered me a job there and then, with no conditions other than passing the medical. The salary would be £1,200, the same as I had just got at Bamfords despite this being a traineeship. Since I had quite a lot of shop floor and other engineering experience by then, he said that the usual two-year training for graduates would be curtailed to one, and I would get my first substantive post in the autumn of 1971.

This would mean that I would be in exactly the same place as if I had passed my A level and had been to Leeds University as I had originally planned. I have often wondered whether it would have been better if I had gone to Leeds, but have concluded that I had such a wonderful, fun and educative time that I do not regret what happened at all.

One of the buses that used to wake us up as newlyweds by idling just below our bedroom window in Uttoxeter was KLB908, Stevenson's 1949 ex-London Transport RTW. Now sixty-eight years old, it belongs to Tim Stubbs who rallies it regularly.

I gave my notice in to Bamfords, saying that my last day would be Friday, 2 October 1970. I spent September writing various reports on things that Keeling needed to know more about. I still have all four of them which look odd today, typed as they are on foolscap paper which, for the benefit of the younger reader, was taller and thinner than the A4 paper we are all used to. They all relate to various aspects of the production process which were clearly inefficient and badly managed. One investigated why there was such an alarmingly high level of warranty returns on the rather primitive single and twin cylinder diesel engines that Bamfords made for the Third World. The answer was relatively simple and had quite a lot to do with employing semi-skilled assembly workers and then assuming that they knew what they were doing without any instruction.

I gave copies of these reports to my BR Training Manager and this had quite significant repercussions, as will be reported in the next chapter. In a sense, they set the scene for the next forty years in that most of my career has been about finding out what customers want, then searching for cheaper and better ways to improve quality and safety. My strongly held belief that you very often can combine cost reduction with higher quality means that I get particularly annoyed by people, often public sector trade unionists, whingeing on about how they need 'more resources'.

I married Diana Crombie, a teacher, the day after leaving Bamfords and, following a honeymoon in Paris, started with British Rail on Monday, 19 October 1970.

Chapter Three

Management training

Monday, 19 October 1970 is a date that I have no difficulty remembering, because British Railways had an obsession about 'seniority' and every form you had to fill in – and there were many – asked for 'date entered service'. On that date, I was told to report to the Training Manager, Terry Kelsall, at Derby Loco Works, which was part of British Rail Engineering. Although I had been taken on as a British Railways Board Engineering Graduate Trainee, we were all actually employed and managed by BREL for the period of our training. As mentioned in the previous chapter, because of my experience at Bamfords it had been decided that I would only do one year rather than the usual two.

My first week in the Loco Works was in the original 1849 roundhouse, then used as the Millwrights' Shop, most of whose work was overhauling steam breakdown cranes of up to 75 ton capacity. This was fairly basic, traditional engineering, much of which was remarkably similar to traction engines with which I had some passing familiarity. It was a good place to learn because there were few spare parts that could be ordered from a catalogue. If you needed it, you probably had to make it or repair it. My Bamfords Toolroom training came in really useful here. However, there was one machine which I had not previously used. It was a 50 ton Massey steam hammer, a smaller version of the huge machines that I had seen forging turbine shafts in Sheffield. I was allowed to have a go. Steam hammers comprise a cylinder with a vertical piston and rod which can be raised and lowered by manipulating the regulator, which is not unlike a steam loco regulator. At the bottom of the piston rod is a striking piece which squeezes the red hot 'job' that is on an anvil. Depending on how you move the regulator, you can bring the striking piece down very gently – I have even seen an egg being held intact – or you can smash it down with immense force and speed. It was a machine you could get to like.

Next stop was the clean room for overhaul and testing of diesel engine fuel injection equipment, the pumps and the injectors that actually put the fuel into the engine. I was only there for a couple of days, but still remember what I was told about 'cleanliness being next to godliness' and what it actually means all these years later. Similarly, a morning spent with a fitter who was one of very few individuals who understood how DMU freewheels worked, because he spent all his time overhauling them, has come in useful.

After that, I spent a few days with a gang who were rebuilding some Class '27' locos in order that they could be used, in push-pull mode, on the Edinburgh–Glasgow service. Here, while helping to refit cylinder heads to a 1250hp Sulzer engine, I learnt about Hylomar, an amazing jointing compound developed by Rolls-Royce that has got me out of engine trouble on rallies in far off places more than once. The Class '27s', incidentally, did not like racing back and forth in Scotland and were retired after only a few years to potter about in the Highlands for the rest of their life. They were replaced by Class '47s' which were rather more successful. Other really interesting places that I visited for a few days each were the Railcar Engine Shop, where hundreds of DMU engines were stripped and rebuilt on a systematic basis each year, and the Loco Test Bay where the main generators of diesel electric locos were coupled to big resistors so the engine could be run up to full power while the loco was stationary.

While under training, I was, quite rightly, asked to produce a series of reports describing my impressions and opinions. I quote here a brief extract of the one I wrote in December 1970:

'A fairly well laid out works bearing in mind the existing buildings and the wide variety of work carried out. A very high standard of housekeeping and cleanliness is maintained throughout the works which is well lighted and heated. Most men are more interested in their jobs than I have found elsewhere and are more concerned about the fortunes of their employer. This appears to stem from the phenomenon of being "A Railwayman". There is an unusually high proportion of skilled men employed. I wonder whether the use of a skilled man is really called for in some of the more routine and simple jobs. A much more marked demarcation between trades exists than I had seen before. Presumably this is partly due to union pressures, but I think that this is something which will become less apparent in the future.'

My training programme was soon interrupted by a most interesting assignment. George Oldham, Works Manager at Crewe, had put in a request to spend £15 million on replacing most of the overhead cranes in his works. In 1970, that was an enormous sum and the request caused an explosion at BREL HQ at the Railway Technical Centre in Derby. The senior manager responsible for such things was a former Western man, S.A.S. Smith, known to all as 'SAS', who had been Works Manager at Swindon. Amid expletives, he had apparently told his people to get hold of a graduate and tell him to demolish the case.

John Forster, who was my rather buttoned-up young training manager, had read the reports that I did for Keeling at Bamfords; hence, about six weeks after starting at Derby Loco, I was called 'down the road' to be briefed by a cheerful, chubby, ex-Doncaster man called Stan Holliday and a lugubrious sparrow-like man from Derby called George Fletcher. Stan was a plant engineer while George was a work study expert, cynical and taciturn, who explained that I should do activity sampling in each shop to determine the frequency of use of each existing crane, while simultaneously assessing the most efficient type to replace it.

I therefore spent the next two months in Crewe Works, a couple of weeks or so in each shop. George started me off by introducing me to the foremen in one of the machine shops so that I could use their office as a *pied-à-terre,* before taking me to the shop representative to explain why I was there. In each shop, after an initial exploration to understand what they did and why, my routine was to walk the length of it, with clipboard, at intervals dictated by a table of random numbers that George had given me. I recorded what lifting activity was taking place. As can be imagined, this gave rise to a great deal of suspicion as to what an earth I was up to, suspicion that was shared by just about everyone from the Works Manager to the shop floor. It was excellent training in human relations and, also, a very good way to study everything that went on in the works. The larger gaps in the random numbers could leave me without any observations to make for up to ten or twelve minutes; thus in the course of a few days, I could spend a bit of time understanding the many interesting processes in a large works that overhauled all parts of many different types of diesel and electric locos.

The cranes were interesting in themselves; the oldest dated from the 1880s and were real museum-pieces with their open commutator DC motors and heavy wrought iron chains. However, they were extremely slow and very noisy because of all their straight cut gears. One 5 ton crane in the foundry dated from 1906 despite being very fast and quite modern in appearance. I suspected that it was being overloaded and thus arranged, when no one was around, to have a crane weigher (like a big spring balance) inserted between the hook and the load. It revealed that it was indeed overloaded, by 100%, and from what the Shop Superintendent could discover, had routinely been so for most of its life.

My report, after discussion with Stan Holliday, George Fletcher and the various Shop Superintendents at Crewe, recommended that rather than £15 million, there should be an investment of about £2.5 million. This would actually achieve a rather better result than the larger scheme promised. My report was adopted in full and implemented over the next two years.

Having learnt a little about locomotives, the next phase was to find out how they were operated and, hence, all M&EE graduate trainees were assigned to traction inspectors for two weeks. I was sent to Crewe and told to report at 08.00 one morning to Chief Inspector Capstick, whose office was on Platform 5. Ron Capstick turned out to be an immaculately dressed, very severe looking little man with a toothbrush moustache and a bowler hat. Like all loco inspectors at that time, he had worked his way up from engine cleaner (with the LNWR in his case) to fireman to driver before being an inspector for some years prior to reaching the pinnacle of his career as The Chief. In fact, he was very friendly, in a rather harsh 'Crewe' sort of way.

He asked what I wanted to get out of the two weeks and, when I told him that I wanted to experience as many types of train as possible and to understand locos and train working from a driver's point of view, he arranged for me to have a very full fortnight with his inspectors. They were from a variety of backgrounds: there was Jack Jones, a Great Western man from Shrewsbury who had his leg pulled because 'those bloody Western engines have got so many corks on the motion that they would float if they fell in the canal.' (Drivers would have to undo every cork in order to oil the engine when they were preparing it.) There was another inspector who had just been promoted from being a driver on Merseyrail… 'Bloody tram driver'.

I had the first of a great many cab rides on a Class '86' electric to Euston and back. Very exciting, fast, tremendous acceleration and the worst, most violent, ride that I have ever experienced before or since. They were so bad that, sitting in the secondman's seat, you had to wedge your knees tightly into the kneehole in front of you just to stay in the seat. Holding on to the arm rests was not sufficient. A few years later the class of 100 locos were all either fitted with much modified suspension or had their maximum permitted speed reduced from 100mph to 80mph.

Slightly tongue in cheek, I had asked if it might be possible to ride in the cab of a Class '52' a which, even then, was under threat of withdrawal. Jack Jones, being a Western man, jumped at the chance and took me via Birmingham New Street, where we joined a Class '45' hauled passenger train bound for Plymouth, which enabled me to see the 1 in 37 Lickey Incline from the cab for the first time. Throughout these accompanied cab rides, both the inspector and, usually, the driver would regale me with tales from the past. They told me about running away down the Lickey with a freight train because the guard had not pinned down enough brakes on an unfitted freight. It was the more frightening for being told as we descended the incline at 50mph. Funny how in all the hundreds of tales of near mishaps that drivers have told me over the years, it was never the fault of the driver! Guards often, signalmen sometimes, firemen occasionally, but never the driver.

On arrival at Bristol Temple Meads, Jack, who revealed that he hadn't bothered to get permission from the Western Region, went straight to the driver of a Paddington train headed by a Class '52' and said briskly: 'Crewe Loco Inspector. I've got a trainee who wants to see a proper engine!'

That did the trick and we were invited on. It took about thirty seconds for the driver to discover that he had a fellow Great Western man with him and they never stopped talking all the way to Paddington. As a boy, I had always rather liked the Western Region diesel hydraulics and here I was, in the cab of the most powerful type on Brunel's masterpiece of a main line. That being so, there was no opportunity to see how the 2,700hp loco tackled hills, but its low speed acceleration away from stops was impressive. However, because of its power it could only exert its maximum tractive effort up to about 17 or 18mph whereas the Class '86' that I had just been introduced to could sustain its, albeit slightly lower, maximum TE up to an astonishing 64mph, hence the extremely impressive acceleration of the AC loco.

The other notable feature of the journey was the Great Western Automatic Train Control (ATC) which was then still installed on all Western main lines. Unlike the BR system, which is still in universal use, the GW system relied on physical contact between the loco and a steel ramp fitted in the 'four foot'. Contact with no current in the ramp meant no green signal ahead, so a horn sounded suggesting a brake application be considered. If the driver did not acknowledge it, the brakes came on automatically. Contact with an electrical current present meant a green signal ahead and a strident bell sounded the all clear. By 1971, many locos that operated across regional boundaries were fitted with both GWR and BR systems. Both provided the driver with the same information, but the older GWR system had various disadvantages: for example, it was on its limit at 100mph and would not have coped with today's higher speeds. On arrival at Paddington, we made our way to Euston and returned on another electric loco.

This fortnight served as an excellent introduction to my railway career and confirmed my view that I wanted to be at or near the actual operations, as opposed to working in an engineering factory which is what Crewe and other loco works were. I have been very fortunate, with only minor exceptions, to have had a cab pass for the following forty-one years. At various times these gave me the freedom of the London Midland, Eastern and Southern Regions, as well as, for a few years, the whole of BR. This has enabled me to understand train operation from first hand experience and, equally important, to understand the thoughts and motivations of train drivers. Almost all of my cab rides have been on passenger trains of various sorts and I have only once, out of thousands of times, been refused entry to the cab. That was in Carlisle when my DMU home to Riding Mill had failed and was being hauled by a locomotive. When I politely asked the driver if I could come with him, he snorted that I could not. However, he had a secondman who immediately chipped in: 'What's wrong with you, you miserable old bugger? Let the man come with us.'

So I did. Of course I did not know what else was going on in his life, but he was probably on a spare turn and hopeful of being sent home after a couple of hours, which would have been common in those days. Instead, he had to go and prepare an engine, take it to the station and haul the DMU to Newcastle before coming back light engine. All of which would have taken at least five hours and possibly much more. To make matters worse, he was driving a Class '25' which was a noisy, hard riding, unpleasant loco to be in.

It was always the practice in steam days for motive power bosses to take a turn driving so that they understood the issues that faced drivers. I continued this practice and have driven several thousand miles over the years, always under the supervision of a qualified driver or inspector. I drove Class '45s' (lovely smooth riding engines with a huge tractive effort) and '50s' before coming to Chiltern and then regularly drove Class '165' and '168' DMUs over many years. Occasionally, I 'had a go', as drivers call it, on Chiltern's heritage DMUs and latterly I drove Class '67s' and the associated DVTs. I am delighted to be able to report that I never had an operating irregularity of any sort and that the worst thing I did was once stop a train unnecessarily at low speed because I failed to acknowledge the AWS quickly enough. There is no doubt that the experience gained has helped considerably when making policy and management decisions relating to trains, safety systems and drivers. It also is respected by the drivers themselves. It soon gets around that The Boss likes to have a go, and it is appreciated.

Next stop on my training programme was the London Midland Region Chief Mechanical & Electrical Engineers (CM&EE) office. The department was located in a large brick built office constructed in 1840 for the Midland Counties Railway and subsequently used

Forty years later, I am still benefitting from my two weeks with the Crewe Traction Inspectors. Here I am driving a Class 67 on a Willesden TMD to Banbury ECS working for Chiltern Railways and I am braking, with my left hand, as we approach Rugby on the down Northampton Loop.

by the Midland Railway and the LMS. The chief, Ken Taylor, was an approachable chap who had started in Gorton Works, Manchester, and worked on the 1,500v MSW electrification before being a leading light in the 1950s and 1960s LM electrification. As CM&EE he was responsible for the technical standards applicable to all maintenance and overhaul of locos, carriages, wagons, plant and electrification systems on the Region, although the actual execution of that maintenance was the responsibility, at that time, of Divisional Managers who also employed Operations staff including drivers and signalmen. There were more than 600 staff in the department and I was to gain an insight into their responsibilities in six weeks.

First port of call was the electrification new works section which struck me as being well run and focussed on the task in hand which, at that time, was the design of what was then called the 'Midland Suburban Electrification'. It is nowadays part of Thameslink, and I remember spending a morning with an engineer who explained the challenges of installing 25kv on the section of line almost under St Pancras where it passes beneath the Fleet Sewer. Because the vertical clearance was so tight, the trains would have to have lower than standard pantograph wells. In addition, because the tunnels were narrower than usual, the coach body ends would have to be tapered somewhat. Even so, the clearance would be so tight that the track would have to be encased in concrete to hold it precisely in place. Of course this information, obtained almost by chance, came in very useful some years later when I was in charge of the Bedford to St Pancras line in the very early days of the new electrified service.

In complete contrast to this well run team was the DMU section which seemed to me to be a complete waste of time in that I could not see how they added any value to the people who had to maintain DMUs. When, later on, I ran a DMU maintenance depot, I was able to confirm that my diagnosis was correct. The section was headed by a miserable bloke who, it transpired, had for years falsified the reliability figures for the LM Region's DMUs. He kept the so-called (because there was no rigorous system of reporting in those days) correct figures locked in the top drawer of his desk. At each inter-Regional DMU engineers' meeting, he reported his made-up figures to the BRB representative for inclusion in the board's statistics. Shocking though this was, it was consistent with the lackadaisical culture that existed in much of BR in those days after twenty-two years of failed leadership and bad management following nationalisation.

There were some highspots, however, after Beeching's excellent report published seven years earlier. People vilify Lord Beeching quite unjustly. Now while the motives and scruples of the minister, Ernest Marples, who appointed him, may be questioned, I believe Beeching did a thoroughly competent, indeed inspirational job which is why I decided in 1963 that I wanted to join BR. He has been unjustly criticised for closing branch lines unnecessarily, most of which carried very, very few passengers and handled freight expensively and inefficiently. OK, he got one or two wrong and closed a couple of lines that should have been developed, but for the most part he was right. What inspired me was the identification of those parts of the business that could have a future if developed and invested in. For example, London commuting, InterCity express, efficient freight handling and transit as exemplified by Freightliner and 'merry go round' trains. I was to be much caught up in this excitement in due course.

I was then sent to the Loco Records and Shopping Bureau. This took up the whole of the top floor and presented a scene which today's youngsters would find absolutely inconceivable. It is not true to say that were in a totally pre-computer age because our payslips were computer generated and came, in bulk, from the bureau at Crewe. However, the office would have been instantly recognisable to a time traveller from the LMS office in 1930… indeed, quite a few of the staff would have been the same. The big boxes of LMS-style individual loco record cards were the same. The cards were the same as the ones the LMS Executive Reorganisation Office (ERO) had designed in 1929. Indeed, many of the forms used throughout the department were still LMS ones, sometimes with a BR heading, but the clue was the ERO number at the bottom in small print. In this office, which had a constant buzz of activity, paper and telex records were received in huge volume. They came from dozens of maintenance depots, fuel points and holding sidings all over the Region. Any time anything was done to a London Midland loco, or there was any report about it, the office would be told. LM HQ Control at Crewe would be in constant touch, as would the nine Divisional Controls. HQ Control would allocate locos to main line trains, passenger or freight, while Divisional Controls would allocate to shunting and local trip working. They would all provide details of the mileage worked daily by each loco. The Regional Control offices at Paddington, York, Waterloo or Glasgow would report anything happening to LM locos at their 'foreign' locations.

The reason this avalanche of information (some of which arrived many days in arrears) was needed was so that the office could calculate the mileage of each loco and programme it for maintenance or 'shopping', which was the term used when an engine went to main works. There were also some subsidiary activities such as receiving, collating and passing on to the relevant engineer, reports of various experimental and trial pieces of equipment.

Another vital task was keeping track of certain safety-critical items, especially wheels and axles. Axles often last forty or more years and it is important to keep track of them individually the whole time in case a defect is discovered in one made from the same batch of steel. Nowadays, this is very easy using computers, but think of the work involved in manual record keeping when each axle could well be fitted to thirty different locos in its lifetime at any one of forty or more places. The activities of the office are all still carried out, but have for many years been done by computer systems into which data is entered at the point of work – the depot or works that carries out maintenance or repair. Likewise, mileages are all calculated automatically when a loco number is linked to a particular diagram. There are, of course, checks to ensure that data being input makes sense.

At this time, all the other Regions allocated their locomotives to individual depots. The theory was that this enabled accountability to be pinned on the depot manager to ensure that his fleet performed as it should. Detractors alleged that the result was more unproductive mileage as there was a tendency for a third party depot, when in receipt of someone else's defective engine, to simply ship it back home for repair, even if home was hundreds of miles away. The LM did not allocate diesel locos to depots, taking the view that it was much more efficient for Control to allocate them to the most convenient depot at any given time. This could result in a loco receiving attention for example at Holyhead, followed by Bletchley, followed by Wigan Springs Branch all in the space of a few days. Having worked both systems, my view is that the pros and cons of each roughly balanced each other out. Having said that, the LMR electric traction people would have none of this common user nonsense and firmly allocated their locos to depots: for example, Class '85s' to Longsight and Class '86s' to Willesden.

After a few more weeks, I was to start my Divisional training and was told to turn up at Furlong House, the HQ of Nottingham Division, and report to Allan Parker, the Divisional Maintenance Engineer. He was responsible, to the DM, for all CM&EE maintenance activities, locos, carriages, wagons and plant in an area bounded roughly by Leicester, Nottingham, Burton on Trent and Westhouses. He gave me a couple of pieces of advice which I have always remembered and tried to follow. Furthermore, I have passed them on to many others. They were: 'Always remember the Foot of the Farmer and the Fish's Head.' In clarification, he explained that the farmer always walks around his farm, frequently, to check what is going on and that anything improper smells – like the fish's head. Very sound advice.

I was then sent, for a couple of months to Etches Park Depot in Derby, which comprised a DMU maintenance shed with an allocation of thirty three-car units and what the LMR called a Fuel and Inspection (F&I) depot which would do fuelling, 'A' exams and minor repairs to any loco sent there by Regional HQ Control. In practice these were mostly Class '25', '31', '45' and '47'. Etches Park was part of the empire of the Assistant Area Manager (Maintenance), Denis Waters. He had a Chief Foreman, Millington, who concentrated on Etches Park. I was put with one of the shift foremen, Brian Gratwich, who was quite happy to explain to me how the place worked and delegated one or two simple tasks to me. After a week or so, he suggested that I might want to talk to his colleague who worked regular afternoons (14.00 to 22.00), explaining that I might find it more rewarding to be on his shift. This colleague, who I will call Frank, to preserve his anonymity, was a very pleasant youngish man who I liked immediately. On the first day, just after 16.00 when 'the hierarchy' – Waters and Millington – left, always on the dot, it became apparent what the plot was. Frank had a mistress who lived a few hundred yards away and, after discussing me with Brian, had decided that, after a little training, he could entrust the running of his shift to me while he attended to her. Thus, what you might describe as a win, win, win situation obtained for several weeks. I thoroughly enjoyed the learning experience. The shift fitters were all very helpful and quite accepting of their temporary boss. Indeed, if they perceived that I was missing a trick, most of them would politely tell me so. They were very happy, also, to explain how DMUs worked and what you needed to watch out for.

I also had nothing but co-operation from the fitters at the F&I which was known as '4 Shed'. This was in contrast to some of the drivers. We had, on each shift what was known as 'a set of men' allocated by the local traincrew supervisor. Nowadays, you would just have a driver, but in those days you would need driver and secondman for the duties, which were shunting engines from one place to another. This was just one example of the inefficiencies that abounded in those days.

One afternoon, the 4 Shed fitter called to say that he had a Class '20' (which was unusual) that needed to come to the main shed half a mile away for brake blocking. Soon afterwards, I saw the afternoon set of men who had just graced us with their presence. I explained that I needed this '20' on No. 3 road in the shed and could they please go and fetch it. 'No,' they replied. 'We don't sign "20s".' Actually, this may have been true because the locos were based at Toton and used exclusively on freight trains which Derby drivers hardly drove. However, this was clearly a try-on, a test of my mettle. Quick as a flash, I retorted: 'OK, take that shunter (Class '08') and haul it up here with that.' I immediately resumed writing the note that was on my desk, but was able, with some satisfaction, to observe the crestfallen look on the drivers' faces. Twenty minutes later, I heard the unmistakeable whistle of the Napier turbochargers on an English Electric engine as the '20' passed my window. I had no more trouble with drivers.

I thoroughly enjoyed my time at Etches Park and learnt a lot. Unfortunately, much of what I learnt was of the 'this is how not to do it' variety. The management of the place by the 'hierarchy' was of a very poor standard. My report speaks of lack of forward planning, lack of discipline, excessive demarcation, material shortages and almost complete absence of proper communication between management and shop floor.

One feature which was common to much of the railway in those days was the nonsense of Carriage and Wagon (C&W) involvement in DMUs. This ridiculous arrangement meant that the engines, gearboxes, radiators, driver's controls and all the electrical equipment were looked after by fitters. The brakes, bogies and suspension were the responsibility of C&W examiners despite the fact that the fitters looked after locos in their entirety. Lest it be thought that this inefficient demarcation, which wasted a lot of time, was the result of trade union restrictive practices, I can assure the reader that this was not the case. That it resulted from supine management is amply demonstrated by the fact that the Electric Traction boys had this all sorted out, and EMUs on the LM were totally the domain of fitters trained to look after both mechanical and electrical equipment.

After Etches Park, I was sent on the first of many BR training courses. This one was specifically for trainees, like me, who were about to be launched into a career in locomotive engineering. As with almost all the BR courses that I benefitted from, it was very well designed and delivered by people who really understood their subject and explained it with knowledge and enthusiasm. In part, I think this was because they were mostly seconded from a supervisory or junior management course and they relished the opportunity to refresh and enhance their expertise and share it with people eager to learn.

I met, for the first time, the other men who were part of my intake and I have maintained contact with many of them ever since. They included John Harden, who was to find himself as my deputy before long; Ian Souter who long ago returned to his native Scotland; Nigel Tilley who spent much of his career at York and retired from there; and Frank Waterland who became BR's expert on the abstruse subject of current leakage when AC and DC traction current systems meet, as at Farringdon, and came with me many times to the Festiniog Railway. John Winter was with BREL and its successors for many years, helping build the first train Chiltern Railways ordered after privatisation. Barry Gardner was a manager at Cricklewood when I was the Area Manager there and John Savage retired from Thames Trains at Reading Depot where he had given a lot of technical help to us at Chiltern with our Class '165' DMUs and whom I met at the Warley Model Railway Exhibition the day before I wrote this.

We spent two weeks being given a very thorough grounding in the theory and practice of diesel locos, electric locos and DMUs. We learnt about: traction motors, field diverts, load regulators, wheel slip relays, lead acid and Nicad batteries, wet liners, indicated horsepower, fuel injectors, overspeed trips, fluid couplings, triple valves, direct admission valves, rolling ring vacuum cylinders and 100 other things.

As we were led through each topic with a series of lectures, tests and practical demonstrations, we built up a picture of why things had been done a certain way, and also discussed many of the developments that would be needed to introduce better, faster, more reliable trains. There was an inbuilt sense of continuous improvement, not as a 'bolt on' but just as part of the normal course of business. We were given, and encouraged to annotate, very comprehensive course notes which I still have and have found most useful to refer to over the years.

Shortly after this, I was sent on a Junior Management Course along with thirty other young engineers. I noticed, for the first time, that civil engineers seemed to think they were a cut above mere shop floor workers. It was very evident in those days that there was an 'officer class' and there were 'men' in a rather military way. Also, there did not seem to be the tradition that I was used to of practical training for Chartered Engineers. As a Mechanical Engineering Manager, I would expect to be able to do pretty well any task that my chaps could do, with the exception of very specialised things. This has stood me in very good stead throughout my career. As for S&T Engineers, I have always thought they are a rum lot. Much of the course was a repeat of management topics covered at college, but there were useful, very practical, exercises in the application of such things as the disciplinary process.

Very soon after, in August 1971, I was told to go for interview for a job on the Locomotive section in the CM&EE office at Derby. At the appointed hour, I met with another trainee, Mike Corbett, who was in for the same job. I was delighted to find out an hour or so later that I had got it.

My first proper job was as Senior Technical Officer, Class '50s', on the English Electric Loco section. Yippee! What could be better? I was to be the (so called) 'expert' on BR's newest class of loco, which bristled with all kinds of new technology and was very much the centre of attention because they were being used to haul crack expresses on the demanding section of the West Coast Main Line north of Crewe. I took over from Simon Fountain who had been promoted to a contractual role which involved managing the leasing agreement between BR and English Electric. (The locos had been leased by BR which thought it a wizard wheeze to avoid the government cash restrictions that were imposed on all nationalised industries. Surprisingly, the Treasury failed to notice this substantial contract for fifty locos ordered in 1966. It was not until 1972 that they pronounced it a scam, which it undoubtedly was, and forced BR to buy them, thus heavily restricting other expenditure that year.)

My boss was a splendid man called Peter Meredith, almost all of whose career had been involved with diesel locos. He had started as an apprentice in Derby Loco Works in 1932 and had seen LMS No. 1831 being converted from steam to diesel, and, as a fitter, had then been involved in building LMS/English Electric shunters in the late 1930s. By the time No. 10000, the first LMS main line diesel loco, was being built in 1947, Peter was a Diesel Inspector and was very much involved in building it and its sister No. 10001. It did not take much to encourage

Peter to talk about the past. He was full of stories about his early exploits and was very proud of his involvement with these two engines. He described the race that was on to finish 10000 before the LMS would cease to exist at the end of 1947. This was achieved with a slim margin of about two weeks. He had many tales of riding one or other of the 'Twins' over the next few years, including how it was impossible to light the Clarkson train heat boilers without singeing your eyebrows. He also helped out on the Southern diesels, 10201, 10202 and 10203, which used the same English Electric 16 SVT engine as the 'Twins,' but had the ponderous plate frame bogie later used on Class '40', '44', '45' and '46'. As I mentioned earlier, this bogie gives a lovely smooth, steady ride but, unfortunately, it does not like going around corners. The result was that all the locos fitted with them had multiple cracks repaired, many had new bogie side frames fitted at great cost and many of the locos were ultimately withdrawn because the bogie cracks were so extensive that CM&EEs dared not run them any further. 10203, which had its engine uprated to 2,000hp, was effectively the prototype for the Class '40' fleet which appeared from 1958.

Meanwhile, the 'Twins' carried on with very little trouble through the 1950s only to be scrapped in an act of vandalism in 1966. Peter was very bitter about this. On very special days, with tears welling in his eyes, he would produce from the cupboard behind his desk the cast aluminium numbers from one end of his old friend 10000. I can see them now. They were tied together with some very hairy white string and were a pathetic memento of an historic loco.

My first boss, Peter Meredith (sitting) and colleague Alan Speed. The cupboard containing 10,000s cast aluminium numerals tied together with hairy white string is behind.

MANAGEMENT TRAINING • 75

The younger of the two twins, 10001, at the end of its short life in November 1965 with a wiring train just outside Willesden shed, which had closed to steam a couple of months earlier.

My boss Peter, in the driver's seat of 'The Fell', as it was always called, with the inventor, Col Fell.

Peter had also spent quite a lot of time with Lieutenant Colonel Fell on the loco that bore his name. This was an unusual diesel mechanical machine which was the result of an approach by Davey Paxman and Col. Fell to the LMS CM&EE, H.G. Ivatt. The deal was actually done after nationalisation, and a joint venture involving BR, Paxman, Shell and Ricardo was formed. The loco, a 2,000hp 2-D-2, emerged from Derby Loco Works in 1952. It had four 500hp Paxman main engines and two 150hp AEC auxiliary engines. The drive was combined in a large central gearbox which drove a jackshaft which, in turn, drove the four coupled driving wheelsets. I saw this gearbox on the works scrapheap when I visited Derby in 1966. Somewhat surprisingly, it apparently all worked quite well, although Peter said it was excessively noisy. He accompanied it on expresses to London and Manchester for about a year.

Peter's boss was the softly spoken and gentlemanly Cec Hughes, who was in charge of all the Diesel Loco sections and had come as a draughtsman from Crewe Works to the Loco Drawing Office in Derby in 1950. As recently as 2013, Cec told me that the reason for his transfer had been that the Derby office had been instructed by Ivatt to design a fleet of locos based on 10000 and 10001. Ivatt retired in 1951 and Riddles, a former LMS man, by then at the British Transport Commission, foolishly convinced them that he should introduce a range of new steam locos, many of which were scrapped when less than five years old. Cec then found himself relegated to drawing tender details for standard steam locos until the job of designing Classes '24' and '44' came along in 1955.

My desk was next to that of Roger Paulson, who at about twenty-seven, was the next youngest on the English Electric Loco section. His arrival only predated mine by a couple of months and he had been an Electrical Inspector in the Loco Works, latterly in charge of the Load Bank which was the place where diesel electric locos could be load tested by connecting their main generators to fixed resistors in the test house. By this means, the engine could be run at any power setting up to the maximum while its energy went into a huge electric fire. It is a good means of testing that an overhauled engine is working correctly although, of course, it does not test the traction motors. Roger, having served an electrical apprenticeship, was really helpful and taught me a lot about the whole subject which I had missed out on at Bamfords.

Alan Chamberlain was in his fifties and was a softly spoken native of the North East who had for many years been an English Electric employee in its Traction Outdoor department, which meant that he worked with customers to commission new locos and multiple units and attend to warranty problems. He was tireless in his help and advice to a very green aspiring locomotive engineer. Like Peter, he was full of anecdotes; for example, one which comes to mind occurred when, in 1950, he was commissioning some new EE 0-6-0 diesel electric shunters, very similar to the LMS/BR ones we had. They had been bought by ICI for its site at Billingham on Teeside and Alan was making a minor adjustment to one when he noticed an ex-LNER 2-8-0 steam loco struggling to pull its train into the ICI yard. It was a cold, misty, day and the rail was quite slippery. To make matters worse, there was a short, sharp gradient at the entrance to the yard and the steam engine just kept on slipping to a stand with its train only half in and with the rear blocking the main line. Alan asked the ICI driver if he would like to show off what his brand new engine could do. Getting the nod, he crossed over to speak to the BR driver and ask if he wanted any help (which he obviously needed).

'That bloody little thing won't be no use,' was the reply.

'Suit yourself,' said Alan, who continued his tinkering.

After a great many more revolutions of the 2-8-0's wheels, without any discernible forward progress, the driver conceded: 'It won't do no good, but I suppose you could try helping.'

As the shunting loco was hooked on, Alan rubbed salt in by suggesting that the steam loco driver just relax and let the small engine do all the work. He took over from the ICI driver, operated the sanders and very gently eased the train right into the yard without a trace of a slip. It proved the benefit of being able to deliver power smoothly in a controlled way rather than in violent fits and starts, as would be the case with a two cylinder steam engine, possibly with a stiff regulator, and a heavy handed driver.

Other members of Peter's section were not so industrious as Roger and Alan. Indeed, I only rarely saw one of them do any work of benefit to the company.

My job was all to do with the fifty Class '50s' which were built by English Electric in 1968/69 and based on its speculative 2,700hp diesel electric, DP2, made in 1962. This loco had used the same body and bogies as the 'Deltics' but instead of having two high speed and very expensive engines, it had a developed version of the sixteen cylinder engine fitted to 10000/10001 and the Class '40s'. Initially it had contemporary electro-mechanical control equipment, but in 1965 it had been fitted with electronic traction control, possibly the first such application, which enabled it to match the acceleration of the 'Deltics', despite their higher power, because the electronic control enabled it to detect when wheel slip was just starting and to adjust the power very quickly so as to make the best of whatever adhesion was available. All new locos and multiple units have had this feature for many years, but it was revolutionary at the time. By the end of 1965, BRB had decided to order fifty locomotives 'similar to DP2'.

I have before me, as I write, a schedule which lists sixty-three items that the LM Region wanted changed on these new locos. Interestingly, they are almost all mechanical and include such things as a stronger crankshaft, better access for maintenance and slack adjusters for brakes. Given the author of the accompanying letter, I am not surprised at the lack of electrical comments, but it is very striking that there is no mention of any of the novel features that the production locos actually had. Electronic traction control has already been mentioned, but others included rheostatic brakes (to extend the life of brake blocks), electronic speed control (effectively cruise control) and an ingenious labyrinth system which was intended to filter the air which entered the engine room and hence the engine via the turbochargers. The majority of items listed were not acted upon.

One serious mistake was not to accept the suggestion that the four turbochargers should be fed with oil from the engine sump rather than have their own very small private reservoir. Later, I designed a modification that did, indeed, see engine oil being fed into the turbos. This was necessary because the very small quantity of oil, especially at the hot (exhaust) end of the turbo, soon overheated and carbonised to a treacle like substance. When you have the rotor running at 20,000rpm, the bearings need nice warm, runny, oil and not some glutinous carbonised treacle. The engine was the ideal source for this oil since the sump contained some 200 gallons of it, all warm rather than hot. Having designed the mod, I went to Crewe Diesel Depot and converted the first loco myself in a couple of days. All the others were done, which resulted in the turbos lasting four times as long and avoiding many very expensive repairs that resulted from the bearings failing and allowing the turbo blades, which are like small jet engine fans, to rub on the casing with noisy and very expensive results.

By now, Ken Taylor had moved upwards to be CM&EE of the British Railways Board and his place as 'The Chief', the CM&EE, had been taken by Freddie Clements, who I was to get to know later. Our boss was the Locomotive Engineer, R.T. (Dick) Ribbons, a rather cerebral and slightly ponderous electrical engineer who had joined BR a few years previously from the Steel Company of Wales where he had been in charge of its fleet of 1949 Alco diesel electric locos at its Port Talbot plant. Quite a number of engineers with diesel experience were brought in by BR in the 1960s. Doug Power, an ebullient Irishman, came from Irish Rail (CIE) and was CM&EE of the Western and then LM Regions. Geoff Passey had been a service engineer with AEC, looking after DMU engines. He retired as CM&EE of the Scottish Region.

I got to see a lot of Dick Ribbons because one of my main jobs was to be secretary of the Class '50' Service Problems Committee, which was chaired by Dick and included fairly senior people from English Electric, BRB CM&EE, Crewe Works and Stoke Division. Since the locos were used on the high profile West Coast line, there was a considerable urgency to lift the performance which, at the time, was unimpressive. My role was really to act as a project manager for Dick and to chivvy everyone until their actions were completed. Much of my time was spent riding on locos to monitor performance and look out for problems. (I rode in the cab and in the engine room of all fifty locos in the course of a year.) Visits to Crewe Diesel Depot where most of the maintenance was done, Crewe Works which overhauled them, and BRB Design office in Derby were all part of my regular routine.

Crewe Diesel Depot always had an air of rushing from one calamity to the next. It was presided over by the urbane and taciturn Doug Fisher who somehow never seemed to be connected to the action. Much more down to earth was the Chief Foreman Bobby Capewell, who was a wild looking individual with straggly hair that had once been red. No matter what, he actually made things happen and was very helpful to the young engineer who, at first, did not know the first thing about the locos. It never seemed that there was enough time to deal with all the locos that appeared on the depot with the result that maintenance was often skimped or not done at all. This, in turn, was one of the main reasons why these engines were very unreliable. Conditions on the depot were inexcusable, as I described in a memo that I wrote in December 1972:

'Yesterday I went to Crewe TMD to help fit experimental equipment to 426. About 70% of the time was taken up in obtaining tools as follows:
1. Electric drill (no chuck key available).
2. Extension cable could not be found. Had to make one up.
3. No working socket outlet found.
4. Air drill. No flexible hose, had to find one in a pile of rubbish.
5. Pedestal drilling machine could not be used because its chuck had been broken.

All this is typical of many visits to Crewe....'

One of the many occasions when I took a Class 50 for a test run to check on its operation. No. 409 in a snow storm at Whitchurch (Salop) 1972.

As you might imagine, visits to Crewe were quite character forming.

One of the many people I got to know was Stoke Division's Alan Baker, who was the same grade (Senior Technical Officer) as me. He was also about the same age, but had started, aged fifteen, as a craft apprentice in 1962 and had, therefore, had five years' experience of steam engines at Crewe. 'Another bloody graduate,' was Alan's opening gambit when we first met. We got on better over the years and in the early 1980s, when he was Depot Manager at Eastleigh, I sponsored him for Membership of the IMechE. He retired as Engineering Director of Angel Trains, one of the rolling stock leasing companies set up at privatisation of BR. He has written several books, including a definitive history of loco builder Bagnalls of Stafford, and countless magazine articles in the railway press.

Things that were commonplace then must seem strange to young people today. For example, although we had dialling phones, they were on an internal BR system with very limited numbers of lines. Local calls in Derby were okay, but there were only a few lines to Crewe and often you could not get through all morning. Forget about trying to call anyone on another Region. It just was not going to happen. If your call was really important, the boss might tell you to use 'The National'. As an example of how out of date the railway could be, The National Telephone Co had ceased to exist in 1911 when the Postmaster General had declined to renew its operating licence. Mind you, using the GPO Telephone System, to give it its proper name, did not guarantee success. You had to speak to the operator and might or might not get connected within the hour.

Many letters were handwritten. This was because, unless you were one of the chiefs, you sent your handwritten letters to the typing pool. Two to three weeks was the average lead time for a letter which, if it contained any technical words (which ours nearly always did), would be full of gaps and typos. You became quite adept at correcting them manually.

Socially, life was good in Room 9 and the adjacent offices. There were lots of youngish engineers who enjoyed their jobs and mostly got on well and spent some time outside work together. It was noticeable, however, that there was a kind of parallel universe in that there were some other people in the office, collectively referred to as 'the clerks', most of whom seemed to take no interest in their jobs, which we tended to think was to their disadvantage. Several times, I observed colleagues explaining a bit about the reason for a task that a clerk had just been given only to be met with a blank lack of interest. On the English Electric Loco section, our clerk was a young tearaway called Malcolm Spiller, who I was surprised to come across twenty years later when he was quite a senior BR accountant.

One lunchtime, one of my friends came tearing into the office. 'Come and see what the clerks have done.' Two or three of us followed him down to the dustbins outside the office which were stuffed full of LMS files, all kinds of things which should have gone to the National Archive or the National Railway Museum. Between us, we salvaged a few. I got one about all the early trials of diesel shunters from 1932 onwards and another which contained a copiously illustrated report by Ron Jarvis of his visit just after the end of the war to inspect dozens of '8Fs' abandoned all over the Middle East which the War Office had offered for sale. I arranged safe keeping of both these files and have had their contents published.

Ron Jarvis was an LMS engineer. In 1938 he was responsible for test running the three-car prototype DMU on the Oxford–Cambridge line. The tests were successful and if the war had not intervened, it is likely that a fleet would have been built. Peter Meredith told me how, at the beginning of the war when Derby Loco Works was being cleared, at great speed, for the repair of damaged aircraft, two spare unused engines for this train were about to be scrapped. He had them covered in a tarpaulin and put into an inspection pit which was concreted over. At the end of the war he identified the location and had them recovered and used on the train, two cars of which were fitted with flat roofs and made into the overhead line maintenance train for the MSJ&A, the 1,500 volt DC line in Manchester.

After nationalisation, Ron was made Chief Draughtsman at Brighton Works. There he was in charge of some very successful projects including the design of the BR 2-6-4Ts, the rebuilding of the Bulleid pacifics and the Class '73' Electrodiesels. By the time I knew him he worked at the Derby Technical Centre and retired soon after. I got to know him then because he was an active volunteer on the Festiniog Railway. After retirement he moved to North Wales and, for many years, painstakingly rebuilt the timber bodies of nineteenth century coaches in his workshop.

One day, one of the clerks, Les Askin, oiled up to me with a suspicious grin on his face. 'Now that you're not a trainee, you'll have to join a trade union,' he said. 'I'm the local TSSA rep.' Unfortunately, I knew that he was right. At that time, BR had a pernicious agreement with the railway unions that there would be a 'closed shop'. This meant that you had to join a union whether you wanted to or not. This did not apply to managers or management trainees but there was an anomaly whereby ex-trainees had to join until they were promoted to a management graded job. Now, I have no problem with people voluntarily joining trade unions, but I strongly object to compulsion. This was another example of the weak and flaccid management style at the most senior levels in BR at that time.

In February 1972 I was sent on a productivity course at the Grove near Watford, which was a large country house that had been bought by the LMS just before the war so as to be able to evacuate HQ staff in the event of bombing. The course was really excellent and equipped us with the means to think logically about how to get 'more for less' in almost any situation. I have found that I have used the principles

8Fs in Egypt photographed by Ron Jarvis in 1946 when he was sent on a shopping expedition by the LMS who wanted to know which ones to buy. This was from one of the files thrown away by 'the clerks'.

Ron Jarvis in retirement in Wales in 1979 looking relieved that I and my gang had not damaged his last five years' work as we jacked and packed it onto the Festiniog Railway lorry.

I learnt there throughout my career. Looking at my notes, which I have often referred to, I see that we had a session entitled 'Project Control: Case Study' delivered by visiting speaker David Rollin from BREL. This is the same David Rollin who set up Interfleet, probably the most successful management buyout, when privatisation came. Additional entertainment resulted from Prime Minister Edward Heath's incompetence which led to many long power cuts that February, one of which occurred during the final party to which we had invited a group of nurses from the local training college.

One morning Peter called me over as soon as I came in and said that Wigan had been on and they were having trouble with a Class '40'. Alan Speed, the Class '40' man, was on holiday, so Peter told me to get myself to Wigan and sort it out. My enquiry as to what was supposed to be wrong with it only resulted in some vague statement about its being low on power. Now on a complex machine like a Class '40', there are a large number of things that could give rise to this condition, so I spent much of the journey, via Crewe, to Wigan running them through my mind. Although I had been in the cab of a '40', I had never been in the engine room. However, from my courses at the School of Transport, I knew roughly how a '40' worked. I also knew that the engine was very similar to the Class '50' which I was quite familiar with.

Having arrived at Wigan North Western shortly before midday, I set off through streets of red brick terraced houses to Springs Branch Depot which was a mile or so to the south. As the Chief Foreman looked me up and down, it occurred to me that this was a set-up job between him and Peter. I suspected that neither had any confidence that I would get to the bottom of a problem that experienced men had been puzzling over for more than a week. I was told that D345 had been 'low on power' for some time, that they had had their best men on it and had found nothing. They did not see what I was going to add to it.

Undaunted, I decided to start at the beginning and draw my own conclusions. First, I asked to see the Driver's Repair Book for 345. It revealed that the loco had been in traffic for about two weeks with low power. The idea of the book is that drivers are supposed to write an accurate description of any problems, together with any clues that might help the maintenance staff rectify it. In turn, the fitter is supposed to explain, briefly, what he found and how he cured the problem. In this case, as was common, neither party had covered themselves with glory. 'Couldn't pull the skin off a rice pudding' or 'low amps' isn't very helpful, while 'NFF' (No fault found) or 'FHD' (For Home Depot) don't convince drivers that much effort has gone into solving the problem. There was, however, one entry which was more thoughtful and helpful. A driver from Healey Mills, near Leeds, had reported that he thought the performance of the loco on his freight train was similar to that which he would have expected from a Class '20'.

That set me thinking. The chaps at Wigan had told me that they had checked all the obvious things. Was the engine running at full speed? Was the Load Regulator increasing the Main Generator Field Current so as to load the engine up and take the full 2,000hp? So what if the engine was only capable of 1,000hp, the same power as an eight cylinder Class '20'? Careful examination of the four engine exhausts showed that the 'B bank' ones were wet with oil, demonstrating that half the engine had, indeed, not been firing. This meant that the individual fuel injection pumps on half the engine were not operating. The most obvious way that could happen would be that the mechanical linkage from the governor had come apart. No, it was all present and correct. As far as I could see, the only remaining possibility was that the 'B bank' camshaft, which drove the fuel injection pumps as well as the inlet and exhaust valves, was not rotating. That seemed a little unlikely since on these English Electric sixteen cylinder 'V' engines there was one camshaft chain, a 1in pitch triplex chain which wound a tortuous route from crankshaft to each camshaft in turn via chain tensioners. Then I remembered that the actual camshaft sprocket was annular – ie, it was in the form of a ring which was bolted with six 3/8in fitted bolts to a hub on the camshaft. Surely those bolts couldn't have broken?

I had a fitter with me to help as required. The Chief Foreman was also watching my every move. 'Take that cover off, please,' I said, indicating a circular cover about 8in in diameter in front of the camshaft sprocket. I ignored the Chief Foreman's protest that this was a waste of time and insisted on having it removed. There it was: no fitted bolts. The camshaft sprocket, copiously lubricated by engine oil, had been turning on its hub for two weeks.

To say that I was relieved (and not a little surprised) would be an understatement. I even got a cup of tea from the Chief Foreman. The moral of this story really is that you do need accurate reporting of faults, together with a logical approach. You also need to make accessible records of what has been previously tried. A fitter in Tyne Yard, according to the repair book, had got close to a solution. He had detected a strange exhaust note. Unfortunately what he did was to replace B3 exhaust joint because he thought it was blowing. The situation, in this case, was made worse by the fact that for most of the two weeks, this LM loco had been working on the Eastern Region. As has been previously explained, different Regions did not communicate well or do much to help each other. This kind of thing would not happen today because of better training and because computerised records are available universally.

One of the features of Class '50s' that prompted more emotion than almost anything else was the rheostatic brake. They were the first diesel locos to have this feature. There were two problems which had been discussed extensively at the Service Problems Meeting:

a) Tyre damage in the form of shelling and spalling which were rather alarming conditions where chunks of steel the size of a man's thumb could fall out of the tyre. Apart from being potentially dangerous, this substantially reduced the life of the tyre because of the heavy cut that would have to be made on the wheel lathe.
b) Sudden jolts experienced by passengers when braking was initiated. Allegedly some passengers had been thrown out of bed in sleeping car trains.

I was asked to set up an instrumented test run to determine just what was going on since these problems were much more severe than experienced on the Class '86' electric locos which were more intensively used and, although having the same maximum speed, 100mph, operated at a higher average speed. Accordingly, on Thursday, 4 January 1973 I found myself waiting at Crewe Station in the new test car *Mentor*, which was coupled to 420. A couple of us had spent the previous day at Crewe Diesel Depot running wires from various parts of 420's control systems to a multi channel data recorder in *Mentor*. As soon as the Class '86' came off the incoming train from Euston, we backed down onto 1S47, 10.11 Crewe to Glasgow, which was air braked.

My report, which I have before me as I write this, details our observations and draws the conclusion that the reason the problems were as bad as reported (which they were) was largely due to incorrect settings of various proportional and other switches. The difficulties arose because the blending of the rheostatic (electric) brake with both the loco and the train air brakes was very crude. The reason that the tyre damage was happening was that as soon as the driver moved his brake handle just a little, the rheostatic brake came full on. This meant that the loco was trying to brake the whole train, at least for a few seconds, until the air brake system caught up. In turn, this meant, particularly at high speeds, that very large amounts of energy were dissipated as heat at the wheel/rail interface as the loco wheels, inevitably, skidded to some degree. This phenomenon also caused a huge jolt which was felt down the entire train (we had an accelerometer in the last coach). A further jolt, in the opposite direction, occurred when the driver moved his brake handle back to the 'off' position because the rheostatic brake then came off immediately, causing the loco to be unbraked while the rest of the train was just beginning to think about releasing its brakes. There is always a delay with air brakes in either applying or releasing. With a short train, that delay is brief, but it is more serious with long trains.

Modern trains have much more sophisticated blending systems than Class '50s' and are so good that passengers do not notice transition. Actually, as we discovered, the '50s' were not too bad if a few simple adjustments were made to various settings. This was another example of neither Crewe Depot or Crewe Works bothering to comply with the instructions which were quite clear and fairly simple.

Having arrived at Glasgow Central, on time, the train was removed so as to release 420 and its partner (we were booked to be double headed and 420 was the second engine) and *Mentor*. We then made a move which would, today, be frowned upon. A Polmadie driver got into the rear cab of 420, the one next to *Mentor,* and propelled it from there for about three miles to a place where there was a triangle to turn the whole assemblage. After several more shunts, we found ourselves inside the former steam loco shed at Polmadie which had been the main passenger loco shed for Glasgow Central. Here we took advantage of the luxurious facilities in the test car to cook ourselves a slap-up meal to the bemusement of local staff who saw this alien object which appeared to be a dining car in the middle of their depot.

Later, we repeated the propelling move back to Glasgow Central, this time with only one loco, as 1M11, 23.00 Glasgow to Crewe, was booked for one engine only. This was *The Night Mail*, the train that had been the target of the Great Train Robbery less than ten years previously. Having come north in the test car, it was my turn to travel back in the cab, so, after *Mentor* had been coupled on to the Mail Train, I made my way to the cab. Here there was much consternation as the armed Post Office guard, who apparently travelled in the cab every night, had not been told of our tests nor that there would be a test car nor that someone extra would be in the cab. A bit of a standoff occurred with the armed guard refusing to allow me in the cab despite my showing him the official notice of our test issued by the Chief Operating Manager, LMR. It was solved by my telling him that if he did not allow me in the cab, I would ensure that the train would not depart.

LM Region test car *Mentor* in its role as a restaurant car inside Polmadie shed as we rested between journeys on our brake tests on 420.

Some miles into our journey, a little before Motherwell, there was a major panic by the PO guard and his colleagues in the train, with whom he was in radio contact. We were stopped at a red signal and the driver was told by the signalman that we would be diverted via a freight route for a few miles before rejoining the main line. Eventually calm returned. We were not raided by an armed gang and, apart from some single line working in the Warrington area, to do with commissioning the new power signal box there, the rest of the trip back to Crewe was uneventful. Unlike 1S47, 1M11 was vacuum braked and, because of even slower brake propagation rates than the airbrake train, the jolting was even worse.

After these tests I personally set up two locomotives correctly and also isolated the rheostatic brake on another two. I monitored all four for some months. The conclusions were that if it was set up as it should be, the rheo brake worked reasonably well and did not cause undue tyre damage or throw sleepers out of their beds. Furthermore, it substantially reduced the cost of maintenance of the loco because the brake blocks lasted about 110 duty hours with rheo brake working, but only about thirty-three with it isolated. Also, the overhaul frequency for the bogie was doubled if the electric brake was not working.

Soon after this, the entire class was transferred to the Western Region so that they could withdraw the Class '52' diesel hydraulics. It was extremely frustrating when the WR CM&EE decided, without making any enquiries, to remove the rheostsatic brake from all fifty Class '50s'. In doing so he unnecessarily wasted several million pounds over the next twenty years or so of their life.

For a year or more around this time, a disgraceful situation was allowed to continue at Derby. The prototypes for both the APT and the HST had been completed and were ready for testing. However, they both sat, unused, in the sidings at the Railway Technical Centre in Derby because ASLEF, the train drivers' union, refused to move them until BR acceded to its demand that both trains be, quite unnecessarily, equipped with two drivers. Instead of taking a firm line, BR prevaricated and eventually gave in to the union. It took the private sector companies twenty-five years later to dispose of this piece of nonsense which they all did in very short order.

I used to come across all sorts of interesting people at work. One such was Ron Pocklington who was working at BR Research. As a young man, he had spent three years at Inchicore Works in Ireland assisting former CM&EE Oliver Bulleid, who left the Southern on nationalisation to build a turf-burning locomotive for Irish Railways. As has been reported elsewhere, it was an utter failure. Ron's verdict on Bulleid was that he was 'barking' and impossible to work with.

One day towards the end of 1972 I was told to go to see Clements, the new chief. When I entered his office, I was introduced to R.H.N. (Dick) Hardy who I had not previously met. Dick had taken over from

	RLY.				RLY.
FROM		TO			

DESCRIPTION		Number of Tickets Required (in Words)		Class (in Words)	Single or Return	Available on or before (in words) Year............
		Male	Female			
SELF						
WIFE*						
CHILDREN 3 and under 15 yrs. of age	Living with and dependent upon applicant and not earning more than 15/- gross per week or the equivalent thereto.	Male	Female			
15 and under 21 yrs. of age						
21 yrs. of age and over living with and entirely dependent on applicant.						

*Erase when issued under authority to dependent Female relative acting as Housekeeper & insert 'Housekeeper'
(See back for conditions).

Even in 1971 we still used an LMS form to apply for priv tickets!

Cedric Rose, who had given me my job with BR. After an initial chat, Clements said that they had decided that it would be a good idea if I broadened my experience by swapping with one of the other Senior Technical Officers, Malcolm Brown, who worked in the Resident Engineers' office in Crewe Works. I did not realise until later that Dick and Freddie knew each other of old. The former, who has written many books and articles about his career, had been a Premium Apprentice at Doncaster during the war and was Shedmaster at Woodford Halse on the GC from 1948 to 1950. Freddie was an LMS, man having started at Horwich as an apprentice in 1935. He was Shedmaster at Neasden, also on the GC, from 1948 to 1951. I was to employ men, later, who had worked for both of them at those sheds.

I started at Crewe, for the second time, in January 1973. This time, I was not working for BREL, but for the major customer. I was one of half a dozen Senior Technical Officers (STO) on the staff of LM Region Resident Engineer Jack Lowe, whose job was to see that the LM Region got the best deal at Crewe. Specifically, this meant seeing that the works carried out overhauls and repairs to the agreed standards, checking that items were not billed unless they had been asked for, and had actually been done to the proper standard. Jack, who was in his sixties, was a wily old bird who had, for many years, been the Works Chief Inspector, so he had turned from poacher to gamekeeper. He knew where most of the bodies were buried. He was assisted by a cheerful individual, Alan Roberts. Alan spent a lot of time reminiscing; often about his time as a technician, testing 10800 which was the third main line diesel that the LMS commissioned. Unlike the 'Twins', mentioned earlier, progress was very slow with this 800hp mixed traffic loco and it was not actually finished until 1950. A series of commissioning runs took place on the long-closed Bedford to Northampton line and, if Alan was to be believed, often included running into a flock of pheasants, one or more of which would be scooped into the cab via the open front facing door. They certainly did not leave alive! Alan had been the first boss at the new depot at Bletchley which opened in 1965 to look after the new fleet of AM10 EMUs. This had clearly not worked out well, hence his position at Crewe.

A fly on the wall would have assumed that the boss was actually Ray York, the clerk who sat with his desk facing the general office where we STOs sat. He would receive all the incoming correspondence and dish it out to us with the bearing and noise of an RSM. Actually, he was typical of a lot of Crewe Works people who tended to be loud and aggressive as a matter of course. I found that the best way of handling that was to give as good, or better, in return.

The STOs were an interesting lot. There was Ben Jenks who looked after electric locos. He told me how, as an apprentice, he had spent two weeks with a fitter marking out the frames for *Duke of Gloucester*, the one-off Pacific built by BR and now preserved. Because of its unique nature, they used manual methods, which included marking where the steel plates needed to be cut by putting a 'centre pop' every eighth of an inch and then drilling a hole through both frames. Brian Thomas was a very quiet, thoughtful, man who, it was said, was the only person on the works who could set up Caprotti valves, which were fitted to *Duke of Gloucester* and some 'Standard Class 5s'. Alas, the last of these had passed through the works some five years previously.

My job was great fun and a wonderful learning experience at all sorts of levels. There were usually about eight Class '50s' on works at any one time and I got the file for each as it arrived. First task was to be quite clear why each loco was there. The options included a Classified Repair, which was a pre-planned event after a given number of miles. There would be an agreed and priced menu of work for this. It could be an Unclassified Repair when some major component had failed early: for example, the engine or a main generator. There was usually an agreed spec and price for these. Finally, it could be a Casual Repair which covered anything else. All of this work comprised jobs that were too big to do in the running maintenance depots like Crewe Diesel Depot. Having read the file, I would visit the Works Production Office and check that their understanding was the same as mine. This is where the first row might start.

Now, there are probably some starry eyed idealists who believe that everything in a nationalised industry was done with the good of the nation at heart. Nothing could be further from the truth. The arguments, obfuscation and deceit that I observed in Crewe Works trumped anything that I have come across between private sector companies. Often one of the guys in the Production Office would hail me to announce that such a job was not in the agreed schedule and would have to be charged for separately. Where he was at a disadvantage was that I had recently finished a complete review of the whole thing and could often quote chapter and verse as to why he was wrong. Next, came one of the best bits as I would spend a couple of hours visiting the so called 'detail' sections where specialised parts were taken after being stripped from a loco. An example would be turbochargers which, on Class '50s', did not last very long for reasons explained earlier. Most of the chargehands who led a gang of fitters were very knowledgeable and interested in getting things right. You could have really interesting technical discussions about how to improve things, which is what many of them were eager to do.

Lunch was usually sandwiches in the office. Sometimes, generally on a Friday, there would be a tap at the window on the side of the office that could not be observed from the works yard. It would be one of the Works Finished Work Inspectors. These were white coated men whose job, on behalf of the Works Manager, was to check that everything had been done to the right standard. On Friday, the Shop Superintendents had one thought in mind, which was to get their quota of work 'sold' – that is, off the works and into service. The reason for the tap would be that a conscientious Inspector (and they mostly were) was fed up of being overruled and told that the loco was going out of the door irrespective of its condition. Depending on the type of engine involved, one of us STOs would be called over to hear the sorry tale which usually involved a foreman being told to go and overrule the Inspector about the need to do various jobs. Now, some tact and playacting was required in order not to drop the Inspector in it. After, maybe, half an hour or so, I would go into the Erecting Shop and, since we had licence to go absolutely anywhere we wanted, I would do a fairly thorough inspection of two or three engines that were almost completed. In the course of this, I would of course 'find' the things I had been told about. Then came the interesting bit when I went to see the Superintendent to tell him that I would not accept one or more of the locos as being finished. Often a shouting match resulted, but I usually got my way.

There was one disgraceful episode where that was not the result. D428 had suffered an electrical flashover on its 850 volt train heating generator which meant it had been shopped for a Casual Repair. This was not done at Crewe Diesel Depot because of the degree of precision needed when reassembling. The engine had been in the Electric Loco Shop for a few days and I had not visited because it was pretty straightforward and there were more important priorities. On Friday morning, I decided to go and have a look at it. Removing the commutator covers from the generator, the inside of the machine was as black as a coal mine which told me that it had not been touched. So I went by the Superintendent's office and asked him when it was going to be looked at. With suspicious alacrity, he told me that it was finished and that he had given instructions for it to be out-shopped. My suggestion that he might care to come and look at it was declined and he maintained that it was going to be 'sold' that afternoon. I told him that it was not and I was going to give instructions that it should not be accepted.

Back in the office, half an hour later, Dick Ribbons, the LM Region Locomotive Engineer, was on the phone for me to say that George Oldham, the Works Manager, had been on complaining about me and

The CM&EE's Inspectorate office in Crewe where I spent a very happy six months in 1973. The authoritative figure on the right is actually Ray, the clerk who used to issue out the work by throwing a loco file on your desk. The actual boss, wily old fox Jack Lowe, is the bald chap seated at Ray's desk. Next to him, standing, is Alan Roberts his deputy and the first boss at Bletchley TMD, which I was running a year later. On the phone by the window is Ben Jenks who ,as an apprentice in 1954 helped cut out the frames of 71000 *Duke of Gloucester*. Vic Dodd, like me a humble inspector, is head down, writing a report for a customer.

The electric Traction shop at Crewe where main generators, traction motors and other big electrical machines were overhauled. This was the scene of my falling out with the Shop Superintendent about work not done on 428.

saying that 428 was fit and healthy. 'Well, Mr Ribbons,' I replied, 'he has been told a pack of lies. If that engine goes out, it will fail in traffic and inconvenience hundreds of people.' I was disappointed that Dick Ribbons chose not to support me. Arriving at the works at 07.30 on Monday morning, there was 428, having failed in traffic on Saturday. The Shop Superintendent concerned went on to become one of the most senior managers in British Rail. In the unlikely event that he reads this, he will recognise himself.

This attitude to quality, which I observed to some degree at Bamfords as well, was one of the reasons that British industry lost many of its markets at home and abroad. I am pleased to say that attitudes are much better now. However, it took the near death experience of losing most of our markets at home and abroad and hence much of our manufacturing industry. I very firmly believe that management has the responsibility of instilling the right ethos and I would never blame workmen or trade unions. Management has to manage.

All of the above was fun, but the even better bit was taking locos out for test runs. We did this with all Class '50s' that had been on works for Classified Repairs. A loco that went out on a test run would have already been tested on the Load Bank where the engine would have been run at various power settings, including full for several hours. I would have witnessed this and observed that various temperatures and pressures were in order. When we went out on the main line, I was in charge and responsible for making sure that nothing unsafe

was done. There would be a Works Inspector and fitter working to my instructions, as well as a driver and secondman.

We had a regular early afternoon train for the test: it was 1D56 Euston to Bangor, which came in hauled by a Class '86' that was booked to be replaced by a Class '40' at Crewe. We came down on top of the train engine whose driver I would ask not to take power unless we had trouble. The line along the North Wales coast is very attractive, especially on a bright day with the sun glinting on the sea. If everything was 100%, I would emerge to admire the view by about Conway. If not, I might be checking and adjusting most of the way there and back. At Bangor, we had about an hour, which gave plenty of time to run around the train and then run around the Class '40' so that we were still at the front. We returned to Crewe on 1A65. If I was satisfied with the engine, it would go straight on to the Diesel Depot available for traffic.

As an alternative to using a service train, we sometimes took two of the LMS Mobile Test Units (MTUs). There had been three of them which were commissioned in 1938 at the same time as a new Dynamometer Car. All were put aside during the war and finished in 1949. They were built in order to scientifically test steam locos so as to optimise their performance but were also used for electric and diesel locos including the prototype HST before being withdrawn in 1976. The MTUs looked like a coach but had separately excited DC generators mounted on the bogies where, on an EMU, you would find traction motors. The excitation came from another generator which was driven by a big AEC diesel engine inside and was controlled from a splendid black marble panel with bare knife switches and other ancient electrical devices. It

The final part of our job in the CM&EE Inspectorate was to take our loco out on a test run. No. 445 has pulled LMS Test Unit 2 as far as the loop at Craven Arms. Ian Cook, in charge of the Test Unit is on the left. I was on the loco, checking that everything was working correctly.

was possible to run the two cars in multiple with one controlling the other. We had a path every week day from Crewe, via Shrewsbury, to Craven Arms where we would recess in a loop before running around and coming back.

Once or twice I was asked to test run Class '47s' and on one such occasion I was on the cab with an old Crewe driver who had not come across the MTUs before. We were climbing the 1 in 97 gradient after Nantwich at a steady 20mph with the master controller wide open, engine roaring and a vertical column of black smoke because the technician, Ian, had wound both cars up to the maximum. The driver was unperturbed, having forgotten that he only had two 'coaches' in tow. It was when we went over the summit, and he found that if he shut off we slowed right down, that he could not believe what was happening. I can still see the look of sheer disbelief on his face.

'Bloody funny coaches, those,' was all he said.

At the end of my six months' secondment, I went to see Dick Ribbons who, having asked how I had got on, rather surprised me by asking where else I would like to go. I had expected that I would naturally have gone back to my job at Nelson Street, but this sounded interesting, so, without missing a beat, I told him that Birmingham interested me, as did electrification. The additional attraction of Birmingham was that it was easy to get to from our new house in Stafford.

So, in July 1973, I reported to Hugh Abbott, the Divisional Maintenance Engineer in Birmingham, and was sent to the Electrification Depot at Soho, a couple of miles north of New Street Station on the line to Wolverhampton. Soho was very close to Winson Green prison and was in a very rough part of the city. One morning I even saw a body being fished out of the adjacent canal. While it was clearly important, I regret that neither overhead line technology nor the associated high voltage switchgear which the people at Soho looked after really caught my imagination. There were not enough wheels and moving bits for me. However, I did make sure that I grasped the basics, which were to come in useful later. I do remember going out with an overhead line technician to measure up for some planned work which involved putting in an up and a down loop with the associated new wiring. This was necessary because a new station to be called Birmingham International was going to be built there.

A much more interesting period followed when I was asked to deputise for the M&EE supervisor on New Street Station. Frank Blackburn was the staff rep for Birmingham Division Maintenance Supervisors and, because of the inept way in which BR conducted its staff negotiations in those days, was required to be released from his normal duties for a month. This was a bit like my supervisory experience at Etches Park, only official! He had about thirty men who maintained the considerable amount of plant on the station and attended to locos, DMUs and coaches which needed attention.

Although New Street handled half the number of trains that it does now, it was still a busy place where something unexpected was always happening.

Finally, I found myself based in the Divisional office in Broad Street, Birmingham, for three months during which I was an 'on call' Carriage and Wagon supervisor. In those days there were, perhaps, 100 or so C&W Examiners in the Birmingham area. Their job was to ensure that the hundreds of thousands of primitive, mostly four wheel, wagons that BR had were in a fit condition to operate safely. In stark contrast to the precise record keeping and preventive maintenance of locomotives and DMUs described earlier, wagons were a complete nightmare. There were literally no records of most of them other than chalk marks on the actual vehicle. Unbelievably, BR did not even know how many it had and most certainly had no method of determining what condition they were in without going and checking each one. (When, a few years later, TOPS was introduced and there was a thorough count, it was discovered that there were about 700,000 more wagons than had been thought.) The job of the C&W Examiner was to make a visual examination of freight trains at predetermined points and to carry out minor repairs on the spot or to mark a wagon to be sent to a repair shop. If you add to this haphazard process the fact that most of the wagons were of crude design, dating fundamentally from the earliest days of railways, it was hardly surprising that mishaps were very frequent. This is where I and others like me came in.

On receipt of a call, I would get into my yellow Morris 1000 BR van and head off through Birmingham to long-gone places like Round Oak Steelworks, site of today's Merryhill Shopping Centre, where I found twelve wagons derailed by a 'rough shunt'. My job was to determine the cause of the mishap, make a plan for rectifying it and instruct the local staff in what to do. While the novelty of such a job would wear off after a while, it was great fun for a few weeks.

The report that I submitted to Freddie Clements, the CM&EE, included comments on the management of the business. I gave an example of a couple of small teams who I thought were exemplary. In both, the leader explained what was wanted, made sure his men understood the task and had the necessary resources and were then encouraged to get on with the job. In general, however, I was not impressed:

'On the whole, the organisation is top heavy resulting in trivial decisions being referred to too high a level. The Field Organisation, we are told, will streamline the management structure and result in 6,000 fewer salaried staff. It is, therefore, disappointing to see the practical detailed application of the scheme failing to do any such thing… and HQ will remain as large and inefficient as now.'

Back at Derby just before Christmas, Dick Ribbons called me in and said I should apply for a management graded job, MS2, which was two grades above mine, at Euston. With the impatience of youth, I had already applied for quite a few promotions, all without success. I had also toyed seriously with going out to Hong Kong to join the fledgling MTR which was just starting construction, but decided not to take up an offer because it was going to be six years before trains would be running.

I suppose I should not have been surprised when, on 11 January, I was shown into the interview room in London to be confronted by Dick Ribbons, my boss, and John Marson, the Euston Divisional Maintenance Engineer. It was clearly a stitch up. There is not any doubt that I really fell on my feet in being allocated to the Class '50' job rather than some other in a less high profile part of the CM&EE organisation. It was, and still is, a fact that locomotives have always been more glamorous than, say, plant and machinery in the context of a railway company. But for that stroke of luck, my career might have been quite different.

I started as Assistant Traction Engineer, Euston, on Monday, 25 February 1974 at an annual salary of £2,815 plus £70 a year London weighting.

Chapter Four

My first 'command'

It was May Day 2013 and I was sitting in the cab of my ex-Darjeeling Himalayan steam engine having lunch, while waiting between trains at the Leighton Buzzard Light Railway, when a lady in her sixties, came up with her husband and asked if I remembered her. Something in her voice seemed familiar and, after a moment's thought, I said:

'Your name is Verna and you were the young personnel clerk who gave me such a warm welcome when I started as Assistant Traction Engineer, MS2, *vice* L. Abbott, in February 1974.'

I told her how she had made me feel so very welcome and that I had told generations of personnel clerks about the positive effect a few well chosen words could have on new employees.

My new boss was the Divisional Traction Engineer, Frank Pardoe, who was a lovely man in his late fifties. He had spent his entire career in electric traction having started as an apprentice in Stonebridge Park Shops in the early 1930s. This was the headquarters of the LNWR third rail electric system which extended from Watford and Croxley to Euston, Broad Street and Kensington Olympia. It was a totally self-contained railway having its own traction power station and overhaul shop at Stonebridge Park. Apprentices, like Frank, were given a very thorough training as electrical fitters and were expected to be able to turn their hand to anything. Frank had got on well and, during the war, was foreman in charge of Mitre Bridge Car Sheds, which were adjacent to the junction where the West London line leaves the West Coast Main Line near Willesden Junction. Later he was in at the beginning of AC electrification on the Euston Division and was the first Depot Engineer at the new Willesden Traction Maintenance Depot (TMD when it opened in 1964, and which became home for many years of the Class '86' and '87' electric locos,

I do not think there really was a need for my post which, I suspect, had been created to accommodate Les Abbott who had been made redundant when the St Pancras Division had been abolished in 1966, but it gave me an opportunity to learn much more about actually managing the operation of a railway and Frank was an excellent mentor both in this job and my next. For example, one of the first things he asked me to do was to represent the M&EE Department at an internal enquiry being held to investigate why a Class '08' and a Class '47' had collided head on at Willesden. It was a low speed accident and no one was hurt, but David Simpson, the very gentlemanly Divisional Operating Officer, was at pains to explain to me how an enquiry should be done and what to watch for.

One of my specific responsibilities was to manage the training team who selected and trained apprentices and provided technical training for maintenance staff, drivers and other operational people. We had a training school behind Willesden TMD and the first time I went there I asked the driver of the Class '501' EMU from Euston if I could ride with him. Seeing my Cab Pass with my job title, he asked if I wanted to 'take it'. Never having been on the 'DC', as it is still known, I declined on that occasion.

At the school we had, in a huge former substation building, an unusual set-up which had been built many years before to help drivers with the transition from steam to, initially, diesel traction. It was the brainchild of Dr Andrews who had been brought in by Sir Harold Hartley who, before the war, was in charge of research on the LMS. Andrews' role, which he continued into the 1960s, was as a kind of Electrical Guru, with a remit to think the unthinkable. He was undoubtedly involved, behind the scenes, in the inception of Nos. 10000 and 10001. At Willesden, he had caused to be created a huge standard gauge model railway. There was a track with third rail the length of the building, about twenty-five yards, on which was a motor bogie from 1918 LNWR Oerlikon stock. Up on a balcony that overlooked the whole set-up there was a driver's master controller. Thus the steam loco driver could drive the bogie back and forth just like a Tri-ang OO gauge train set. Surprisingly, no one appeared to have run into an end wall!

A Class 501 just outside Euston having come on the 'DC' from Watford. I was offered a drive the first time I ever got in one.

The depth of technical knowledge imparted to trainee drivers was considerable and enabled them to deal with quite a lot of faults that arose on the line. This changed soon after as operators took over and decided that all this technical nonsense was unnecessary. I think this change can be linked, at least in part, to the decline in punctuality that occurred over the next few years. Not that the engineers were blameless, as one of my instructors, Frank Rolle, was there because of past misdemeanours rather than any training ability. He had been in charge at Marylebone Diesel Depot and had made such a mess of it that he was taken from there and made an instructor at the same rate of pay. BR had a very bad habit of finding jobs for people who actually should have been shown the door. I was to discover and rectify further problems at Marylebone before long.

Next door to my Training School was Willesden TMD which, in 1974, had 100 Class '86' electric locos and was just receiving thirty-four Class '87s' which were being built at Crewe when I was there the previous year. These new locos had been ordered for the newly electrified northern section of the WCML. They replaced many of the Class '50' diesels which then went to the Western Region. The boss at the TMD, successor to Frank Pardoe, was Albert Laing, a red-headed man in his sixties who had started as an apprentice at the Bow Loco works of the North London Railway. He was a steam man through and through and I am not certain he knew one end of an electric loco from the other; however, his deputy, Bill Sargeant, and his supervisors more than made up for that. Among the team were Rolling Stock Inspectors (RSI) Keith Sargeant, Bill's son, and Peter Daw who retired in June 2016 after nine outstandingly successful years as Engineering Director of LOROL, a job I had recruited him to. RSIs were the technical brains of the depot, the men who were mobilised to solve tricky problems on locos. Most of them had been trained at Stonebridge Park like Frank and all had a very good understanding of things electrical and mechanical. Despite quite a bit of leg pulling at my constant questions, they were all very helpful to me.

The Divisional Maintenance Engineer's office was in the former Railway Clearing House (RCH) office in Eversholt Street just beyond the end of Euston Station Platform 1. There are some similarities between the role of the RCH and that of modern day ATOC, but after twenty-six years of nationalisation, its role had finally disappeared, hence its office being available. One morning, feeling rather guilty because my train was quite late, I was stepping out quite briskly towards the office and did not pay much attention to the tall, slightly stooping elderly gentleman who I overtook.

'That is a very firm stride, young man.' The voice was that of Divisional Manager Geoffrey Huskisson, who seemed to know who I was even though I had not met him. I was to get to know him quite well later on.

A big organisational change had been planned called 'The Field Organisation' and the essence of it was that some power would be transferred to Area (local) level while Divisions and Regions would be abolished, to be replaced by 'Territories'. The idea was to substantially reduce the cost of HQ overhead and to empower local managers to make more efficient local decisions. The first phase, at Area level, was planned to come in at the end of May 1974. It then became clear why I had been encouraged to come to Euston as I was told to go to Bletchley to fill the new post of Area Maintenance Engineer from 21 May. Some of my new responsibilities had been carried out by Brian Harrison who was reckoned to be a 'hard' manager and, thus, just the man to be moved to Cricklewood Depot where anarchy ruled as a result of several years of weak management. As it turned out, the BR Board, chaired by ex-Labour Transport Minister Richard Marsh, (described in one obituary as 'cynical, superficial, lazy, hopeless, idle') flunked the decision to carry on and complete the changes because of resistance by the trade unions. It took the best Chairman BR ever had, Bob Reid (the first), to show, some years later, that the management and not the unions were in charge.

I thought my new role was perfect and could have been designed just for me, taking advantage, as it did, of all the learning and experience of the last eight years since leaving school. At the age of twenty-five I found myself at the head of an organisation that had responsibility for the safety of thousands of people every day and for the smooth operation of a substantial part of the WCML. I had a team of 180, the majority based at Bletchley TMD, but with some at Marylebone and other smaller places. I had to manage a budget of nearly £2 million a year and had a good deal of autonomy, provided that I stayed within the law and complied with prescribed technical standards. I could, and did, hire and fire and, as a soon-to-be Chartered Engineer, was expected to make professional judgements backed up as I saw fit by expert opinion.

Bletchley TMD, which had opened in 1965, had an allocation of forty-nine Class '310' EMUs used for Euston and Manchester commuter services, thirty-five four-car Class '115' DMUs which ran GC line trains and had their light maintenance done at Marylebone, a handful of single and two-car DMUs for local branches, and a few Class '08' shunting locos. Also based at the depot was the Overhead Line gang who had eighty miles of the WCML to look after. In addition, the Plant team saw to everything from station lighting to lifts at more than fifty stations and depots. Finally, there was a rag-bag of Carriage and Wagon (C&W) people thinly spread to deal, mostly, with freight trains at long-closed places like Wycombe West Yard and Stewartby Brick Works.

In addition, I had to deal with any derailment or mishap involving trains anywhere on my Area. There was a breakdown train at Bletchley

All 49 Class 310's (one had been written off after an accident) were allocated to Bletchley and worked commuter services to Euston, Birmingham New St and Manchester Piccadilly. Here 075 is seen at Stoke-on-Trent on a Manchester to New St service in 1974. We got them back every fourteen days for maintenance.

which, until just before I arrived, had a 30 ton steam crane. In my previous job I had helped introduce MFD powered hydraulic jacking equipment which took the place of the crane and, once the crew got the hang of it, was much quicker and easier than a crane for most jobs, especially under the 25kV wire which invariably had to be moved before you could start using the crane.

I now reported directly to John Marson, the Divisional Maintenance Engineer, although, in practice, my previous boss, Frank Pardoe, was a tremendous source of wise advice, including how to handle Marson! The only other manager was my deputy John Harden who had been appointed a few weeks before me. I had first met him three years previously when we both attended the Derby course on Diesel and Electric Traction. John was a very bright man, but I sensed that he was not at his happiest getting results through other people which, of course, is what management is all about. I enjoyed working with him for two years, but he then left for a more technical role elsewhere which, I felt, was more his cup of tea.

The real character at Bletchley was the Chief Foreman, Adam Blaikie. Adam had joined the LMS as an apprentice in the steam shed at Ayr just as the war started. As fitters were demobbed in 1946, he found himself without a job and so transferred to Camden, which was the passenger loco shed for Euston. In common with other London sheds, it had been bombed, was a filthy run down place and had perpetual staff shortages. Adam, who was a big rough and ready man, thrived on this and was soon made up to chargehand and, in the mid 1950s, was promoted to be Mechanical Foreman at Bletchley steam shed. There, reporting to the Shedmaster, he had the job of managing the fitting staff and keeping 1E's locos and Derby Lightweight DMUs up to the mark. By the time I met him, he was about fifty and most of the fitters would follow him to the end of the earth. He was rough, gruff, swore continuously but absolutely upheld the interests of the company and had a heart of gold, as anyone who needed help found out. Conversely, he had a very sharp tongue for malingerers and administered to them summary justice that would certainly not stand up in today's employment tribunals.

In the '70s there were still far too many derailments. They almost always involved short wheelbase wagons like these at Hemel Hempstead in the morning rush hour. With a very stiff, short wheelbase, they were very sensitive to minor track imperfections that do not bother bogie vehicles. The Pennsylvania Railroad had high capacity bogie coal wagons in 1898. Why were we so far behind? Overhead Line Inspector Roy Broadhurst, in the foreground, is organising his team to slew the 25kv wires so that our 30 ton steam crane can get to work.

One particularly nasty accident between the slow line platforms at Watford Jct happened when someone, unknown, pushed a BRUTE trolley onto the down slow track in the early hours. The 03.28 Euston to Bletchley staff train was booked to be formed of one of our Craven 2-car DMU's which normally worked from Bletchley to Bedford. This was because of frequent OLE isolations during the night in the London area. It was braking in order to stop at Watford when it was derailed to the right by the BRUTE. Unfortunately, seconds later 85.022, at the head of a parcels train, hit it at 75mph with such force that the leading DMU car was knocked clean off its bogies and its driver was killed, as was a secondman riding in the loco. 85.022 was repaired and lived another fifteen years. There wasn't much left of the DMU.

    He could have made the life of an inexperienced young manager very difficult. He did not. He did everything he could, almost all of the time, to guide and help me to understand and get to grips with my new job. Adam had been elected as the Staff Representative for the Maintenance Supervisors and had his own novel way of discharging this duty. Rather than representing their views to the management – me – he chose instead to tell them what to do, which was nearly always whatever was right for the company and them if they cared to think about it.

    Frank Moran, my Chief Overhead Line Supervisor, was Liverpool Irish and, like many of his chaps, after years in the construction industry, had helped install the early LMR 25kV overhead in the 1950s and had migrated southwards as new construction headed for Euston. He had been the chief at Bletchley since 1966 when the line was energised. Frank had reached the time in his life when the prospect of retirement and more time on the golf course appealed. If there was a

Carriage and Wagon Examiner Derek Antwis re-seats a wagon spring after yet another derailment.

The right hand, single track, bore of Linslade tunnel was the location of the 10ft diameter ball of overhead wire after the de-wirement caused by the p-way department forgetting that the line had been electrified.

real problem, like a mile of overhead line coiled up in a 10ft diameter ball in front of a loco in Linslade Tunnel, as happened in my first year, he was superb. Other times he needed some motivation.

Sam Abbott was my Carriage and Wagon Foreman. He had started as an apprentice coachbuilder at nearby Wolverton Works in 1925 and had worked, briefly, on the Wolverton and Stoney Stratford tramcars, which were the largest trams ever run in the UK and were steam hauled the couple of miles to deliver men to the works. The tram closed in the General Strike of 1926 and never reopened. At the end of his apprenticeship, Sam suffered the same fate as many of his contemporaries in that he was dismissed because of lack of work. The railway companies all did this, having been happy to receive a man's work when paying at the apprentice rate. They also had the temerity to 'summon men to report back as and when there was a job for them'. For Sam and his contemporaries there was the opportunity of well paid work at the Ford factory at Dagenham, which opened in 1931. After a year or so in digs there, he was 'summoned' back to the LMS, working as a coach repairer at Cricklewood Carriage Depot for some years. He remembered that the foreman there used to mark starting and finishing time by striking a buffer heavily with a hammer and sending out a sonorous tone.

Eventually he got back to Wolverton and spent the entire 1950s doing a job which seems inconceivable today. Each morning he booked on at Wolverton, then got on his motorbike and headed for Verney Junction, erstwhile terminus of the Metropolitan Railway and a wayside station on the LMR Oxford to Cambridge line. The line from there to Quainton Road had been closed to all traffic in 1947. Instead, it was used to park five miles of coaches which were only used for six weeks each year. Sam's job was to make his way through all these vehicles in ten months to repair any internal or external fittings ready for next summer.

In contrast to the above, all of which was reasonably well organised, the Plant Maintenance outfit I inherited was a complete shambles. The supervisor was Bill Carty, an Irishman in his sixties with as much blarney as I have ever come across. Our first falling out was when I asked him to come and see me at Bletchley one day. Bill said he was far too busy.

My C&W supervisor, Sam Abbott, was a steady old boy.

The Wolverton and Stoney Stratford tram, owned by the LMS, which Sam had once worked on as an apprentice in 1925.

When I enquired about the nature of his 'busy-ness', I was told that he had a huge number of returns to send each week.

'Right,' I said. 'I'm coming to see you on Tuesday. I want you to lay out on a desk a copy of every return you send.'

I wish I had kept a copy of each form Bill alleged he was filling in each week. There were thirty-four and they included printed examples from the Great Central, LNER, GWR, LMS, BR (E), BR (W), BR (M), Railway Executive, BRB, reflecting the fact that Marylebone had, at various times, come under the auspices of most of the above. I quickly sorted through and told him to continue with four which looked sensible and junk the rest. He had thirteen men on his payroll, some of whom I suspect never appeared and several who did but failed to contribute anything useful. I quickly reduced that lot to a team of three led by a splendid and talented tall Jamaican fitter, Bill Husbands, who looked after all the stations and depots from Marylebone to Banbury, dealing with anything from station lights to a Coles diesel electric mobile crane.

I was immediately faced with a very urgent and serious challenge in that our EMUs had taken to casting off their brake pads all over the railway. When this happened, the steel carrier on which the pad was mounted was forced against the brake disc, which resulted in serious wear to both items and poor brakes. It was so bad that if you travelled in the cab anywhere on the southern part of the WCML, you could see Class '310' brake pads all over the place. When a train came into the

The starting grade in the C&W dept was 'oiler'. Colin Payne, son of chargehand Reg Payne, is learning the ropes with a colleague.

depot, which it would normally do every fourteen days, what should have happened is that the worn carriers would be replaced by new ones and scored brake discs replaced. Since there were no spare carriers and very few spare brake discs, this did not happen. Instead, a new pad was fitted despite the fact that it would fall off again in short order.

Clearly this was a very serious problem and some drastic action was needed to get a grip of it. Since new carriers were not available in any quantity (normally they would last many years, hence the low stock), the only option was to consider repairing the damaged ones and to discover why the problem had happened in the first place. My previous spell at the CM&EE headquarters at Derby came in useful here as I knew the Regional Metallurgist, Tom Evans, who immediately helped me put together a repair procedure for the damaged carriers. Within a couple of days I had Wolverton Works turning out repaired items that were as good as new. In a case like this, it is vital that you identify the root cause of the problem. In this case it was, quite simply, fitters failing to apply locking wire to the two bolts which held the clip that secured the pad on at one end. Within a few weeks we got everything back to normal but not before some excessive hours had been worked.

The Traction part of the organisation, under Adam Blaikie, had several supervisors including four Rolling Stock Inspectors whose

Class 310 disc brake pads. The bottom one shows how they were coming out of service. The cast steel carrier has been rubbing directly on the steel disc....which it obviously is not supposed to do. Above, our repaired item. You can see the weld where a plate has been attached to the carrier after it has been milled to a standard size.

job was to help out with technical problems that might be beyond the capabilities of others. Two stick in my mind in particular.

Jimmy Brown was a small softly spoken Glaswegian who usually had a twinkle in his eye. He wore a blue smock coat and was hardly ever seen without a battered brown trilby. He could charm even the most awkward fitter into doing his bidding and was very technically competent. Tommy Weir was a short Ulsterman with a bald pate that he did not cover. While technically excellent, you would not ask Tom to sort out anything to do with humans!

Both had been instructors during the late 1960s when drivers needed to be weaned off steam and diesel on to the new electric locos. I travelled a lot in those days with loco and EMU drivers and was very impressed by the quality and consistency of driving. This said a lot for the training that Jimmy, Tommy and their colleagues had given. They were also the people who would go out with our

One of our 2 depot drivers, Pete Sirrett, with his brand new Ford lorry. His job was to collect parts from, mostly, Derby and Wolverton works so we could maintain the trains. Pete was one of the most helpful people you could find. A Cockney, he had been a lorry driver since before the War and in 1939 had driven several loads of artworks from Buckingham Palace to a secure store in the Manod slate mine in North Wales.

The Class 115 DMU's came to Bletchley for all the bigger exams, 6,000 mile and above, and also for engine and gearbox changes, which were all too frequent in those days.

breakdown crew whenever it was called. The crew were all volunteer fitters or fitter's mates who were on call and would attend at the depot very quickly if they were off duty. They were pretty busy as there were still a lot of old-fashioned wagons around that caused most of the derailments.

To try to keep these derailments to the minimum, there was a regime of examination of freight trains at start of journey and after 100 miles or so. The people who did this were called Carriage and Wagon Examiners, generally unskilled men who had been found to be trustworthy and conscientious. It helped if they had at least some mechanical aptitude but you really did need to be able to rely on their being where needed to examine a train thoroughly in all weathers and often at night.

Sam, my C&W foreman, was not a very confident man and, having been a coachbuilder, was not all that comfortable with mechanical things, so he always asked if I would conduct interviews for prospective C&W examiners with him. Unlike in the Traction part of the organisation, there was little formal training available for these people so we probed their technical understanding in some detail at interview. I remember that one of the questions I always asked was: 'Please tell me eight defects that could cause a "hot box" on a wagon.' Many wagon derailments started as hot boxes. The hoped for answer was:

1. Lack of oil in the axle box.
2. Absent or defective lubricating pad under the axle journal.
3. The bottom of a split type axle box missing.
4. Excessively worn guard irons, allowing the axle box to jam.
5. Wagon overloaded.
6. Wagon unevenly loaded; too much weight on one end.
7. Underframe twisted, thus overloading one or more axle box.
8. Broken spring, thus causing uneven loading.

Most of the rest of the interview was aimed at trying to understand how reliable the candidate really would be.

It might be worth explaining that the axle boxes comprised a bronze bearing, with a white metal coating, which sat on the smooth end of the axle (called the journal). Under the journal was an oil reservoir and there was a patented cotton pad arrangement which fed the oil upwards. This type of box was, in those days, fitted to the majority of wagons and to a very significant number of passenger coaches, many of which were allowed to run at speeds of up to 90mph. If maintenance was good, as was almost always the case with coaches, they performed perfectly reliably and safely. Indeed, they had one advantage over roller bearings in that their rolling resistance was lower. Wagons, however, were different in that the maintenance was very haphazard and the quality variable at best. As far as I am aware, at the time of writing, there are now no oil axle boxes in regular use on the main line. The only vehicles with them would be steam locomotives.

Not long after I arrived at Bletchley, I decided to pay a call at my nearest Railway department which was Wolverton Works. I had, of course, already been in the 'backdoor' to get the brake pad carriers repaired, but now decided to go and say hello to the Works Manager. He was Geoffrey Tew, a GWR man who had been much involved with loco performance before the war. Indeed, I have a proposed high speed profile for a new GW 'King'-hauled service from Paddington to Birmingham signed by Tew in 1939. He had become Wolverton Works Manager in 1955 and remained there until he retired in 1975.

The staff were terrified of him, which was partly because he almost never came out on the shop floor, partly because he was intensely shy and tended to communicate in short, gruff sentences and grunts. His office was certainly guaranteed to enhance his reputation, as I shall describe. I had been told all this and was, therefore, looking forward very much to meeting him. On entering his office, you did not immediately see him since it was very long, maybe twenty yards, and full of all kinds of wooden models laid out on a long table. Lurking behind all this lot was Geoffrey, sitting at a huge desk. There is no doubt that anyone coming for a bollocking would not really have needed it by the time they had been intimidated by this set-up. I found him to be charming, once you got him warmed up a bit, and could begin to see why he was such a stalwart of the hunting, shooting and fishing set in Buckinghamshire. He had a wife who was a doctor, much younger than him and an absolutely stunning blonde.

One of the features of the depot that I felt uncomfortable about was the fact that one of the cubicles in the gents', uniquely, had a Yale lock as it was supposed to be for managers only. It came off very quickly, as I have always believed that managers have to earn respect, not try to take it in that way. I made sure that all the lavatories were cleaned regularly and properly, not just the managers' one.

I have already mentioned Frank Rolle as having been moved to become an instructor at the Willesden Training School. He had been, as Assistant Area Manager Marylebone, responsible for Marylebone Depot and the maintenance of what we called in those days the GC line fleet of Class '115' DMUs. The thirty-five units, built in Derby in 1960, each comprised a Driving Motor car at each end, each with two 238hp Leyland-Albion engines, and two trailers, one of which was 50% first class. These were substantially built vehicles, 64ft long, whereas most DMUs were 57 footers and they felt much more solid than, for example, a Craven or BRCW unit which always felt as if it was going to shake itself to pieces at speed. The powerful Leyland Albion engines gave these trains very good acceleration, providing that they were all working. That is where the problem lay. They needed rather more love and attention than their much more common 150hp cousins.

A London depot which had difficulty getting staff, any staff, let alone well qualified people, was not the best place to look after them.

The situation was complicated by the fact that, although Marylebone and the line to Aylesbury (less 14.5 miles belonging to London Underground) was by then part of the LMR, the route out to High Wycombe and on to Banbury was part of the WR. It was, therefore, Humphrey Todd, Divisional Manager at Reading, who was harangued in the press for frequent cancellations and trains breaking down and told to tender his resignation by the passengers from Gerrards Cross who, as I can testify, can get very cross indeed. This whole affair came to a head in 1973 just before I went to Bletchley, and my one time boss, Frank Pardoe, was drafted in to solve the problem despite, or perhaps because of, the fact that Marylebone Depot came under the auspices of his colleague, the Divisional Carriage and Wagon Engineer, Harry Noden.

Frank decided that the Electric Traction Department could rise to the challenge and show the C&W people how to do it. Bletchley Depot had the capacity, skills and determination to be part of the solution. Marylebone would continue to do the 750 and 1,500 mile examinations which needed to be done between peaks or at night, while everything else – 3,000, 6,000, 12,000, 24,000, 48,000 and 96,000 mile exams and all major component changes (engines, gearboxes, wheelsets, final drives) – would be done at Bletchley. Bletchley would also supply a fitter to work six nights a week at Aylesbury to make sure that that the twenty-odd units that were stabled there all got off in the morning without any delays. Each weekday evening, at the end of the peak, three units were coupled together and driven across from Aylesbury to Bletchley via Calvert, Claydon LNE Junction and Winslow. Each morning, three units would go back in time to work morning peak trains to Marylebone. The staff at Marylebone Depot was reduced to a handful of thoroughly competent individuals, and one of the shift foremen, Bobby Breingan, was promoted to be the boss.

When I arrived, this was just about working, in that cancellations and train failures were at much more acceptable levels, almost all exams were done when due (which was very far from the case before) but everyone was working flat out, with lots of overtime, and some individuals were making superhuman efforts to keep everything going. The incident with the Class '310' disc brake pads showed me how fragile it all was. Clearly this could not continue. The obvious solution, to recruit more fitters, was not really an option because there were very few suitable men with the right training and experience looking for jobs. Those that were could get better paying ones mostly not involving shifts. Nearly all our fitters had been BR apprentices, who had received a substantial amount of training in both mechanical and electrical work, with the result that they were good at diagnosing faults and carried out their work quickly and accurately, and we

Marylebone depot was run by Glaswegian Bobby Breingan who had got fed up of the trade demarcation and other restrictive practices in Clydeside shipyards. He was a fitter and told how when detailed to fit a bracket he might have to wait four hours for a driller to come and drill the holes in the structure. As a fitter he was perfectly capable of doing it himself. He came south to find work on the railway where this kind of nonsense did not happen. It is no wonder that we lost our shipbuilding industry. I was to see this at closer quarters in my next job.

needed these skills. I determined, therefore, to do two things: to take on several apprentices for the longer term and to improve productivity by analysing and re-planning the work we did.

I took on seven apprentices in August 1974. Five of the seven still worked for me when I retired 37 years later: Brian Green and Ian

Punter at Chiltern's Aylesbury Depot where Punter was a supervisor, Garry Foster, David Nelmes and Vince Heffernan at Willesden TMD, by then run by London Overground. Heffernan even had a son as an apprentice at Aylesbury. Alec Simmons left after his apprenticeship, but not before achieving the distinction of becoming the first BR employee to be disciplined (by me) for not wearing one of the newly introduced high visibility vests. It was a couple of years before these lads made serious inroads into the workload, but they were very useful from then on.

My training as a Production Engineer had led me to believe that there is no situation or process that cannot be improved and speeded up by analysing it and asking 'why?', 'why?', 'why?' until you get to the bottom of every process. I had spent some time watching and asking, and decided that I needed some help. I obtained this in the form of a couple of very competent work study guys who had been trained at the BR school at Watford where I had attended a short course. We, thus, talked the same language and got off to an excellent start. The staff and supervisors at Bletchley were entirely supportive of what I wanted to do since the long hours were getting to be too much, however much some of them liked the extra pay. They also appreciated that I was determined that we would keep the newly won work and they saw the recruitment of extra apprentices as a very positive move.

The principle of what we did was very simple and was, later, used by the two guys at many other BR Traction Maintenance Depots and formed the building blocks which we used a few years later to establish BR's computerised Rail Vehicle recording and planning system – 'RAVERS' – derivatives of which are still in use forty years later. In essence, the task was to identify every individual maintenance task, what it involved, what tools and equipment it needed, how long it took and to document this in a logical way. You might expect that this had already been done. Well, it had in a sense, in that the best supervisors worked all this out themselves. What we were really doing was capturing all the best ideas and documenting them. In effect, this meant that every shift could be as effective as the best had previously been. Because of the way that the two guys worked very closely with both supervisors and shop floor, the new system was easily accepted and was able to help us bring the workload situation under control quite quickly.

In early 1976 I had a visit from Dick Hardy, who I had first met when he and Freddie Clements fixed up for me to go to Crewe three years earlier. He sent a message that when he came he would like to see a fitter called Jack Stowe, who had been at Woodford Halse Shed on the GC when Dick had been Shedmaster, some twenty-five years previously. I remember being somewhat surprised that Dick remembered him although, as I got to know him better over the years, I realised that Dick had an encyclopaedic knowledge of everyone he had ever worked with.

The result of his visit was that I was nominated to go on the BR Middle Management Course at the School of Transport at Derby. This was a well run course which set out to equip us with basic tools of management. In this respect it was useful, but the feature that really stands out after all these years was the visit from David Bowick, then BR's Chief Executive, who joined us for dinner and then spoke to us, as a group, afterwards. You might have noticed that I have made the odd uncomplimentary comment about British Rail's leadership and direction already. Bowick's session was astonishing. First, you had a job to hear him at all despite the fact that we huddled closer and closer. Secondly, it was the most wimpish, lily-livered speech I have ever heard, before or since. And this bloke was supposed to be our leader! Fortunately he was not around for much longer.

Once a month I was called to a Divisional Managers' meeting along with all the Area Managers, AMEs and Divisional Heads. They were held in the former LMS boardroom in Euston House, home, at the time, of the LM Region General Manager's office. We sat at the splendid oval board table which had a polished mahogany top, deep carved edging and discreet bell pushes at each place which had once summoned a flunky. Alas, by this time, there were no flunkies to be had. The meetings were chaired by Geoffrey Huskisson, the DM, and were remarkable chiefly because of the certainty that, at some point, he would explode in a rage which caused his face to erupt in a thunderous deep purple just as he smote the table with his fist. Equally predictable was the cause of this outbreak; it was always something said either by Phil Dunkley, Area Manager Rugby, or, more often, by Arthur Spicer, Area Manager Marylebone.

Dunkley, who later ascended to the prestigious Area Managership at Euston, was a puzzle in that I never really understood what his crime was. Spicer, on the other hand, was about sixty and obviously overpromoted, which he confirmed with every stupid, negative statement he made. There were many stories about Arthur Spicer, mostly related by drivers, several of whom told me that it was always a waste of time looking for him after midday; also that the Area was really run by the ever cheerful Assistant Area Manager, Operations, Bill Crowcombe, known universally as 'laughing Bill'.

Another concerned Alfie Bryant who was the drivers' LDC Rep (staff representative) at Aylesbury. Alfie was a neat, compact man with a toothbrush moustache who, in those days, always boned up his shoes until you could see your face in the toe caps. One cold winter morning he was sitting in the cab of a DMU in the up bay at Aylesbury wishing that the unreliable 'Smiths' heaters were working but having resolved to take the train despite the cold. Spicer turns up in his dark suit and long BR issue black coat and sits down on the secondman's side a couple of minutes before train time. After a moment or two he announces:

'Brrr… it's bloody cold in here, I think I'll go in the train.'

BRITISH RAILWAYS			BR.33063		
DATE 6/8/76 TIME 0810	CAR/ LOCO No. 51657 HOME DEPOT		K 609978		
	DEPOT WHERE LEFT				
REPORTED BY	A BRYANT DEPOT AYL				
DEFECTS. Leave a clear line between items	ACTION TAKEN BY M'TCE STAFF		CHECK or DEPOT No.		S.M's or H. & M.
2 BOLTS MISSING FROM CAB STEPBOARDS (S.)	✓				
WINDOW WASHER N/BS.	✓				
DET BOX SEAL MISSING	✓				
SIGNATURE of SUPERVISOR		DATE 6/8 TIME	DEPOT		

Driver Alfie Bryant could be the bane of fitters lives. The annoying thing was that he was usually correct. This is a page from a DMU repair book which was carried in every cab in those days. One day when he drove over to Bletchley in his Reliant Robin for an LDC meeting, the fitters got their own back on him by placing a repair book in the car and listing the many defects they found.

As he walked towards the warm first class in another coach, he turned and noted that Alfie was trotting along behind him, driver's black bag in hand.

'What are you doing, driver?'

'Well, if it's too cold for you, it's too cold for me, Guv'nor.'

Yet another train cancelled, and to hell with the passengers.

When, twenty years later, I returned to Aylesbury I was more than a little surprised to discover that Alfie was then a Traction Inspector. This was never going to work and he, sensibly, decided, a few months later, to retire at the age of 60. Within weeks he was back, bored with retirement and we re-employed him as a driver until he retired again at 65. He fell on his feet again and started another career as a part time guard for the heritage DMU shuttle from Aylesbury to Princes Risborough, a job which he relished and did very well, always with a smile and an excellent rapport with his regular passengers. He retired for the third time in his late seventies.

Every now and then, the phone rang and Huskisson's secretary told me in her posh Edinburgh accent that Mr Huskisson was wondering what I was doing later that morning. I soon realised that what this meant was that the old bugger was fed up with all the halfwits he had to deal with and would like to come out and have a nice long lunch in a country pub. The first time this happened I had come to work in my smart new yellow BR liveried Morris Marina van which I felt was not appropriate for taking the Divisional Manager to a pub, so I borrowed John Harden's car and picked Huskisson up at the station.

As might be expected, I was a bit apprehensive at first because he was a formidable figure and I had seen the fist come down on the LMS boardroom table a few times. I need not have worried as I found him to be a charming and entertaining companion who always bought me a nice lunch and just wanted to talk in a relaxed way. I think he had just had enough of work and the many incompetent and lazy people he came across. I got to be quite comfortable in his presence and, perhaps, overstepped the mark a little when one day in the car I described a rather stuffy individual as 'like a colonel in the Indian Army'. At this he turned towards me rather formally but with a slight suspicion of a smile: 'Young man, I was a colonel in the Indian Army.' He retired in 1977 but we corresponded until his death a few years later and he was always interested in what I was doing and often asked for my views on recent developments.

Class 52s were in their last few weeks by the time this one came onto Bletchley TMD in 1976. It had been on one of their last workings, the Westbury to Leagrave stone train, when it ran into a tractor at an occupation crossing. Swindon Control told us not to do any repairs at all because it would be scrapped. I had to insist on our repairing the damaged air pipe because we could not move it out of the way otherwise. That won it a reprieve for a few days until, no doubt, some other minor incident precipitated its demise.

One of my many pleasures was celebrating long service or retirements with men who had spent their entire career on the railway. These chaps had all started with the LMS in the '20s, except for Tom Parker who had started with the L&NWR in 1918. I always found it very moving that these chaps had spent their entire working life in one job, often in one place. Of course, they had seen many changes, mostly for the better, as a steam shed was a pretty inhospitable place to work. Ron Felce, second from left, had a steel plate in his head and Ernie Dimmock, on the right, had lost an eye. Both as the result of accidents at work.

One of the special pleasures in a very enjoyable job was celebrating the career of someone who was retiring. In those days, they would almost always have spent their entire working life on the railway, apart, perhaps, from military service (OHMS as the staff clerks would describe it on the record card that they had for everyone). Before 1982, when staff records were computerised and a huge disservice to social history was performed by throwing away all paper records, I, as the manager, could research the retiree in some detail. He would often have applied to the railway company shortly before his fourteenth birthday, and a selection of fascinating documents would be found. Often there was a school report or a letter of recommendation from his headmaster. If he had started with the LMS, which most had, the application form would have included the question: 'Are you good with horses?' Anyone who had been in employment, by any

It was a sad day when Geoffrey Huskisson retired. Monthly Divisional Managers meetings became quite boring.

IF A CERTAIN GUEST OF HONOUR WILL PERSIST IN CALLING FOR THE WAITER IN HIS USUAL MANNER — LET US BE THANKFUL THERE IS NO TRIFLE ON THE MENU!

of the railway companies, in 1926 had a line describing their actions in the General Strike. If they had worked, there was an entry in red ink: 'Remained loyal to the Company.' This was used subsequently in determining promotion. The record card, although brief, told you a lot about a man's career. Usually, one card sufficed for the fifty or more years that a man was a Railway Servant and it would show his progression by listing all his rates of pay (usually including a 'war wage' dating from 1916 but not consolidated until 1968). It would also show any disciplinary offences. Once, at a retirement presentation, I mentioned an incident in 1946 when the miscreant had been given a day's suspension for throwing snowballs. He was still trying to plead his innocence! The oldest retiree I had was Tom Parker who had joined the L&NWR in 1918 at Bletchley as a labourer. He retired, aged seventy-one, in Bletchley, as a labourer.

If one were to describe what the railway felt like from my perspective in the mid 1970s, I would start by pointing out that the aftermath of the Beeching closures was still being experienced, although some were not actually in his original 1963 plan but had been added later. For example, for most of the time I was at Bletchley, the line to Bedford was going to be closed. That it was not was largely down to the efforts of a Bletchley doctor, Peter Jarvis, and his daughter Hilary, who, along with many others, used the line to get to and from school in Bedford. They successfully argued that the local roads were too narrow and indirect for a bus service to be practicable.

Commuter numbers into London were slowly falling, and continued to do so until 1984, and much of the railway felt under threat as a result. On the other hand, Bletchley TMD was an important part of the WCML support infrastructure. At that time, everything had been renewed and a very good fast, reliable train service ran. It was not as frequent as now, but it worked very well and we were all proud to be part of the team that ran it. It demonstrated that a high quality, fast, fairly frequent InterCity service was a winner.

However, there was very limited vision, as is exampled by my boss, John Marson's, reaction when I expressed disappointment that the BR Board had just announced it would not safeguard any of the trackbed of the closed Great Central route. Having told him, as we stood at Calvert on the GC one sunny day in 1974, that I thought the decision was shortsighted and would be regretted, I can still hear him saying: 'Do you *really* think so?'

Some really stupid decisions were taken by quite senior people who seemed to lack brains. An example: all the AC electric locos had been built with two pantographs, which was sensible because pans can be damaged, for example, by pieces of wire hanging down in their way. If you have a second pan, you can swap over and often continue. Someone decided that it would save a lot of money if the second pan was removed. Quite how this was supposed to save money is not clear to me since we had both pans, and the suggestion that cost would be saved by reduced maintenance was nonsense since you could only wear one out at once. At a stroke, electric loco reliability, and hence train punctuality, was reduced for no measurable benefit.

Freight was largely a disaster, with hundreds of thousands of archaic, uneconomic and unsafe four-wheeled wagons in use but doing less than five journeys a year. A huge opportunity had been lost in the 1955 Modernisation Plan when millions were wasted in perpetuating this nonsense rather than taking the first steps to develop a modern network. This was almost certainly because the best managers had left at nationalisation and those remaining either had no imagination or chose not to challenge conventional wisdom.

I certainly perceived that the company was not being led by the firm hand that I felt it needed. Too many decisions were fudged because of lack of a clear strategy and an inclination to give in to the trade unions. Richard Marsh, the former Labour Transport Minister, was the uninspiring Chairman for my first few years in BR and was replaced by Peter Parker in 1976. Parker certainly encouraged railwaymen to be proud of what they were achieving and started to put BR on the 'front foot', although it took his successor Bob Reid to actually start putting words into action.

Rule 1.2.2. of the BR Rule Book said: *'Employees must not report for duty under the influence of intoxicating liquor or of any drug that might impair the proper performance of their duties. They must not consume intoxicating liquor or any such drug while on duty.'*

Despite this, drinking at lunchtime, sometimes to excess and sometimes during working time, was practised by a sizeable minority of managers. Nor were these habits confined to managers. At one time I used to travel home from Euston to Stafford in the late evening, always in the cab with a Liverpool driver (because that was the train that happened to stop at Stafford). Invariably, around Tring, the driver would put the master controller in 'EO', which was the equivalent of putting a car in neutral, and enabled him to leave his position and go back to the urinal inside the loco without the Driver's Safety Device bringing the train to a stand. I would find myself alone in the cab of a driverless loco doing 100mph with 500 people behind who had every right to assume that the driver was doing his utmost to look after their safety. Now, obviously, I knew how to stop the train or sound the horn, but I have no reason to suppose that this did not go on routinely. To give some reassurance, the AWS would have stopped the train in the event of a signal that was not green being encountered; however, if

The new BR Chairman visited many parts of his new 'empire'soon after he arrived. Bob Long, Asst Area Manager, and I hosted Peter Parker for a staff meeting in his second week.

anything untoward had happened, like a freight train derailing, the missing driver would not have been there to act.

You might well ask why this was tolerated. In fact, it was much worse: when the new Euston Station opened in 1966, there was a staff bar, the Griffin Bar, named after the first Area Manager, under the concourse. When I asked why this was, I was told that it made it easier for the traincrew supervisors since they did not have to send a runner around several pubs if they needed to get hold of a driver. It took Bob Reid to crack down on all this nonsense a few years later but not before a Freightliner train, which had stopped in a loop on Beattock, ran back, wrong line, down the hill for about twelve miles because the driver had got out to relieve himself and had failed to secure his train. Fortunately, it did not hit anything. You will be pleased to know that a modification called 'SSF' was introduced on all locos and multiple units a few years later, which meant that it was impossible to run the vehicle at more than 6mph with the master controller in 'EO'. If you try to, the brakes will come on.

I, and most of my contemporaries, took a very serious view of this laxity. I made it very clear at Bletchley that the Rule Book would be complied with and transgressors would be disciplined. Therefore, when a 'little bird' tipped me off that one of the Shift Supervisors, when on late turn, had a habit of leaving his post and visiting the Staff Association Club for a drink while on duty, I felt the need to act. A couple of weeks later, I was returning from London at about 21.00 when he was on duty and decided to look into the club on my way home. Sure enough, there he was, pint in hand. A simple request to come and see me at 09.00 the following day was all that was needed at that point. I dismissed him.

I had been working towards full membership of the Institution since starting at college in 1967. I had achieved the academic qualifications at Stafford and now had the requisite practical and management experience to be accepted as a Member when I was twenty-seven. I was very proud to be able to use the letters 'CEng MIMech E' after my name, denoting that I was now a Chartered Engineer. This meant that I was recognised as competent to exercise skill and judgement in connection with engineering design, manufacture and maintenance. In practice, as I have told a great many young engineers, the most valuable skill is to know what you do not know and when to seek advice from someone more knowledgeable. I have used this skill to judge many non-engineering situations and determine who is bullshitting and who knows what they are talking about.

I was an active participant in IMechE activities and I well remember a visit to the Timken Roller Bearing factory near Daventry in 1976. A coach was arranged and I chatted to a young chap who sat next to me. He had just started as a railway journalist after some time with English Electric so we had some experience in common except that his interest was in 'Deltics'. His name was Roger Ford.

I was also a regular attendee at meetings at the institution's HQ in Birdcage Walk in London. Under the eye of a splendid full length portrait of founder George Stephenson, I have listened to excellent papers on many subjects including the new InterCity 125 train just about to go into service on the Western Region. One memorable paper by Freddie Beasant, Traction Director at Brush, described a demonstration his father, an engineer with Bristol Tramways, had set up for him. After service hours, the current had been switched off and a tram placed at the top of a steep hill with another at the bottom. The one at the top was allowed to run down the hill causing, to the delight of the young Freddie, the other to rise about 60% of the way up the hill.

At about this time, I started going on the annual IMechE Railway Division outings to other countries. These were excellent, not only because you got to see behind the scenes at other railways, but also because there was the opportunity to talk to senior and retired engineers who were all very willing to tell you about their experiences. These included Terry Miller after he retired as CM&EE, BRB, Colin Curtis who had been with London Transport buses since 1946 and had spent much of his career developing the Routemaster, and Gordon Hafter who retired as Director of Mechanical Engineering for the Underground.

Not long before I left Bletchley, Adam Blaikie brought his youngest son Robert to 'see where Dad worked'. Robert was twelve and had a bright red woollen jumper. I said hello and chatted to the boy for a few minutes. Some twenty-five years later, when I was in my office at Aylesbury, the phone rang and it was the boy in the red jumper, by now a Traction Arranger at Willesden TMD, asking if I remembered him and if I could offer some advice as he was about to be made redundant. Shortly afterwards he started as a supervisor at Aylesbury. A few months later, I got a really nice card from his mother, Eileen, who thanked me for helping him and added that Adam, who had died many years before, would have been very proud of what I had achieved since working with him. I value that card.

I really enjoyed my first 'command', which lived up to all my expectations, and more. I had the opportunity to lead my own team and to understand a lot more about how machines, organisations, people and life work and interact. It had been a time to experiment with many of the skills that I had been taught over the previous few years. I also enjoyed being part of the community and dealing with other businesses and local politicians. My wife, Diana, was a teacher in Bletchley and taught some of the children of my employees, which could be interesting.

However, there came a time, after I had been there for about two and a half years, when I felt that a new challenge was needed. In early 1977, the main opportunities were on the Eastern Region, which was

In the long established tradition, I thought it would be a nice idea to get some of my staff to pose on a loco when I left. On the extreme right is Cyril Ropke, member of the breakdown gang, shop rep and originally a boilersmith who was made redundant from Caerphilly Works in South Wales. There, in the '50s and '60s, blue asbestos was used to insulate boilers. Cyril, like many of his contemporaries, later died an unpleasant death of mesothelioma as a result.

preparing for a major upgrade to its ECML services involving the introduction of InterCity 125 trains, which was very exciting. I saw a couple of advertisements for Depot Managers, one at Bounds Green in London and the other at Heaton in Newcastle. I rang a friend, Steve Hoather, who was the IC 125 engineer at Eastern Region HQ at York. He told me what was going on, explained that both depots were substantially new and that if I applied for Heaton I must be mad. I applied for and was interviewed for both.

I was not sorry when Dave Perry, brother of Cliff, who was Depot Engineer at Bristol Bath Road at the time, got Bounds Green. I was delighted to have the opportunity to savour the challenges in Newcastle, from where my ancestors came. My last day at Bletchley was Friday, 22 April 1977 and the following Monday I started the only job that I ever applied for. My son Alastair had been born three weeks earlier.

Chapter Five

Launching HSTs at Heaton

Heaton Depot had just been completed and formed an important part of the project to introduce the new InterCity 125 trains on to the East Coast Main Line. As its manager, I was to be part of a team which included Dave Perry, who had been appointed to run Bounds Green Depot in London, Jim Walkden, who ran Leeds Neville Hill Depot and Kevin Loney, who ran Craigentinny Depot in Edinburgh, together with Operations people at Eastern Region HQ at York, in each of the three ER Divisions and the Scottish Region. It was a tremendously exciting time and there was a huge enthusiasm to make the whole project successful. I already knew what a fabulous train the IC 125 was, having followed its production at Derby and Crewe, travelled in the prototype, and listened to several presentations on it at the IMechE.

I was welcomed to Newcastle Division by Bill Gilpin, Assistant Divisional Traction Engineer, which was the same role that I had held at Euston three years previously. Bill was a rather wild looking individual who clearly had suffered a few reverses in his life. I soon learnt that he had been the Depot Engineer at Gateshead, which was the largest diesel loco maintenance depot in the North East, but had been relieved of his command. As I came to understand a little of what went on in this far flung part of England, it soon became obvious that Bill, who had a reputation as a 'hard man', would have been seen as rocking the boat unduly. This view was further advanced when, a couple of years later, I discovered that as a young chargehand in the steam shed in Workington, he had scandalised the establishment because he put his own father, a fitter, on a formal disciplinary charge for some misdemeanour.

Bill and I took to each other immediately and I found him to be a constant source of information, help and encouragement. He seemed to positively revel in helping someone who he, correctly, perceived as prepared to stand no nonsense from anyone. He had been very much involved in specifying the newly completed £7 million depot and its *modus operandi* and was very anxious to seek my approval for what he had done. Having been shown around it all by him and having had the flow process for dealing swiftly and effectively with the servicing of complete rakes of coaches explained, I told him that I thought he had done a great job, given the constraints of the site. It was about three miles north of Newcastle Central Station and in the fork where the formerly electrified line to Tynemouth and Whitley Bay deviated from the ECML. He was very apologetic that my job had been advertised so late, with the result that most of the key managers and supervisors had already been appointed. He told me that he had argued strongly that my job, as the boss, should have been filled first so that I could choose my team but he had been overruled by others who, in his opinion, did not understand management. As I got to know those concerned, I tended to agree with his judgement. Bill had, however, been involved in the selection of the team and, with one or two exceptions, had not done a bad job.

My deputy was a prematurely grey, mild mannered and softly spoken locomotive engineer called Colin Cleminson who, having spent all his career in and around Newcastle, was an invaluable source of local information. My Operations Assistant, Bob Ellison, was an inspired choice; he was approaching sixty and was full of enthusiasm for the exciting new adventure that we were embarking upon. Bob had been a driver for 'Monty', General Montgomery, at El Alamein and had driven a Humber 4x4 staff car many thousands of miles in the desert. Joining the LNER in 1946, he had worked his way up through the grades of Goods Shunter, Passenger Shunter, Goods Guard and Passenger Guard before being promoted to the rank of Inspector and then rose to be Chief Inspector at Newcastle Central. He had been a union rep at various times and knew all the tricks and scams, who the rascals were and how to get things done. He was a tireless supporter and an enormous help, especially since my operational knowledge was a little limited.

Real-time management was delegated to one of five Shift Managers who had total control of all activities, engineering or operational, on their shift. They were all youngish engineers, newly recruited and from a variety of backgrounds. Dave Panks was a bluntly spoken Yorkshireman who at first appeared very macho and confrontational, until you realised that was just how people from his part of the world projected themselves. He was quite soft actually. Malcolm Bundy, always full of enthusiasm, had started as an apprentice in Derby Loco Works in 1966 and had worked his way on to the Management Training Scheme. Colin Precious hailed from Hull where he had quickly progressed from the shop floor to become a technical instructor, teaching his former steam fitter colleagues about new diesel locos. Geoff Errington, from Edinburgh, was the most academic of the crew and often got knotty problems to work through. The final member of the group was Ken Deighton who was almost old enough to be father to the others who were all about my age, twenty-eight. The reason for having five was that we needed one of them there continuously. With five, and careful rostering, you can achieve this and allow for holidays and a modest amount of training and the odd day off sick. They all had different experience and ability and, even though only one was on duty at any one time, they worked together as a team really well, allocating tasks among themselves according to their abilities.

Heaton staff looking their best for Peter Parker's visit to officially open the depot. L to R, Malcolm Bundy, Production Manager (PM), Gordon Fairburn, chief clerk, Owen and Jim Robson, clerks, with Ken Deighton and Colin Precious, PM's.

Bob Ellison had done a good job in recruiting Operations Supervisors whose role was to make sure that the flow of trains did indeed run smoothly and safely. They included Bram Yates, who always came to work dressed immaculately, complete with dickie bow, which must have looked even more out of place at his previous posting of Healey Mills freight sorting yard. Another very useful member of the team was a former Traffic Management trainee in his first job, John Holroyd, who went on later to be Operations Manager for the very large Scottish road haulage and logistics company W.H. Malcolm.

The concept of Depot Manager was a new one for the Eastern Region and I, formally, reported to two bosses. Ralph Lewis was the white-haired patrician Divisional Operations Superintendent who was always there if you wanted advice but did not, otherwise, trouble himself with what he regarded as a purely maintenance depot. Alan Clothier had been a Western man but had been appointed as Divisional Maintenance Engineer at Newcastle at just thirty-five in 1965, and also left me very much alone except for such unwelcome intrusions as I shall report later.

Both, however, had various lieutenants who I saw much more of. Martin Idale and Mike Donnelly were both young and vigorous managers who were very helpful in various ways, often in helping to demystify the sometimes illogical ways of the Operating Department. This was much more than can be said of their boss, Les Binns, who sat, organisationally, between them and Ralph Lewis. Les appeared to spend his entire working hours in his office behind the portico at Newcastle Central Station, puffing on his pipe and writing pithy comments in green ink on correspondence that crossed his desk. He was the example I thought of most often when I reflected on the fact that BR had too many unnecessary layers of management. Surprisingly he was later promoted as we shall discover presently. Clothier's deputy was Derek Reeves, the Divisional Traction Engineer, the equivalent of my former mentor Frank Pardoe, who was often to be seen driving himself to work in the cab of a DMU from Darlington, where he had lived for his entire life, his father having been Works Manager at the Loco Works. The most useful person to me was his assistant Bill who we have already met.

Another regular contact in the Divisional Office was the young Training Manager, Michael Woods, who later became Area Manager at Dartford and then, after a spell in the Office of Rail Regulation, where he saved me £500,000 on the cost of building Warwick Parkway Station, became a consultant. In this role, I was his first customer. At the time if writing he is a wise old bird at RSSB.

I was quickly brought into the planning meetings at York HQ for the whole ECML HST launch. There was very much a team spirit among the engineers (of various persuasions), the operators and the marketing people. We oversaw the whole plan, contributing to all aspects of it, and then went away to deliver our part of it in the knowledge of how it fitted into the big picture. There I met, among others, Dave Perry, my opposite number at Bounds Green, pipe smoking Jim Walkden, boss of Neville Hill, and Chris Kinchen-Smith, his able deputy. I learnt a lot from this multidisciplinary approach and have used the experience many times.

For several months my routine was to leave home, in Bletchley, on Sunday evening and catch the sleeper from King's Cross to Newcastle. In those days, all the sleeping cars were BR Mk 1s which were quite comfortable but did have various quirks. For example, on occasion you would open the door to find a steam-filled room resulting from a leaking gland on the radiator valve. Electric heating had not, then, reached the Eastern Region. Shutting the valve generally assured a steam-free, if cold, night. Further adjustments might be necessary if you could not sleep because of excessive track noise coming from holes in the floor around the heating pipes. Stuffing the towel into the holes was the solution here. Of course, such defects were my fault as the cars were allocated to Heaton for maintenance and I would personally mark up the job card for attention. One advantage of having the sleeping cars at Heaton was that, when they arrived at Newcastle, the two very jolly sleeper cleaning ladies joined the empty stock and rode on it to the depot. This meant that I could get half an hour's more sleep than other passengers and, also, a cup of tea from the ladies!

On Friday, I usually left mid-afternoon and rode in the cab of a 'Deltic'-hauled express to King's Cross. Having been on the English Electric loco section at Derby a few years before, many parts of the 'Deltic' were familiar except, of course, for the two amazing engines, each of which had no fewer than thirty-six pistons and made a huge noise that was very noticeable in the cab.

A very interesting sight, observed first hand from the 'Deltic' cab, was the rebuilding of two tunnels on the ECML. These both required the floor to be lowered in order to provide room for larger containers and for future electrification. Rather than close each tunnel completely, which I suspect is what would happen now, a system of working was devised which involved single line working through the tunnel while the track was removed on one side and the floor was lowered. There was a fence down the middle of the tunnel to allow work to take place while trains were running. The single line working was carried out most efficiently because there was a signal box in a Portakabin together with points and signals at each end of the tunnel. All train movements were timetabled, taking account of this operation. When one tunnel was done, the entire kit – signal box, points and signals – was moved to the second tunnel where it was reused. This is a really good example of effective team working across departments with a common goal. Just the sort of thing that the civil servants and lawyers, who do not understand how things work, prevented by forcing an unsuitable method of privatisation later on. In so doing, they increased massively and unnecessarily the cost of the railway.

During the week, I lodged at Monkseaton, on the coast, with a taciturn Gateshead driver Walker and his wife, Ann, who provided B&B in their large red brick Edwardian semi. I travelled between there and Walkergate Station on a DMU on the line which had formerly been electrified and which now is part of the Tyne and Wear Metro. The DMUs were unkempt, dirty and plainly were not being looked after properly at Gosforth Depot, which had a very poor reputation. You could see why.

When I started at Heaton, we had about 130 of the planned complement of some 350 staff that we would need when the depot was fully commissioned. Meanwhile, the task at that time was to maintain several hundred Mk 1 and Mk 2 coaches. The newer ones, all air-conditioned, were made up into regular sets and used on 'Deltic'-hauled ECML trains; older ones formed regular Newcastle to Liverpool sets while there was also a very large itinerant fleet of shabby miscellaneous coaches which were used all over the Region and which no one loved. They would often turn up only a few hours before being booked to work a football, or other, special. Because every depot had the opportunity to shovel them off elsewhere, it was not uncommon to find them months out of date for important safety-related maintenance. You had no forewarning of this, only a foreboding, because the entire maintenance recording system comprised chalk marks on the coach itself. I am pleased to say that this entirely unsatisfactory and unsafe situation does not now exist with the modern railway. Indeed, it did not exist then on the other Regions, all of which had rather better systems. In this, as in so many other areas, I found the Eastern Region far behind, but trying hard to catch up.

One of my first jobs was to move maintenance and cleaning of these coaches into the shiny new and very well equipped depot. It was still being done in litter strewn old sidings with rotten sleepers, rough walkways and no shelter from harsh North Eastern winters. There was provision for steam heating the older coaches and this comprised a steam main, supplied from a fixed boiler, which ran under six sidings at the point where the back of the train would come to a stand. Now, in order to be able to couple the rear coach to this system, it was necessary to stop the train, which was being propelled by a locomotive 200 yards away, quite precisely. Officially, what was supposed to happen was that the shunter, in charge of the move, would be on the ground close to the steam pipe and would communicate with the driver by hand signals, or lamp at night. There were no radios in those days and this system suffered from the obvious defect that it was not easy for the driver to see the shunter in favourable conditions, and actually impossible until the last minute with a long train because of a curved approach to the sidings.

As is often the case, the men on the ground had, long ago, devised a far neater, but frighteningly dangerous, alternative. The shunter would instruct the driver to propel the train in and stop several yards short. At this point, he would remove the vacuum pipe (known locally as a hogger) and put an empty Coke can over the end. The driver would then blow up the vacuum and the can would thus be held in place. Having, then, instructed the driver to push back, the shunter would perform the potentially lethal action of going behind the moving train to kick the Coke can off. This, of course, destroyed the vacuum and stopped the train immediately. Thinking about what might have happened if he had slipped on a wet sleeper or missed the can is just too awful.

As soon as I became aware of this appallingly dangerous practice, I had no alternative but to stop it immediately. Fortunately, I had an alternative in that the new shed was now ready and the layout was such that trains could be hauled in loco first. I very quickly found out why this had not been done already. We had twenty Carriage and Wagon Examiners whose duties included changing brake blocks and adjusting the brake rigging. They point blank refused to move into the new shed despite the fact that it did not snow in there, it was heated in winter and they did not have to lie on their back in a mixture of oil and faeces to adjust the brakes. Apart from the fact that no one had bothered to discuss this with them, their very practical objection was that when standing in the inspection pit beneath the train, they could not get enough leverage to pull the brake rods up tight. By then we had several very good maintenance supervisors who I engaged to work through with the examiners how best to ease their task. Having always worked for 'operating' types before, this idea of a supervisor actually understanding their task and wanting to make it easier was a novelty – one that they liked. So opposition to the move gradually melted away, perhaps helped by their seeing that I had absolutely no intention of backing down.

The C&W staff and most of the other grades, wholly male in those days, almost always communicated any grievance that they had via their representative (usually elected by the employees, rather than appointed by the trade union). The women cleaners, however, took a much more direct approach which I rather preferred. An example was the morning that I arrived at the depot at about 07.30, as usual, to find a small deputation of women from the night shift. Two of the older women spoke for another in her mid twenties who, they alleged, had

Electrician Alan Hampton attending to a Mk 2 coach.

been molested by their chargeman. According to them, at about 02.00, she had been bending over a bucket in a brake van when he had put his hand up the back of her dress. The chargeman, Youssef, was a very smartly dressed man who was something of a perfectionist, no bad thing for a cleaning supervisor, you might think. He was the head of his family, owned several corner shops in Newcastle and had previously been a passenger guard at Newcastle Central. There, he had impressed Bob Ellison very much with the very efficient and polite way that he did his job. So much so that Bob had invited him to come to the new depot at Heaton to help set the standard that would be needed for the forthcoming HSTs. The existing cleaners, many of whom had worked in very poor conditions and without proper discipline or supervision for years, were, therefore, experiencing a bit of a culture shock.

This was at the back of my mind as I listened carefully and without interrupting for several minutes as they told me what had happened. I then said that I would need to hear Youssef's side of the story before considering what action, if any, I might take. I saw him separately and he denied that any such incident had taken place. Indeed, as he remarked, having four wives, he was not in need of additional female company. Here we have an interesting situation where several women were all assuring me that an unsavoury incident had taken place while the alleged perpetrator had no supporting witnesses and swore that they were lying. I had no clear evidence as to who was telling the truth and recognised that this needed resolving quickly so I told them all to go home, it being long after the end of their shift by now. I said that I would see them again at 07.30 on the following day.

My next move was to discuss this with Bob Ellison who undertook to go and make a few enquiries. Later that day he reported that the word on the street was that the cleaners had been plotting for several days how they could rid themselves of this very correct chargeman who had a peculiar idea that they should be present for their whole shift rather than skiving off half way through as they had been used to. I suspect that the women thought that they had devised a killer plan. However, the following morning I told them that I not only did not believe them, but that I fully supported the firm line that Youssef had taken both on standards of work and timekeeping. It was immediately obvious from their reaction that I had successfully called their bluff. They did not quite say 'fair cop', but their demeanour told me that they knew their try-on had not worked. Youssef had no more such accusations while I was at Heaton.

The other manager I inherited was the Chief Clerk, who provided me with admin, financial and personnel support. He was a big man with a lazy eye which made him look rather menacing. He was another who knew most of the scams and tricks of the trade. In fact, he was quite a 'wide boy'. Now this can be a useful trait in a Chief Clerk but only if you grow to fully trust him, which I never quite did. While he was boasting about some stunt he had pulled on someone else, I was always left wondering what else he had done without telling me. A pity, because as I have found both before and after, this kind of role if done well can be a real strength for a manager who is trying to do the right thing and not necessarily trying to be universally liked.

I had noticed that one of his clerks appeared to leave early every day and enquired what was going on there. The reply, which spoke of administrative incompetence over many years, was astonishing. It seems that the North Eastern Railway, which clearly had the level of profitability from coal which leads to profligacy, had, during the Great War in 1915, seen fit to grant some of its clerks a thirty-five hour week, unlikely as that may seem. Later on, the LNER wanting to rescind this wanton concession, had decreed that it would only apply to the post of the clerk so advantaged. If it had applied to the person the practice would have literally died out over time. Since it was the post it continued until BR bit the bullet and abolished it but incredibly said that the person in such a post could keep the thirty-five hour week whatever job they moved to. Thus a new depot in 1977 was stuck with a piece of nonsense from 1915.

The old Mark 1's still needed looking after, here by one of our 'C & W'semi skilled electricians.

We were all reminded of the need for eternal vigilance when an incident that could have ended in a very serious way occurred. When a locomotive couples on to a train or an additional vehicle is added, it is mandatory to do a brake test, the purpose of which is to check that there is continuity of the brake pipe from end to end. This is particularly important with an air braked train because it would be quite easy to leave one of the brake cocks, at the end of a vehicle, closed. One particular Newcastle driver was well known for being cantankerous and unhelpful to his guard. Having brought his 'Deltic' light engine to our yard, he had it coupled on to his train by one of our shunters and then, because he was late, shouted at the guard and somehow persuaded him not to bother with a brake test.

Surprisingly, he managed to stop at Durham and Darlington without noticing anything amiss. It was when he overran the platform at York by a couple of coach lengths (the

Newly delivered
254.001, the first East Coast HST, on an early training run in Newcastle.

Supervisor Kenny Harper, one of the team who had trained the new fitters, checks the AWS cable under a power car.

signal was 'off') that he realised what had, or rather had not, happened. He went charging down the platform very publicly berating the useless guard for not doing a brake test. One of the brake cocks between engine and train was closed, with the result that he had only had the engine brake even though he had been doing up to 100mph. The platform inspector at York soon found out what had happened and the foolish driver found himself in deep trouble.

While all this was going on, the real task was to prepare for the imminent arrival of the new HSTs, the first of which, 254.001, arrived in late June. These splendid new trains called for altogether different treatment from that historically meted out by those at Heaton. We had calculated that we needed more than forty skilled fitters and electricians to look after the fleet that we would soon have custody of. Ideally we should have had dual trained men who could turn their hand to anything that needed doing, as the London Midland Region had had for many years. Here, unfortunately, was another example of the Eastern Region being behind the times. I did not have the luxury of the time I would have needed to win this argument either with the trade unions or with the management who were actually the source of the problem.

I, therefore, spent much of my time during the early summer of 1977 recruiting skilled fitters and electricians. One beneficial, to us, side effect of the collective suicide being committed by Tyneside shipyard workers was that hundreds of them replied to job advertisements. I got several Maintenance Supervisors to help me with this task and, between us we devised a series of filters through which to put the applicants. We soon found that the long-serving men who had never worked anywhere but the shipyard were no use to us at all in that, because of trade demarcation, their skill range was far too narrow. Maintaining trains calls for someone who has a good appreciation of how the whole complex machine works and can turn his hand to anything that needs doing either on a scheduled or a repair basis. There were quite a large number of applicants who fitted this profile very well. Typically, having completed their apprenticeship, they had opted for the excitement of a life at sea. This usually meant starting as a Third Engineer in some small rusting tub where the fancy title

HSTs can be coupled either to themselves or to a loco using the sort of emergency coupling that I am demonstrating.

Stores supervisor Charlie Pomeroy is much taken with his new side lift fork truck. Air-con modules for HST trailers are on the right.

Getting the first trains out at 04.30 on a winter morning could be 'interesting' in a Tyneside winter.

masked the fact that they were called upon to do any difficult, dirty, hot, unpleasant job that arose. I listened to lots of fascinating stories of removing piston and con rod from a six cylinder main engine under sweltering conditions in order to run it on five cylinders because that was the only way to escape the rocky tropical shore that you were drifting towards in a storm. These guys, having had a baptism of fire after a pretty good basic apprenticeship, were just who we wanted.

Incidentally, the invariable reason why they had returned to the shipyard was that their girlfriends actually wanted to see something of them.

Almost the first thing I had done at Heaton was to send several of the Maintenance Supervisors, who did not yet have much to do, on instructor courses so that they could teach the new recruits the intricacies of HST maintenance. This worked very well as the new guys were eager learners, and it also earned the Supervisors the respect of the very talented fitters and electricians. Oh, and because of their previous experience, they were eager to get on with the job and turn their back on the nonsense of demarcation.

Monday, 7 November 1977 was the day selected for British Rail Chairman Peter Parker to come and officially open Heaton Depot. He arrived in the cab of a brand new HST which had brought him from Central Station and came right into the main building. My job was very simple: I took him and led him around the length and breadth of the building, introducing him to staff as we met them. He was very good with people and had the ability to make even the most humble feel important. He was a bit lost for words, however, when my Senior Technical Officer, Gordon Nicholson, tried to explain how the HST power control circuits worked!

Senior Technical Officer Gordon Nicholson was better at repairing electronic equipment than explaining it to our resolutely non-technical chairman.

After about forty minutes of this, the Chairman asked if there was somewhere private that we could go so that he could freshen up. As it happens, we had a salaried staff toilet, just the sort of thing I had got rid of at Bletchley, so I took him there. An astonishing transformation then took place before my very eyes. It was if he turned a switch in his brain. Gone was the confident, affable controlled Chairman, for I saw before me a man who needed to recoup his mental energy and to be reassured about how he was doing. Who was he seeing at the forthcoming press conference? What he should say? I was amazed, but tried to calm and reassure my Chairman, realising that, at heart, here was an actor for whom the real world was his stage. Then, after a couple of minutes, he flicked the switch and there was Peter Parker, Chairman of the British Railways Board. But I now knew this was just the character he was playing. As it happens, the press conference was tame in the extreme and Parker was soon on his way, leaving us to introduce the HST fleet into service from the forthcoming timetable change.

During the late summer and autumn, each new HST, having been commissioned, was immediately put to staff training of either drivers, maintenance or catering staff. Astonishingly, the plan was to have no fewer than twelve of the latter on each train, using two catering vehicles. (Remember this was before anyone had any idea of the profitability of the business. Costs and revenues still only came together on the Chief Executive's desk.)

After a whistlestop tour of the depot, the chairman heads to his press conference. L to R, Geoff Myers, Eastern Region GM patting his head, Peter Parker, Divisional Manager John Thompson, and one of my two bosses, silent Ralph Lewis, the Divisional Operating Superintendent.

One of the newly arrived ex-Gosforth DMUs on the jacks repairs.

One wizard new wheeze dreamt up by the marketing Johnnies was to have beer on tap in the bar. As you might expect, there was a meter on each tap to show the volume dispensed in order that daily stocktaking could be undertaken. This, however, reckoned without the scale of corruption that was endemic within train catering in those days. These were the days when chief stewards bought their own bread and had sandwiches made up on the train and bought crisps and snacks from the cash and carry and, in each case, pocketed the proceeds. Much more profitable (to them) than selling the official stuff.

It was really not surprising, then, that one of our maintenance people came to me, tears in eyes, to report that 'some bastard' had been vandalising our wonderful new trains. The meter was a bit like an old fashioned odometer on a car. It had quite clearly been smashed by someone hitting it hard with a screwdriver. Other acts of vandalism, always to catering equipment, followed soon after. Our people just could not believe how anyone could do this to such a beautiful new train and they were really upset. I was straight on the tail of the Restaurant Car Manager, a Glaswegian, full of bullshit, who I never saw completely sober. Unfortunately, he was on leave so his young deputy, Theo Steel, got the full force of my considerable anger. I suspect he did not know what hit him. Nor did the vandalism stop.

The HSTs went into service one set at a time from late autumn 1977 and, for such a complex train, were remarkably trouble-free. They were an immediate success with passengers and really transformed their whole experience, despite the worst efforts of the catering staff. The fact that they are still in front line service forty years later shows what fantastic trains they are, designed, of course, under the auspices of the old steam man, T.C.B. Miller.

Heaton Depot had been designed with the capability of maintaining the fleet of DMUs which would be left over after the new Metro had taken over services from Newcastle to 'The Coast'. They were transferred from Gosforth Car Sheds in early 1978 along with those staff members who wanted to stay with BR. I think it would be fair to say that the more adventurous and forward thinking fitters decided to stay at Gosforth and be in at the start of a new venture.

We tried to make the new arrivals feel at home in our immaculate new depot. However, nothing seemed to suit their staff representatives. After one particularly tedious meeting which had lasted eight hours, simply because the Shop Committee insisted on going around and around over the same ground and asking the same silly questions in numerous different ways, I was rather more glad than usual to get home. I was half way through supper with my wife when the phone rang in the hall. It was Alan Clothier, the Divisional Maintenance Engineer, one of my two bosses. I was immediately suspicious when he started off by asking me whether I thought I might have been a bit hard at the consultation meeting today. What? How did he know about the meeting? What had it got to do with him?

It was obvious what had happened. He had just been called by a 'Big Man' called George Arnold, the AEU District Organiser, who was on local TV most nights criticising industry and, very successfully, helping to close down much of the once proud engineering and shipbuilding industry on Tyneside. Why he thought throwing thousands of people out of work advanced the cause of socialism was never clear to me. Clothier was terrified of him.

I was in no mood for compromise so I gave it to him with both barrels: 'Look, Mr Clothier, you pay me to run the depot. I have made some perfectly reasonable proposals which have been discussed at very great length. After taking account of their views I have told them that I am going to implement the necessary changes. I will not have trade union officials telling me how I am going to run my depot.' With that, I put the phone down on him. I heard nothing more of the matter and went ahead and implemented the changes to working practices shortly afterwards. It was plain that our friends from Gosforth had always been allowed to do as they pleased in the past.

The DMUs from Gosforth were in such appalling condition that, even though the required availability was not very high, we had difficulty, for a while, in covering all their booked afternoon diagrams. There was a small silver lining to this cloud in that we had a set of three Mk 1 coaches whose duty was finished by about 15.00 and, after the introduction of the first HSTs into service, there were several 'Deltics' with no booked work. Consequently, a train composed of a 'Deltic' plus three coaches left the depot at about 17.00 each weekday and worked an all stations train from Newcastle to Hexham. The ride home in this extremely lively train was very rewarding!

Divisional Managers' meetings were pretty boring after Geoffrey Huskisson's at Euston: no smiting of the table and shouting at idiots. At least Huskisson did it all out in the open. In Newcastle, the DM, John Thompson, was calm and collected in his meetings. Privately, however, like some other rather insecure people, he could be an out and out bully who destroyed, to my knowledge, the careers of at least two managers who were unable to stand up to him. The two most senior, and very competent, managers were Neil Clark, a civil engineer who as Area Manager Newcastle, was my closest and very helpful contact. Neil went on to be one of Her Majesty's Railway Inspectors and, after retirement, was Chairman of the North Yorkshire Moors Railway until 2014. The other was 'Gentleman' Dick Taylor, AM Freight, based at Tyne Yard. There were also three or four more junior AMs who still seemed to me to be running yesterday's railway.

One day in early autumn 1978, Mike Casey, the Eastern Region CM&EE, brought his fellow CM&EEs to Heaton to show it off. The party included Maurice Maguire (Southern), Dougie Power (Western), Vernon Atkinson (Scottish) and Freddie Clements, my old boss on the LM. Part way through the tour, Clements took me aside and whispered that he would like me to come over to Carlisle as Area Maintenance Engineer. Carlisle was a much bigger job than either Bletchley, where I had also been Area Maintenance Engineer, or, indeed, Heaton. It was graded accordingly and also had the merit that it was the only place within travelling distance of Riding Mill, where we lived, that I could move to with a promotion.

So I left Heaton in November 1978, just eighteen months after arriving. It had been a very exciting, fast-moving job, the overriding purpose being the preparations for the introduction of the transformational new HST service. Everyone involved in this was caught up in the excitement and we made fast progress, swiftly navigating around the inevitable problems that arose. The downside was the constant battle with the men who came from Gosforth along with their scruffy, badly maintained DMUs. I do not blame the individuals, although some of them could be trying in the extreme. The fact is that they had been allowed to become that way because of years of bad management – management that should have set clear boundaries with respect to what was and was not acceptable behaviour and performance.

I had been warned about all this and chose to take up the challenge anyway. This was absolutely the right decision and I have no regrets whatever about my all too short stint at Heaton. I was quite prepared for the resistance to change that came from certain quarters and had no problem with the loneliness that always comes from being 'the boss'. Indeed, it suited my temperament as I have never worked well when having to do the bidding of others. However, I did have some feelings of relief when Freddie Clements approached me because I perceived a level of stress building up within me. It manifested itself in a constant 'tight' feeling in my stomach which made me think that I was heading for an ulcer.

I took some time to analyse the situation and concluded that it was caused, in large part, by the fact that I was not given the support that would have been appropriate by my boss, the Divisional Maintenance Engineer. Bill Gilpin and many other middle managers could not have been more helpful, but that is not the same as the support and encouragement that you sometimes need from your boss when things get really difficult. I had enjoyed that support from Frank Pardoe in my previous job, but it was sadly lacking at Newcastle because there was a long history of management not standing up to powerful trade unions.

I resolved to set a personal strategy to make sure that, whatever the difficulty, I never got into this position again. With one or two close shaves, I am pleased to say this worked well for the rest of my career.

Chapter Six

On the border: Carlisle

My journey to work in Carlisle started, as before, from Riding Mill Station in a two-car Cravens DMU. However, it now involved a ride of just over forty miles over the very top of England, much of it at an exhilarating 70mph, with windows and luggage racks vibrating loudly. One morning in my first week, it was a little more exciting when, sitting just behind the driver, I happened to glance up to see a huge snowdrift which we hit moments later at full speed. Its top was about level with the bottom of the driver's windscreen and it extended for about fifty yards. There was the most almighty bang and then a complete blackout as the entire vehicle was encased in snow for a few seconds. Then it was back to normal as the driver and the few passengers wondered why we were still on the tracks.

That same day we had a Freightliner train hauled by a Class '40' slip to a stand on the Settle and Carlisle Line because of snow. The conditions were so severe that we could not recover it and sent some fitters to drain the coolant, then abandoned the whole train for six weeks, ploughing past it with the snow plough to create a route for single line working.

Next, I got a call from Mike Carrier, the Operations Assistant to David McKeever, the Area Manager. Mike was very worried because, for the first time since electrification in 1974, snow was building up at Shap Summit on the West Coast Main Line. He feared that it would soon reach the point where an Independent Snow Plough (one pushed by a loco) would be needed and he, as a good Operating man, could not find any relevant instructions in the Rule Book. Over to me…

In such circumstances, the green Electrification Rule Book referred the reader to the 'Electric Traction Engineer' which, in the absence of any such gentleman, as a result of organisational changes, appeared to be me! I simply did what any engineer would have done, which was to understand the intended operation, considered the risks attached, and wrote out a safe and practical procedure which entailed getting the Electric Control Operator at Cathcart, near Glasgow, to open his circuit breakers, on both lines, for the relevant section. This caused the 25kv line to be isolated but not earthed. This meant that it was not safe to touch because several thousand volts could have been induced as a result of the proximity of 400kv Grid lines. This did not matter because all we were going to do was deluge it with snow. No one need go near it.

The alternative, conventional, approach would have been to get Overhead Line Maintenance staff to fight their way through deep snow at each end of the electrical section to isolate and earth the line.

This would have risked injuring these men and caused substantial delay for no discernible improvement in safety. Mike Carrier's father, Frank, had been one of the senior designers in the LMS loco drawing office in Derby and had, among many other things, helped implement William Stanier's designs, including the '8F', 'Black Five' and the Pacifics. Mike has published a book about his father.

I soon found out why Freddie Clements had poached me. My predecessor had left under a cloud having let many things slip. One of my first symbolic actions was to dispose, fairly publicly, of the substantial liquor store in my new office.

As Area Maintenance Engineer, on a salary of £6,834 a year, I had three senior assistants. Bill Hodgson was an energetic and relentlessly positive fifty-four year old who had been running the shop temporarily. Bill was a local man who had been an apprentice fitter with the LMS and had been Loco Shedmaster at Kirby Stephen before steam engines departed in the mid 1960s. He had then been put in charge of the Carriage and Wagon Department in Carlisle which had doubtless required the major shake-up that Bill would have administered. He knew everyone and could talk anyone into doing anything. Everyone

My very able and helpful deputy at Carlisle, Bill Hodgson beside *Leander*, which was stabled overnight at Carlisle Upperby between turns.

liked and respected him, as did I. He taught me a lot and simply could not have been more helpful.

Cyril Hampson, in charge of maintenance of plant and the 25kv electrification from Lancaster to the Scottish border, could not have been more different. He was about the same age as Bill, and I had known him in Birmingham where he had been the Chief Distribution Inspector (which means that he was in charge of a small team who maintained 25kv substations). Cyril was one of those unfortunate people who simply could not bring himself to be the bearer of bad news. This resulted in some people getting away with murder because they knew he was unable face them up and stop them. Others just did not know where they stood with him.

Nick Kaye was an LM Region former Management Trainee the same age as me. We knew each other beforehand and got on very well. Nick needed very little of my time as he was quite capable of managing his team of, mostly, very competent and conscientious loco maintenance staff.

This was a very different job from Heaton. I had 450 staff spread over a huge area from south of Lancaster to the Scottish border. It was almost a day's job to get from Carlisle to Barrow in Furness and back, before you started to think about doing anything with the handful of employees there. Carlisle feels a long way from anywhere and very much had, when I was there, a 'border town' feel. You did not have to scratch far to find a strong feeling of dislike of the Scots and all their works, and this was not solely as a result of trainloads of drunken Glaswegians passing through during the football season. It came out in all sorts of little things and was clearly institutional and of long standing. The place was also old-fashioned in all kinds of social senses, perhaps as much as fifteen years behind the South East in attitudes. It would be interesting to know if this is still the same now that social media, for example, is universal.

Despite me having some far flung-troops, most of my 450 men (there were only a couple of women typists – and graduates at that) were in Carlisle. Kingmoor was a fairly new Traction Maintenance Depot which had replaced half a dozen steam sheds. It looked after an allocated small fleet of DMUs which operated over the Cumbrian Coast Line, and diesel locos from LM, Eastern and Scottish Regions which arrived in the adjacent yard on freight trains. Electric locos showed up from time to time, usually when they had failed.

Upperby, where I used the old Shedmaster's office, had been a big steam loco shed until only ten years previously. By 1978 all that remained was the ex-LNWR carriage shed where we looked after twelve WCML coaching sets and repaired around 500 individual coaches each year, which other depots could not handle. The majority of these repairs were to the motor alternator sets fitted to modern air conditioned coaches. The extent of these problems came as rather a surprise since the same items had rarely caused any problems at Heaton. However, a little thought soon caused the realisation that the ECML coaches had, electrically, an easy life. They either had a Class '47' with its modern, well regulated and constant 850v DC supply or the idiosyncratic arrangement of the 'Deltic'. Rather surprisingly, these locos had not been built with Electric Train Heat (ETH) in mind, despite its use on the LMR by the time they appeared. When they came to be converted, they were arranged so that, when idling, the two DC main generators were coupled in series for ETH purposes. This just about gave 400 volts, which was right at the low end of acceptable. When the driver took power and the engine speeds increased beyond a certain point, the MGs were put in parallel causing the voltage to fall right down, only to rise steadily to about 750 volts at full power. Contrast this with 1,000 volts AC relentlessly supplied from an AC loco on the LM. The worst part was, however, that at every neutral section, about every twenty miles, the supply switched off, only to return with a bang seconds later. No wonder the LM went through MA sets at such a rate. Incidentally, the proper solution to this situation, a solid state inverter, only eventually materialised in 2014, many years after most of these coaches had been scrapped.

There was also a combined Plant Maintenance and Overhead Line Maintenance Depot housed in the former loco stores building. The relatively new locomen's hostel, where drivers and firemen from Birmingham and Glasgow would have lodged, looked over us from high above and had become a hotel.

Currock, which until 1926 was a loco shed, had been a wagon repair shop ever since. It was an absolute hive of activity ruled, with a rod of iron, by Tommy Elliot, the Chief Foreman. He had a works hooter to signal the start and finish of work. Woe betide anyone who disregarded its stentorian tones. Like Upperby, Currock was kept busy by dint of selling its services enthusiastically to whomsoever had a need. In neither case did geography help, but this was much more than made up for by a willingness to go the extra mile and take on anything. A good example of this was a contract to refurbish more than fifty DMU cars which, being maintained in an awful depot in Manchester, Newton Heath, were in a terrible state, possibly even worse than the ones I inherited at Heaton. The men at Currock had never done anything like it before, but soon learnt new skills and got on with the job, producing a very creditable result at a fraction of the price BREL would have charged.

Also part of the Carriage and Wagon team were about a dozen examiners at Carlisle Citadel Station who provided twenty-four hour, seven days a week cover for examining passenger trains, all of which stopped there. These were a real throwback in that not only had examination of passenger trains ceased at most other places, but they actually still used long 'wheel tapper's' hammers to test every wheel

Currock wagon shop, part of Bill's department, was a hive of activity.

(on the side away from the platform) for cracked tyres and, what is more, they illuminated their way with acetylene hand lamps. I thought I had just stepped back fifty years!

As far as I could determine, there was no one else still tapping wheels, many of which were by then solid and hence had no tyre

Fitter John Todd machining a pair of shunting loco wheels for the Army.

One of the many Newton Heath DMUs that the Currock chaps smartened up. Jimmy Harkins is on the left. He was an excellent general handyman/carpenter who turned his hand cheerfully to anything he was given. In steam days, he had been employed as a 'floor board' carpenter, i.e. a bit rough and ready.

to crack, and the incidence of cracked tyres on coaches was almost zero anyway. Acetylene had been used for lighting for many years, including on early cars because it gave out a powerful white light. It worked by putting calcium carbide into a chamber at the bottom of the lamp and then attaching above it another chamber which contained water that was set to drip on to the chemical below, thus producing acetylene which, when mixed with the right amount of air, gives off a brilliant white light. What makes calcium carbide so dangerous is that if there should be an unintended fire, dowsing it with water makes it much worse.

Changing all this was made quite easy because the men were some of the nicest, most reasonable chaps I have ever come across. I decided to spend a night with them to find out what really went on, during which time I certainly discovered why they liked their lamps so much. The fact that I had bothered to do this meant that they knew they could not bullshit me as to what actually went on. We very quickly found an amicable way of substantially reducing the cost of this largely unnecessary operation by redeploying some of them and allowing others to retire early.

While at Carlisle Station one day to agree these arrangements, I was called to an up express which had just arrived from Glasgow. It comprised a Class '87' electric loco hauling a full brake van and eleven coaches and would have come most of the way at 100mph despite the fact, as it turned out, that the handbrake on the leading vehicle, the brake van, was full on. The resultant flats were more than a foot long, resulting from all eight wheels having been dragged for so far without turning. I told the platform inspector to have the loco remove the van, but on no account to release the handbrake. To have done so would certainly have caused a derailment. The power of the locomotive was such that the driver had not noticed this problem. Indeed, the train was on time.

Louis Richardson was the supervisor in charge of Workington wagon shop. He was as strong as an ox and had, for many years, been a carriage and wagon examiner based at Appleby. He thought nothing of cycling ten miles over the moors to Shap with a couple of cast iron brake blocks hanging from his handlebars by a piece of string.

An important part of my job was to reduce costs by improving productivity throughout my organisation. I have just described one, fairly easy, achievement but others were not so straightforward. I had been very interested in this whole subject of 'doing more for less', or 'working smarter' as it tends to be described now, since the days of Dennis Smith's lectures at Stafford. My interest had been stimulated further by the productivity course that I went on in 1972, and I had taken a lead on the London Midland Region, when I had been Area Maintenance Engineer at Bletchley. While I was there, a BRB initiative called 'Re-incentive Schemes' was launched for workshop staff in maintenance depots. It implied, mostly correctly, that the original

'Incentive Schemes', basically payment by results, were so corrupt as to be meaningless. I had used the considerable 'carrot' of all the extra DMU work from Marylebone to do a deal with the staff. As a result, Bletchley Depot was as efficient as anywhere you would find in terms of work output per man hour. I was pretty surprised to discover that my predecessor had done absolutely nothing in this respect. I was even more surprised, three years later, to discover that nothing whatever had been done on the whole Southern Region; but that will have to wait.

As I have already implied, Bill Hodgson had ensured that the Carriage Depot at Upperby and the Wagon Shop at Currock were hives of activity. This left the Traction Maintenance Depot at Kingmoor, the Plant and Machinery Maintenance team and a few minor outstations to attend to. Kingmoor was fairly straightforward because almost all the work had been measured and there was plenty of work measurement and method study data available from other depots (including Bletchley), who did the same work. The main task here was to negotiate out a series of allowances and scams of one sort or another that had been allowed to creep in with consequent increases in unit costs. Nick Kaye, with a little help, was well able to deliver on this tedious, grinding task that required many meetings with staff rep 'Pop' Carruthers and his colleagues. ('Pop' because he sometimes went off like a bottle of pop... which could relieve the tedium somewhat.)

The Plant and Machinery group was totally different, first because the chaps had to look after a huge range of machinery including lifts, pumps, retarders, fuelling installations, floodlights and fork lift trucks to name but a few, all spread about a large area. Secondly, the management in the form of my P&M Engineer, Cyril Hampson, and his two foremen, were really not in control of their activities and had no clue about concepts of measured work or planning. In addition, one of the staff reps was a particularly tricky individual, Ken Rivers, who was a van driver. In this role, he saw far more of what went on as he delivered men and materials to far-flung sites and he had the ability to poke his nose into anyone's business and did so, continually. Thus you have the nightmare situation of weak and ineffective management who had no idea about what was going on, together with a strong, well informed staff rep who knew everything and everyone. It will come as no surprise that everyone from Cyril down was afraid of Ken.

Clearly this situation demanded, and got, a fair amount of my time. To give just one example of the sort of thing that was going on, I will describe what happened when Cyril came to me, one day, to ask me to authorise overtime for two fitters and two fitter's mates for six weeks. The task which, allegedly, gave rise to this extra work was the overhauling of a set of pneumatic retarders on the 'hump' in Carlisle Yard. I should explain that the enormous Carlisle Hump Marshalling Yard was one of many foolish 'investments' that the old guard squandered the 1955 Modernisation Plan money on. It was finished in about 1966 and was obsolete from day one. When I was in Carlisle, more than half of it had been closed, but one hump and its associated control tower remained.

After a wagon had been pushed over the top of the hump, it ran by gravity down a steep slope to whichever track the hump operator determined. On its way, its speed could be reduced by a retarder that comprised a pair of steel beams about 10ft long, which were forced together by a series of air cylinders, thus gripping the rims of the wheels of the wagon. It had been determined that this retarder needed overhauling, a job which comprised removing the whole assembly in many parts, taking it to the workshop three miles away, replacing a number of large steel bushes and rubber seals, then refitting the whole lot. This was all going to take six weeks, during which part of the hump would be unusable and provide a substantial boost to the earnings of the men concerned.

After getting nowhere with my challenge to my manager, I decided to take myself off to site with Frank Heaton who was the mechanical chargehand and seemed to me to possess more sense than all his bosses put together. I first observed that, since half the yard was closed, we could rescue an identical retarder from the closed half and overhaul it so that the reduction in sorting capacity was only for a few days while the equipment was swapped over. Then I challenged Frank to get it done over a Bank Holiday long weekend when the yard was closed anyway. I authorised three days' overtime, rather than the six weeks that had been asked for. Frank called me on the Sunday evening to say that they had finished in two days.

After a lot of hard work, I had reduced the P&M team to half its size and taken on more work. When it was announced that I was leaving Carlisle, Cyril Weber, the other plant rep, who was an electrician, came to see me. He surprised me by saying that he wanted to congratulate me because, although he did not agree with it, he had noted that I had achieved the job I was sent to do!

There was another P&M Depot at Carnforth presided over by a delightful man called Bob Bamber who demonstrated exactly how such a team should be managed. He had a similarly wide range of responsibilities from maintaining Civil Engineer's tampers, which are a box of tricks, to little stations most of the way up the Cumbrian Coast to St Bees.

I was travelling one morning in the train to Carnforth, accompanied by my wise old Head of Admin, Stan Jarvis, who had been the Shedmaster's Chief Clerk when Upperby Shed was open. As we passed through the beautiful Lune Gorge, I asked Stan what he was writing.

Chargehand Frank Heaton, on the left, could turn his hand to most things.

'The minutes of the meeting,' he replied.

'Yesterday's?' I queried.

'No, the one we're having this morning.'

You need a wise old bird like that sometimes. He knew exactly who would say what and when. He did not have to change them and we did agree a new Incentive Scheme because Bob Bamber had done his job.

The Overhead Line gang at Carlisle were presided over by a very experienced Chief Supervisor, Doug Butroid, who was a contemporary of my Chief Supervisor at Bletchley, Frank Moran. They had worked together on new construction in the 1950s and 1960s and were thus very well placed to look after the equipment. Doug had obviously had a full report about me from Frank!

ON THE BORDER: CARLISLE • 153

The retarders that were expected to provide large amounts of overtime.

Bob Bamber, boss at Carnforth, just got on with quiet efficiency.

I did not have to spend much time with them, mainly because the later design of OLE, installed in the early 1970s, was much more reliable. I did, however, enjoy one short episode when the first of a new type of truck was delivered for the use of the Overhead Line gangs. It was quite a lot bigger than the large vans they were used to and was much more suitable since they spent most of their working time, day or night, in their vehicle either travelling to site for a patrol or an incident, waiting for permission to take an isolation for another department, or eating. It also enabled them to carry more spares, thus reducing the number of trips back to the depot. Our chaps would not have objected to the new trucks were it not for the fact that their Liverpool equivalents had refused to drive the new vehicles on some spurious grounds but, no doubt, actually calculated to get management to cough up some unnecessary allowance. They claimed that they were 'too tiring' to drive. Bill Hodgson and I had a great day driving this brand new 7.5 ton truck around the Lake District, pronouncing when we came back that we thought we might allocate it to the Carriage and Wagon mobile team who went out all over the place to deal with defective wagons. Problem solved, the Overhead guys were not about to lose their truck to the C&W!

After I had been at Carlisle for about six months, I was nominated to go on an Area Managers' course at The Grove at Watford, where I had been for my productivity course some years previously. The idea, I think, was to prepare you for the most senior Operating roles within BR and there were a dozen or so of us who did, indeed, reach these heights. Quite why dear old Ron Neil, sixty-four year old Area Manager at Victoria, was there is anyone's guess. He certainly did not know! However, I learnt a lot from a kindly old man who was almost at the end of a long career in the Operations Department. He had become a junior Station Master with the Southern Railway in 1939 and had worked his way up to the pinnacle of his profession, the head of one of the big London stations.

Brian Scott, who became the last General Manager of BR Western Region before privatisation, was another member of the group. He was Area Manager at Bescot which was a 100% freight job. Two of our lecturers, who were almost all internal, come to mind: Tommy Greaves was the BRB Head of Traction and Traincrew. In English that meant he was the professional head of drivers and he told us that we all should be driving trains regularly. I did not need telling twice. The other was John Mayfield, newly appointed as BR's Chief Internal Auditor. As you might imagine, we had a rather boring lecture only enlivened by my asking him how the board satisfied itself that it got value from its huge Audit Department. This perfectly reasonable question, I thought, was treated as practically treasonable and caused me to think very deeply about how to construct organisations that were self checking without excessive use of expensive and unproductive auditors. I later employed the results of this thinking while still retaining a very small mobile audit function.

I was starting to get more involved in outside activities. Freddie Clements, the CM&EE, called me one day and told me to put myself forward to fill a forthcoming vacancy on the Railway Division Board of the IMechE. When I protested that this would mean quite a lot of time away because the meetings were in London, I was told that this was OK. I found the monthly meetings interesting and also learnt, as Clements would have realised, that other members, some of whom were very senior, did actually listen. It was still, however, with some trepidation that I thoroughly disagreed over some matter with Iain Gardiner, then BR's most senior engineer. We got on famously after that, which taught me a lesson.

One benefit of being in London until the evening was that I started returning north on the sleeper to Barrow-in-Furness, which enabled me to have an excellent full English breakfast at the Duke of Edinburgh pub opposite Barrow Station and then spend some time with my chaps there before working my way back to Carlisle via some of my other far-flung troops.

For many years in various jobs, I would see the apprentices, talk to them about what they had learned and discuss with them the contents of their log books in which they were supposed to write up everything they had done and to draw conclusions from it. I was again driving my steam engine, this time on the South Tynedale Railway near Alston in September 2014, when a man called up to me that he had been one of my apprentices at Carlisle all those years ago. Perhaps I did do some good.

Around this time, steam-hauled excursions were becoming more acceptable to BR and we had regular trips usually with Carnforth based locos which would work their way up the Cumbrian Coast Line to Carlisle on the first day, stay overnight at Upperby and then do a return trip to Skipton on the second

Several different steam locos appeared during the summer. Me by LMS Jubilee Class *Leander*.

John Duncan, Chief Rolling Stock Inspector, was the brains at the Diesel depot and was also the fount of all knowledge on steam locos. Seen here beside ex-Southern Railway No 850 *Lord Nelson* in Upperby yard.

day. Since my chaps did the daily 'fitness to run' examination, I was professionally responsible for the safety and performance of these trains. For this reason, I chose to ride on the footplate from time to time. After one Carlisle to Skipton and return trip on 850 *Lord Nelson*, an ex-Southern 4-6-0, I got a very shirty letter from one David Ward. He was the LM Region Passenger Marketing Manager and was fairly senior. He had found out that I had been in the cab of the loco and informed me that I had no right to be there.

David should be credited with doing a great deal to get steam-hauled excursions running again in the teeth of much opposition from very senior people at the board. However, he did have a tendency to be rather prickly. I replied, in rather more measured tones, to say that since I had the professional responsibility of ensuring that locomotives running on the railway were safe, I considered it my duty to ride on them from time to time. Furthermore, I would not seek his permission to do so. I heard no more.

As I mentioned in Chapter Three, I first came across Dick Hardy, whose job it was to make sure that BR got the best out its engineering graduates, at whatever level, when I was sent to Crewe Works in 1973. He spent a lot of his time meeting those of us that were on his books, if possible at their workplace. He had been to see me at Bletchley and, my diary tells me, he came to Carlisle on 28 August 1980, arriving at 11.55 with a request that Nick Kaye and I meet him in the Station Hotel for lunch so that he could depart, on the footplate, of course, at 13.58 with 4472 *Flying Scotsman* to Skipton. Brief though the meeting was, he used his time to the full and had detailed knowledge of a great many people. In my case, that lunch probably prompted him to tell me to go for interview at Waterloo the following January with Maurice Holmes, the Deputy General Manager of the Southern, and Maurice Maguire, the CM&EE.

My last day at Carlisle was Friday, 30 January 1981.

ON THE BORDER: CARLISLE • 157

We borrowed the replica of *Rocket* from the National Railway museum and gave rides at our open day.

In total contrast, the APT derailed in 1980. at Carnforth at 100mph because one of the fancy hydro-kinetic braked axles broke. Fortunately it stayed upright and within gauge and thus did not hit another express which passed almost immediately.

The APT engineers were very sniffy about my plan to bring the new axle in hanging from a JCB bucket. However, they did not have a better idea.

More old boys leaving after a lifetime. In Carlisle especially, I went to far too many funerals of those who did not make it to retirement.

Chapter Seven

Change agent on the Southern

I arrived at Croydon on 2 February 1981 and was given the snappy title of 'Assistant M&EE (General)' at the not inconsiderable salary of £11,155 pa plus £459 pa London allowance. I reported directly to the Chief Mechanical and Electrical Engineer, Maurice Maguire, who of course I had met several times. Despite that, I was not his choice and it was made very clear to me by Maurice Holmes, the Deputy General Manager, that I was there to act as a change agent and to drive the modernisation of the department, which was seen as very insular and staid. Maurice Maguire was pleasant enough but took very little interest in what I was doing. He had joined the Southern Railway Electrical Engineers Department in 1946, straight out of the Army. By 1981, he was in his early sixties, worn out, unwell and just looking for an easy life.

I very soon found out the department's reputation was richly deserved. There were two ways of doing anything: the Southern way or the other way. There could be absolutely no debate as to which was right; this was not healthy and resulted from very few people coming in from other Regions and absolutely nobody coming in from other companies.

The Deputy CM&EE and Rolling Stock Engineer, Jim Vine, was a large, scruffy, individual who never tired of repeating the mantra that 'Southern is best'. He was deeply suspicious of me, no doubt suspecting that I had been put in as a change agent. However, we had to work together and did so with a sort of 'armed truce' until, later in 1981, David Blake came as the boss when Maurice Maguire retired. Vine then realised that his number was up and became a great deal more helpful. I had known David previously as a fellow Area Maintenance Engineer. He ran Shields EMU Depot in Glasgow when I was at Carlisle and we got on extremely well, having much the same outlook on life.

Meanwhile, my priorities seemed to be:

1. To introduce the so-called Re-incentive Scheme which had been on the go since I was at Bletchley seven years previously. That indicates the priority which the SR gave to BRB directives.
2. To work out how and where we were going to maintain the new Gatwick Railair trains that were coming in 1984.
3. To produce a strategy for introduction of the Class '508' EMUs on the Central Division.
4. To deal with the Training Officer who had gone off the rails. Then find a replacement.

Before I got stuck into any of these I thought I had better go and find out how the Southern's CM&EE Department worked. Since I reported directly to the CM&EE, I was in the fortunate position of being able to call just about anyone in the 5,000-strong department and tell them that I was coming to see them and discuss their job, how they did it, and solicit their views on how the whole outfit could be improved. What I discovered was that the managers in Head Office at Croydon, for the most part, rarely left their desks and did not, therefore, understand what was going on outside. Meanwhile, the managers outside had low levels of delegated authority and were pretty frustrated both by this fact and the results of what they considered to be stupid decisions. The other Regions had all, several years before, delegated much more authority to local level and had, by and large, equipped their managers to use it effectively.

One interesting result of rarely seeing their bosses was that many of the local managers were very ready to 'spill the beans' and tell me what was really going on. This brought me up to speed quite quickly. I was also helped in this by the fact that I inherited a team of fifty work and method study practitioners. Goodness knows why anyone thought you needed that many and my first instruction to Allan Hardy, the boss, was: 'You lot had better do a method study on yourselves and radically reduce your numbers.' As a matter of fact, they did that with remarkably little fuss.

As in previous jobs, I had a cab pass, in this case for the entire Southern Region, which I generally used as I travelled to depots as geographically spread out as Ramsgate and Bournemouth. As usual, drivers were happy to have someone in the cab to talk to, although I was always very careful not to distract them in complicated areas or when approaching yellow or red signals. My main impression was just how slow much of the Southern was, compared with other parts of the country. The exception to that was the South Western Main Line out of Waterloo.

The need to introduce the Re-incentive Scheme was most urgent in the Electrical Department whose employees maintained substations and their smaller brothers, Track Paralleling Huts, and high and medium voltage cables, including all the many track bonds needed on a third rail network. There seemed to be a view that because there were, inevitably, different layouts in each place, it was not possible to measure the work and, in any case, only an electrical engineer could understand it. In lunchtime discussions with some of the senior engineers, I remember being told things like: 'During the war we had a problem with that in Balcombe Tunnel, so we can't change it.' Or: 'When we electrified the Brighton Line (in 1933!) we decided against doing that.'

Of course, I delighted in telling them that while I did not know anything about their business, which was only partly true, I did know that there had been a few advances in technology in the previous forty years. However, I was strongly supported by Phil Perry, the Electrical Engineer, who, like me, reported to the CM&EE and, as an ex-rolling stock man, was as keen as I was to drag the department kicking and screaming into, well, the 1960s as a start.

Similarly, my now slimmed Productivity team soon showed the local managers that method study is a technique that can be applied to any activity. I had several teams out on site, usually in a mobile office that was an old (often pre-grouping) passenger coach that had been adapted to make a very cosy office. There were still enough disused parcels bays to be able to locate the coaches more or less where you wanted to. I used to visit the guys pretty regularly, usually combining it with a visit to a nearby Traction Maintenance Depot. Over a period of about eighteen months we demonstrated that the work could be done with about half the number of staff if there was rather better planning and management control. We then helped the managers, who had never done anything like this before, to implement the changes.

The Productivity team were a splendid set of guys, the 'Lancing Mafia' as I called them, since most had started in Lancing Carriage Works as apprentices and had known each other for years. They had all received excellent training at the BRB Work Study Centre at The Grove where I had been in 1971. Some of the practices we observed were 'interesting'. I decided to go out one Saturday night on a cable laying train to find out what went on. The job was to lay a couple of miles of high voltage cable which was to go in concrete troughs in the cess, at the side of the track, and was to be done from a train. When I arrived on site, just after dark on a warm summer evening, I found a Class '33' coupled to a train of flat wagons on which were mounted 6ft diameter wooden cable drums. The method of working, once the train had reached the relevant site, was for a bunch of labourers standing in the cess to hang on to the end of the cable while the loco moved forward at about 3mph. Additional men were positioned along the cess so that they could catch hold of the cable and guide it down.

In safety terms it was a nightmare, starting with the fact that most of the navvies were Irish labourers who had been rounded up from local pubs at throwing out time (22.30 in those days). They were used to working on the track but may not have done this task before. They were shouted and bawled at by Irish gangmasters who had probably had as much Guinness as they had. Add to this the fact that it was often pitch black with ineffective mobile lighting and you have all the ingredients for serious accidents. Indeed, on the night I was there, something caused the cable drum to jam which meant, as the loco continued relentlessly, the cable tightened and flicked one of the navvies, who was hanging on to it as instructed, up into the air, over a bridge parapet and into the River Wey beneath. No doubt the anaesthetic properties of the alcohol helped because he just swam to the bank, clambered up and carried on working as if nothing had happened. There would have been no paperwork.

Other teams from my Productivity section worked with local management in Rolling Stock Maintenance Depots. This was much more straightforward because measured work already existed and it was really an updating process together with supporting the local managers in negotiating out a few restrictive practices. Overall, this part of the department was being reasonably well managed. The much bigger task was in the Plant and Machinery Department. This, rather like at Carlisle, was out of control. Probably this was why my friend Chris Kinchen-Smith, who had moved from Neville Hill HST Depot to the Southern at the same time as I came south, was moved from Chart Leacon to sort it out.

Chris and I shared a flat at Tunbridge Wells for six months. We selected the location because it was roughly equidistant from Chart Leacon where Chris was the boss of the Repair Shop, really a mini main works for overhauling EMUs, and Croydon. The first part of my journey to work was via Tunbridge Wells West and Eridge on what is now the preserved Spa Valley Line. I suggested to him that he might find the LM Region Plant and Machinery Management System, PAMMS, which I had originated at Bletchley in 1974, useful. It was a fancy name for a basic work measurement and planning system that helped managers manage in a rather challenging area. Nowadays, lots of consultants make a lot of money selling 'Asset Management Systems'. That is what PAMMS was. It had been spread across the LM Region so I took Chris to one of the bigger depots in Manchester.

The second, and most interesting, part of my job was leading the strategy for the Region's train maintenance and stabling depots. At that time, EMUs were outstabled overnight at no fewer than 180 locations, all of which were visited during the night by cleaners and Carriage and Wagon examiners. The latter would adjust brakes and replace brake blocks while lying on the sleepers under the train in all weathers. Now this may or may not have been a good way of going on for the previous fifty years, but it certainly was not going to work for new disc braked trains that were soon going to be replacing the existing cast iron brake blocked trains which, although some were fewer than ten years old, were essentially prewar designs.

Most pressing was the need to find somewhere to look after the new Gatwick Railair service that was to start in 1984, and to work out where the Class '508s', which were then planned to come in on the Central Division, would be maintained. When I arrived, there was a basic plan, which had not been worked up in any detail, to maintain and clean the Gatwick trains in the 1926-built Selhurst Carriage Shed. This was a large building with many tracks but no pits. It was used for stabling suburban EMUs, mostly former Southern Railway Class '405' – 4-SUBs in Southern speak – and their slightly newer cousins

Line closures were still going on in the early '80s. When I was flat sharing with Chris Kinchin Smith, my journey to work started in a DEMU from Tunbridge Wells to Eridge. Here such a train is taking Grove Junction onto what is now the preserved Spa Valley line.

Class '415' or 4-EPBs. The conductor rail stopped just outside the open end of the unheated shed. Incoming trains coasted in after leaving the third rail. To leave, a power cable hanging from an overhead trolley was plugged in to a socket on the train which was, thus, powered up and able to be driven out. One of the many traps for the unwary was that a train so powered, or one that had been drawn forward so that its first pick-up shoe was on the conductor rail outside, had live pick up shoes and bolts on each shoebeam. This meant that a cleaner walking down the narrow space between trains had to take great care to avoid electrocution.

For several reasons this did not seem an ideal environment to maintain the trains, quite apart from the fact that a place would have to be found to stable the EMUs displaced. The trains, which were going to replace Class '423' – 4-VEPs, the last of the slam-door stock to be built – would comprise a Class '73' Electrodiesel loco, eight Mk 2f air conditioned coaches plus a Motor Luggage Van converted from an EMU passenger vehicle. This meant that they had a cab at each end and so did not have to run around after each journey. With 1,600hp at one end and only 500 at the other, they were hardly overpowered but they would probably be OK on the Brighton Line, which was limited to 60mph out as far as Croydon in those days and was not much faster for the rest of the way. The locos all lived at Stewart's Lane, which was an old steam shed tucked away behind Battersea Power Station. There was also a wagon shop and a large carriage shed a bit like the one at Selhurst except that it had pits on four of the roads.

One of the local managers whose confidence I had won was Keith Parsons who ran the show at 'The Lane'. He suggested that it would make a great deal of sense to base the trains at his depot, especially as it was the intention to keep the locos semi-permanently coupled to the coaches. This would mean that if there was a problem with the loco, there would always be someone who knew them intimately nearby in the loco shed. I made a few other checks and realised that this made a lot of sense, especially since the work we would have to do would be a lot cheaper than at Selhurst and, because Stewart's Lane was much closer to Victoria, empty mileage would be lower.

It was quite easy to convince my Operating and Divisional colleagues that this made sense. The slight difficulty that I had was that I knew that Jim Vine was not a fan of Keith (unjustly in my view), so I had to take care to present the proposal as one that Keith was not very happy with. Result: Jim agreed immediately!

Everything was ready for the launch of the service in May 1984, and the newly configured trains started running non-stop between Victoria and Gatwick Airport every fifteen minutes. Just to remind the engineers not to be complacent, the locos, which were twenty years old at the time and had been almost trouble free, took great exception to one of the gaps in the conductor rail just outside Battersea Park Station, the first station out from Victoria. The Class '73s' on full power were drawing much more current per pick-up shoe than the hundreds of EMUs which passed uneventfully over this particular gap every day. At least one loco was damaged by the heavy arcing, which was much worse than had been experienced with them elsewhere. The solution, which was quickly found, was to fit a much larger arc guard to the loco and to make some small changes to the conductor rails. The lesson from this is that whenever you change the duty of a machine it may behave differently. Beware! After this the trains continued to run quite satisfactorily until replaced by new 'Darth Vader' Class '460' EMUs some seventeen years later. These were also maintained at Stewart's Lane.

Over the three years that I was at Croydon, my team initiated and, in many cases, project-managed improvements and enlargements at several depots, including Slade Green, Grove Park, Brighton, Wimbledon, Fratton, Bournemouth and Waterloo, tucked away under the station to service the Waterloo and City Line then owned and operated by BR. All of these were in recognition of new trains coming in the next few years and to allow about half of the 180 stabling points to be closed.

Keith Parsons, Depot Engineer at Stewart's Lane where he looked after the fleet of Class 73s.

After the Gatwick Express project, the top priority when I arrived in February 1981 was how and where to look after the next batch of Class '508s', which were then expected to come to the Central Division to work inner suburban trains out of Victoria and London Bridge. The '508s' were directly descended from the 'PEP' experimental train that had run trials on the Southern for several years in the 1970s. The first production version was the Class '313', which was introduced in 1976 on the new Great Northern Electrification scheme.

The '508s' were forced on the Southern by the British Railways Board when the SR had sought authority for some more 'VEPs', Class '423', to replace the remaining 'SUBs', Class '405'. The Southern hated them – because they had new-fangled disc brakes, because they had autocouplers, but most of all because they were designed at Derby. All previous SR trains had been a product of Lancing or Eastleigh Carriage Drawing Office, the CM&EE technical section initially at Tooley Street

The EMU shed at Stewart's Lane, typical of many on the SR, which we upgraded for the new Gatwick Express trains.

next to London Bridge Station, latterly at Croydon and English Electric. Passengers, on the other hand, welcomed the new, light, airy trains with their smooth riding air suspension.

It is probably of interest to explain the longstanding relationship that EE had with the Southern. The Southern Railway, like most other railway companies of the day, tended to manufacture its own rolling stock. Before the Brighton Line electrification of 1933, almost all new electric trains had Metropolitan Vickers (MV) electric traction equipment. Herbert Walker, the very forward looking General Manager of the Southern, promoted at that time a rolling programme of electrification as a means of reducing cost and making the Southern more attractive to passengers. He envisaged all principal lines east of Reading and Portsmouth being electrified. It was decided that there were considerable benefits to standardisation of electric traction equipment and, therefore, both MV and English Electric were invited to discuss a ten year agreement to 'design, develop and supply electric traction equipment'. In the event, English Electric (EE Co.) was selected, as Alfred Raworth, the Electrical Engineer, New Works, favoured them.

The agreement was to cover the design, development, supply and back-up for all electric traction equipment for electric rolling stock, including locomotives. It would provide the SR with guaranteed contract prices for all items of equipment on an agreed schedule, initially at a price per pound weight! Any significant developments beneficial to the railway were to be notified. Priority was to be given to production for the SR. In return, the railway would keep EE notified of all forward programmes 'in good time' and there would be regular meetings between the engineers of both companies to ensure a full exchange of information. There was a view that the agreement stifled development. On the other hand the railway wanted, above all, standardisation with thorough reliability and would not countenance change for change's sake. This, of course, led to all suburban type rolling stock having identical performance to the 1915 LSWR trains and timings were virtually unchanged until new trains were procured after privatisation. The 1937 Brighton Main Line stock had a slightly inferior performance of 5.5 nominal hp/ton compared with 7hp/ton for the earlier Brighton Line trains. (A 1964 Class '86' with typical train on the West Coast Main Line would have more than 10hp/ton, a 'Pendolino' very much more.)

The agreement was renewed for another ten years in 1946 and again, but for five years, in 1956. The English Electric Co. was very proud to have beaten its competitor Metro Vick, and all staff who had dealings with the contract were made very aware of its importance. Very senior staff from both sides met regularly and Lord George Nelson (boss of EE) took a personal interest. This information has come from letters to me in 1992 from Arthur Tayler, who joined the SR Electrical Engineer's office at Tooley Street in 1942, and Fred Pinto, who was then one of EE's sales and contracts engineers. They agreed that what really made the contract work was a very close liaison throughout, a pride in getting it right first time and that the customer was getting value for money.

An example of the trust that existed was that the Southern Region, in 1951, decided to extend the scope of the contract to include the Hastings diesel electric 500hp multiple units. Word went out within EE that 'we must not let SR down' – especially since all the other Regions had opted for diesel mechanical multiple units. Arthur explained to me, however, that the new DEMUs were allocated to the Locomotive Engineer of the SR as opposed to the Electrical Engineer and that the loco people who normally dealt with steam engines were rather fed up with having the 'piss taken out them' by the electric traction boys for being old-fashioned. As a consequence, they played a silly trick in that, although the DEMUs and EMUs had identical EE jumper cables, the loco chaps had the 'Forward' and 'Reverse' wires swapped around. As a result, if you tried to run an EMU in multiple with a DEMU, they would each try to go in different directions. Regrettably, the same piece of nonsense was perpetrated by ex-SR people, by then working for Network SouthEast, who did the same trick when Class '165' DMUs were ordered for the Chiltern and Thames lines in 1988. Thus, Chiltern,

Great Western and London Overground Classes '165', '166', '168' and '172', while happy to work with each other, will not multiple with any other DMU in the country.

After much argument, the BRB agreed to transfer the forty-three Class '508' units to Merseyside, who were delighted to have them so that they could replace their prewar LMS EMUs. They were replaced by a new build, the Class '455', which used a variant of the very successful Mk 3 loco hauled coach body as its basis. The BRB, rightly, insisted that autocouplers and disc brakes be fitted. However, Southern was allowed some say and, in true Southern Railway tradition, incorporated some parts recovered from 'SUBs'. The traction motor armatures were all recovered from the EE507 motors of the older trains. Also reused were the Westinghouse DH 25 air compressors. Indeed, these had a very long life, as I once saw in Eastleigh Works a Class '455' compressor which had been made in 1917. It must have been originally fitted to an LSWR 3-SUB EMU which, itself, probably incorporated parts of pre-1900 coaches. However, there was one bitter twist in that the Mersey system only required three-car units. Thus the SR was forced to retain one trailer car from each four-car Class '508'

One of Bullied's 4-SUB's at Clapham Junction. Known to drivers as 'Marys' because, when the prototype appeared in 1941, it was bigger than anything previously seen, like the *Queen Mary*. No. 4672 was one of the last built, in 1951, and almost certainly donated its traction motors to one of the new Class 455s.

The PEP train was a BR (i.e. not SR) initiative to design a thoroughly modern commuter train. It gave birth to the hated 508s.

and incorporate it into a new Class '455', so there was an ever present, and still existing, reminder of the hated BRB-designed trains.

A further batch of '455s' was then planned for the Central Division to replace the remaining 'SUBs' that still worked inner suburban services. However, the new trains required very different maintenance facilities from the ones they were to replace. As has been explained, much of the work on them was done in the open in sidings that had no facilities other than narrow platforms to enable cleaners to access the carriages. Brake adjustment and brake block replacement was done on electrified sidings. Modern disc braked trains will run quite large mileages between attentions, but they do need depot tracks with both centre and side pits so that there is easy access for brake pad changing.

It fell to me to find a suitable location on the Central Division that would cater for its needs for many years. In this task I was assisted by a legendary figure called Dick Mythen, who headed a team of project managers. Dick was a tall, balding man in his fifties who always wore a slightly quizzical smile and who delighted in talking in riddles. For all that, once he realised that I had got a rough idea about a few things, he was a tower of strength and, such was the pace of change over the next couple of years, effectively managed rolling stock depot modernisation projects in more than twenty places simultaneously.

We started by agreeing with Phil Evans, who worked for the Chief Civil Engineer as our interface man, a set of depot design standards for the new trains that would come in over the next few years. I drew

508.017 at Ewell West. The car park, to the right, was formerly Hardwickes yard, which had contained many traction engines in various states of repair.

One of the, then new, 455s that replaced the 508s when they went to Liverpool.

The view from my office in Southern House, which was fitted out with SR malachite green carpets. Selhurst depot is in the background. The sidings on this side of the depot were just about to become the site for the present day maintenance shed.

extensively on my experience at Heaton for this and, it seems, these standards have stood the test of time. The new Class '455' depot was built alongside the existing Repair Shop which did, and still does, overhauls, modifications and repairs to, mainly, Central Division trains. It was completed on time and on budget in 1984 just in time for the first new '455s'.

I spent a fair bit of time getting all departments to agree where and how depots were to be improved. One of the more interesting challenges was to find a place to put the maintenance depot for the proposed new Channel Tunnel scheme. This was not the scheme that was eventually authorised but one of several that had been proposed over the years, only to be shelved. This scheme did envisage the London terminus being Waterloo, as actually happened some years later, but with the train maintenance depot being on the Southern Region. We were asked by the BRB to help them find somewhere handy for Waterloo, which was a pretty tall order given that the trains were to be sixteen cars long. We came up with two sites, the first of which was near Longhedge Junction on the low level freight lines between Clapham Junction and Stewart's Lane. This was a very tight site which we put to one side in favour of one in Clapham Yard, which is between the Windsor Lines part of Clapham Junction Station and the South West Main Line section.

Part of the depot would have extended alongside the Windsor Lines almost as far as Wandsworth Town, which is the next station. Another unusual feature, necessitated by having to shoehorn the depot into a very cramped site, was that there would be a long headshunt extending towards Waterloo between main lines. Just after achieving a workable layout, the whole scheme was terminated by the government as a result of the ASLEF strike in July 1982.

British Railways had a difficult relationship with the drivers' trade union right from the start. There was a long strike in 1955 which could not have come at a worse time in that lorries were by then available that could seriously challenge rail for the freight market. As a result of having to shift to road, many shippers found that they did not need rail after all. This was made worse by a lamentable lack of investment in modern types of wagon by all the railway companies for most of the twentieth century, thus increasing costs. At the time of the strike, many drivers were in the National Union of Railwaymen, NUR, and chose not to support their ASLEF colleagues, which left a sometimes bitter legacy for the next thirty years.

The Beeching closures, and those that followed through the 1970s, hit driver numbers and morale hard. Many drivers and firemen were made redundant and large numbers of drivers were 'put back' which meant that they were acting as firemen or secondmen. This continued through the 1970s and into the 1980s. Of course, there really was no valid reason to have a secondman on diesel or electric locomotives except for some special circumstances. Ray Buckton, the ASLEF leader, knew this, which is probably why he was so stubborn in insisting that any train that exceeded 100mph should have two drivers. There was, of course, absolutely no logic in the argument, it was simply a 'peg to hang their hat on' which ASLEF deployed because they had let slip the opportunity to double man the LMR AC electric locos which only had one man in the cab.

When the BRB wanted to introduce the prototypes for both the APT and the HST in 1972, it had every intention of having only one driver in their cabs. ASLEF had other ideas and a two year stand-off resulted during which neither train turned a wheel. Eventually the BRB gave in, resulting in totally unnecessary double manning for more than twenty years until the privatised companies swept the nonsense away. This was British Railways at its worst, kowtowing to the unions who then had it on the run until it all came to a head in 1982.

This was the time when Prime Minister Margaret Thatcher, fresh from defending the Falklands from the Argentinians, told British Rail to stiffen its backbone, something it should have done years before. So when a perfectly reasonable proposal that drivers' shifts should vary, a little, in length in order to match work requirements was rejected, BR was told to stand firm. This resulted in a strike by ASLEF. Thatcher, whose hero US President Ronald Reagan had just sacked all his air traffic controllers and replaced them, told BR that it could do the same.

As one of the managers privy to some of the decision making, I and colleagues were very seriously worried that the PM was on the brink of closing BR down entirely. Perhaps a very much smaller commuter network might have reopened on totally different terms. Before this happened, however, cracks appeared in the drivers' determination. First, a few brave individuals ignored picket lines and came to work. One, Owen Edgington, worked for me later. I will pick up his story in the next chapter. Then an entire depot, Aylesbury, returned to work en masse. The strike quickly crumbled then and 'flexible rostering' was introduced. Before too long, secondmen were removed from freight trains. As a postscript, when, some twelve years later, one of the Aylesbury drivers transferred to Euston because he wanted to drive express trains, he had acid poured over his car. Some people have long memories.

Another of my responsibilities that I very much enjoyed was training. The Traction part of the department had traditionally taken skills training very seriously. There was a truly excellent Apprentice Training School at Selhurst where some twenty lads per year spent two years learning all aspects of electrical and mechanical craft skills. The training, under Chief Instructor Charlie Barr, was very thorough and meant that the Traction depots had a steady supply of excellent craftsmen. Many of them, of course, went on to be technicians and managers. For example, one is currently the Chief Executive of a train leasing company. To follow through, there were also 'Module Controllers' who ensured that the remaining two years of the apprentice scheme were effectively managed.

The boss of the training department, reporting to me, was none other than the Jack Brooks who had spent a week showing a bunch of schoolboys around the department in 1964. Unfortunately, Jack had rather lost his way, with the result that I had to gently ease him towards early retirement. I do not think he realised that the fifteen-year-old he had met before was the person showing him the door. I certainly did not tell him. He had an excellent, very enthusiastic, deputy, Ken Powell, who I had no hesitation in promoting.

One area which I took upon myself was the introduction of a Management Appraisal System. As in so many areas, the Southern was behind the times and had no such system in place. The essence of such a system is quite simply to enable managers to make clear to their staff what is expected of them, and then to give feedback on how they are performing. Equally important is the opportunity for the manager to get some feedback on how he or she might get more out of their employee. Such a system may also be used for assessing what pay

My ever cheerful training manager, Ken Powell, in our instructional train, former 'Mary'055, which was fitted out inside with class rooms and examples of equipment that staff would need to understand. It went, under its own power, to depots throughout the region and is seen here at Streatham Hill depot.

increment, if any, might be appropriate, but that has always been very much a secondary consideration in my view.

All this seems simple and commonsense. Indeed it is, but for many people it is uncomfortable. The fact is that many do not like having a full and frank discussion face to face about such things. I set up many sessions with, in total, about 180 managers in the department and we discussed why this was important and, using some role play, considered how to make a start. Hopefully it was useful.

I was also asked to look after graduate trainees who were allocated to the department, such as Clive Burrows, later Engineering Director for First Group, and acted as mentor to such people as Tony Wrighton, who became Engineering Director of East Midlands Trains before leaving for Australia, and Carolyn Griffiths, a fiery young lady who, after helping set up the Singapore Mass Transit, then the Sheffield Supertram, later became Her Majesty's Chief Inspector at the Rail Accident Investigation Board. I was also asked to present quite frequently to various management courses at The Grove and to help recruit graduates to BR's various training schemes. With a delicious piece of irony, I was asked by the Depot Engineer at Eastleigh, Alan Baker (remember 'not another bloody graduate' when I first met him at Crewe in 1971?), if I could help him find a way to become a Member of the Institution of Mechanical Engineers. He had run up against a brick wall since he did not have a degree. I was, by then, a Fellow and devised a plan for him which worked.

Various miscellaneous tasks came my way, such as being the Southern rep on the BR Re-railing Committee. This was another opportunity to modernise and introduce new technology aimed at improving performance and reducing costs. Our principal achievement was to get acceptance of the use of what the Americans call 'Hi-Rail' vehicles – road vehicles that can also run on rails. We introduced Hi-Rail lorries that carried hydraulic jacks and other tools and could often get to site much more quickly than a breakdown train and at much lower cost. The only snag was that there was no provision in the Rule Book for such vehicles that could join or leave the railway mid-section. Consequently, I found myself persuading operations colleagues that these were not the work of the devil and helping them draft revisions to the Rule Book to permit and regulate their use. Nowadays, Hi-Rail vehicles are used by the hundred, mainly for work on infrastructure. I was also responsible for getting rid of the last remaining Southern steam cranes at Brighton and Hither Green.

In the early 1980s, there was still a lot of activity aimed at further trimming the network by closing sections which were not seen as important. There was absolutely no concept of preserving corridors against future needs. One route which was closed shortly after I went to Croydon was the Sanderstead, Coombe Road and Elmers End line. I thought that this was particularly stupid as it had the potential to play a significant part in providing a duplicate to the Brighton Line, especially if the Uckfield to Lewes section was reopened. It is true that some further provision would have been needed at the London end, but existing corridors through suburbia should be seen as a valuable asset.

One route where I was actively involved in decision making was the Tunbridge Wells to Hastings line. It had been a nuisance ever since it had been built in the nineteenth century because the contractor for several tunnels had, fraudulently, built them with too few rings of bricks. When this was discovered, the solution was to insert two additional rings inside. This may not have mattered at the time, but by the 1930s it was an embarrassment, and indeed the 'Schools' class of 4-4-0 steam locos had to be built to a restricted loading gauge in order to fit. Later, the first DEMUs, referred to earlier, were built with very narrow bodies, as were some of the Class '33' diesel locos, known as 'Slim Jims'. We looked at many options, but there was a strong school of thought that the line should be closed south of Tunbridge Wells, which would have left Hastings with a much longer route to London, via Eastbourne and Lewes. Eventually it was decided to keep it open, electrify it and single through the tunnels. My contention that we could, thus, use standard stock which, being electric, would be cheaper to maintain, helped swing the argument. The hawks had to be satisfied with closing Tunbridge Wells West to Eridge, now the Spa Valley line.

Dick Hardy nominated me to go on a pilot course at Manchester Business School. This bespoke course was an intense, but shortened version of an MBA. It was very helpful for me as my subsequent career increasingly moved into business management. It was also pretty exciting in another way in that it coincided with the Falklands war which was graphically reported on TV.

A sad day came when Dick Hardy decided to take early retirement, which was celebrated at a very crowded event on 1 December 1982 in the boardroom at '222', BR's HQ at Marylebone, now the Landmark Hotel. After a career in Motive Power, which was his enduring love, and a spell as Divisional Manager, Liverpool, Dick really found his niche as the successor to Cedric Rose who had employed me. Their job was to ensure that young mechanical and electrical engineers were developed and placed into the most suitable jobs. Dick's legendary memory for people, their strengths and weaknesses, meant that he was really effective in this job.

In April 1983 I was invited to the Crewe Dinner as a guest of George Curry, then Director of LAMA, the Locomotive and Allied Manufacturers' Association, predecessor of today's Railway Industry Association (RIA), a trade association for railway equipment manufacturers. I knew George because his son Nick had been in my class at school for several years. George had lent us quite a number of railway films for the school railway society. The Crewe Dinner had been started by Francis Webb, the Chief Mechanical Engineer of the LNWR in the nineteenth century, for his Premium Apprentices. It has grown to be an annual dinner in London for those who trained at Crewe. It has been held every year, apart from during the Boer War, First and Second Wars, and is a splendid reunion for many present and retired, sometimes long retired, engineers. I have been a member for many years by virtue of my, albeit short, training there in 1970.

In September 1983, the government, after trying for two years to find a replacement for Peter Parker as Chairman of British Rail, reluctantly appointed the man who many, including me, consider was the best

Chairman BR ever had, Chief Executive, Bob Reid (the first of two BR Chairmen with that name). To add insult to injury, he was initially only appointed for three years instead of the usual five. Later, he told me that he had been called in by Nicholas Ridley, the Transport Secretary, and told in extremely plain English that he had 'better bloody well perform'. Perform he did. He started by setting out his stall in the BR staff newspaper, *Rail News*, and said that we must:

1. Step up the pace of change.
2. Develop a whole new set of attitudes.
3. Sharpen our marketing skills.
4. Improve the product.

He said that BR's weakest point was the way it dealt with customers. Its strongest was the popularity of rail as a means of transport.

'My immediate task is to make sure that all our managers have understood that the Corporate a Plan that we published in August represents the *minimum improvement* in performance that we are committed to achieving over the next five years.'

His predecessor, Peter Parker, was a popular figure but, as I have shown earlier, was an actor at heart – an artist, good at crafting fine words. He was not, however, a strong leader. Bob Reid had joined the LNER Management Training Scheme in 1946 having been a tank commander during the war. He knew railways inside out and was passionate that they could, and would, succeed. He was not seen as passionate because he was an intensely shy man who used few words. As sometimes happens with such people, he came across as very fierce and intimidating. However, if you got to know him, which I did a few years later, you very soon realised that he was a very kind, considerate and thoroughly nice man. He did not, however, suffer fools gladly and he, quite rightly, was very intolerant of those he thought were not pulling their weight. He also ruthlessly stamped out the trappings of the old order that had allowed senior managers to rest on their laurels in 'officers' messes'.

In 1987, not long after I had been appointed as MD of Red Star Parcels, the Chairman held a semi-social event for senior managers. He sought me out and congratulated me on my promotion and went on to give me a little advice. One of the things he said was that every senior manager needed a mentor. He told me that his was an American called Cortland Linder and that he had learnt a lot from him. Furthermore, I should go and see him. On investigation, it turned out that Mr Linder was a retired shipping magnate who had had a very colourful career and who lived in Up State New York.

A few months later, when I was in the USA on business, I made the two hour car trip north from New York and sat for a very pleasant couple of hours looking out, through huge picture windows, over a beautiful wooded valley chatting to my Chairman's seventy-seven-year-old mentor. He revealed that he had told Bob that if he wanted to fundamentally change BR, which he clearly did, he ought to reorganise it on business lines. He should identify what businesses BR was in, put someone in charge of each one and then let them get on with it.

This, of course, is exactly what Bob did. He decided that the businesses were: InterCity, London and South East, Other Provincial Services, Freight and, finally, Parcels. Not long after becoming Chairman he announced the appointment of so called 'Sector Directors' who were, respectively, Cyril Bleasdale, David Kirby, John Welsby, Colin Driver and Mike Connelly. Each one had a secretary but, initially, no one else. No real explanation was given as to how it would all work, so everyone was going around asking what it was all about. That, of course, was the idea. Each director had to work out what to do and then negotiate with some very strong characters who did not want to lose power. The Chairman just told them to decide what to do and get on with it. Brilliant.

Towards the end of 1983, my boss David Blake, although still the Southern Region CM&EE, was spending much of his time at the BRB HQ in Marylebone Road. He was one of a very small team of senior people charged by the board to improve efficiency, management accountability and reduce costs. I found myself chairing, on his behalf, several inter-regional groups to 'put some flesh on these bones'. This included the Computer Systems Group, which was charged with working out how the M&EE function nationally could improve its efficiency by the use of IT, which had hitherto been restricted to big data processing applications such as payroll and TOPS. I set up several initiatives, including one eventually called Rail Vehicle Records – 'RAVERS' (see Chapter Four) – which, in effect, automated places like the Derby Records Office, which I had visited as a trainee.

The other initiative came at the issue a different way. I asked Ian Gotts, one of the mechanical engineering graduate trainees that I mentored, to set himself up on the shop floor at Slade Green Repair Shop, near Dartford. It was a workshop organised to do lifts and minor repairs to suburban EMUs and was, at the time, entirely run on pieces of paper and record books. Bert Kennard, the manager, was very supportive of my plan to put this bright lad with PC on the shop floor and just see what happened. After some initial suspicion, ideas came tumbling in from all sorts of people who could see how it might make their work easier. It was a real 'bottom up' process. Ian left BR soon afterwards, joined Arthur Anderson, now Accentia, and spent several years managing the installation of large government IT schemes at the Department of Health and Social Security.

David Blake asked me to help him with plans for getting rid of the Divisional layer of management and beefing up the Areas. This was

The Southern was quite keen on using old passenger trains for departmental purposes. Unit 023, formerly a pre war 2-HAP, is seen at Hassocks taking EMU stores from Selhurst to Brighton Lovers Walk depot.

music to my ears as it has always seemed to me that policy should be determined at the higher level of an organisation, but execution should be managed as locally as possible. While involved in this work, it occurred to me that I would rather fancy one of the new, enlarged, Area Manager jobs as this would broaden my experience of management in other fields. I mentioned this to David and, shortly afterwards, was called to interview at Euston House, the LM Region HQ. I was interviewed by David Rayner, then the thrusting, up and coming Deputy General Manager, and by David Maidment, the rather bookish Chief Operating Manager. The job under discussion was a really interesting one: Area Manager, St Pancras.

For three years I had been living in Hurstpierpoint, just north of Brighton, with my family, now four with the addition of Victoria who had been born in Hexham Hospital, Northumberland. She was born on the day that Margaret Thatcher came to power, 3 May 1979, in, of all places, the Labour Ward. Travelling daily to Croydon or, sometimes, one of the London stations, there was no sense of who was in charge. Most of the time it worked pretty well, if slowly, but you just did not get a feeling that there was anyone whose only reason for coming to work was to make my journey special.

Another oddity long gone. This Class 33 is taking the boat train along the former GWR tramway to Weymouth Quay.

It seemed to me that it did not have to be like that. I thought that I could change it and that it would be a lot of fun to do so. I was aware that the line from St Pancras to Leicester had been very seriously considered for closure in the early 1970s but, instead, it had been decided to completely modernise the southern end as far north as Bedford. It was, effectively, a new railway. Electrified, track replaced, stations rebuilt, resignalled and, most controversially, planned to be the UK's first Driver Only passenger railway. If any service would benefit from a much more customer focussed approach, this must be it.

I started at St Pancras in early September 1984.

Chapter Eight

Learning the passenger business: the 'Bed Pan Line'

My predecessor, Denis Walker, could not wait to retire, which he did two weeks after I arrived at St Pancras. He was worn out after all the annoyance caused by five years of major disruption, while his railway, Bedford to St Pancras and Moorgate, was completely renewed.

As Area Manager, now earning £17,310 pa plus London allowance, I was responsible for running the trains safely, on time and within budget while delighting my passengers. Actually, I made up the last bit as it was not in my objectives in those days! These trains were InterCity Expresses (mostly HSTs) to Leicester, Nottingham, Derby and Sheffield; the new 'Midland Electrics' or, as the press called them, the 'BedPan Line' from Bedford to St Pancras and Moorgate; along with an odd remnant from Midland Railway days. The drivers called it the 'Ponderosa', nowadays known as Gospel Oak to Barking and part of London Overground.

This job turned out to be a fantastic opportunity to work out the way in which many parts of the railway could and should link together to provide a safe, reliable and pleasurable journey for our passengers. As such, it was invaluable experience for my involvement with Chiltern Railways that was to come at privatisation.

I had drivers at St Pancras and Bedford, a modern power signal box at West Hampstead and one old-fashioned manual signal box at Dudding Hill on a freight line. I was in charge of twenty stations ranging from the grand, if a bit tired, St Pancras to unstaffed Cricklewood which had not been busy since the trams came to that part of London in 1904. The railway was running reasonably well and Denis was right to be proud of his considerable achievement. However, there were lots of loose ends. Punctuality was a bit 'fragile', station car parks were, for the most part, gravel surfaced and prone to flooding in heavy rain. Station shops were inadequate and many ticket offices were small and inefficient, meaning that passengers often had to queue too long to buy a ticket.

In addition, the argument about whether Driver Only Operation (DOO) was really safe had not quite been put to bed. It was a fact of life and had been for about four months but there was a continual stream of letters from passengers and others expressing doubts. I grew quite practised in replying comprehensively to university professors who never seem able to express themselves with anything that resembles brevity. My considered opinion, then and now, is that provided that the system has been properly thought out and implemented, DOO is

St Pancras in 1984 represented the 'all new' railway after the slow and pedestrian Southern.

actually safer than using guards for despatch. There is also a significant reduction in station dwell time. This opinion is based on the experience of managing such systems for more than twenty years. It is reinforced by my personal experience of driving trains, both with and without a guard over many years.

This was in many ways a very different type of job for me, but one that I very much relished because of the opportunity to put the passenger at the heart of everything we did. To help me do this, I had a team comprising: Operations Manager Les McDowell, a very serious and conservative young man for whom the Rule Book was all. He was a safe pair of hands who was not going to let anything untoward happen, but did present a bit of a challenge on occasions when I felt that there just might be a better way of doing something. I had not been there very long when he sidled up one day, with an embarrassed look on his face, and asked me if I knew that certain of his staff were calling me 'Mr Car Park'. He was a bit shocked when I told him that I was delighted to hear that since, once we had sorted out the train service, car parks (lack of and state of) was our passengers' top complaint. Les was, initially suspicious when I said to him that I thought the Rule Book was unduly restrictive in that if, for some reason, you needed to have a loco on each end of a train (if you wanted to turn it all around on a triangle, for example) you had to man both engines. I explained to him that, while this was necessary on a vacuum or unbraked train, it was quite unnecessary on a two piped air braked train. The rear loco can simply be considered as another braked vehicle as if it were a coach. As with the Roadrailers on the Southern, the solution was to persuade the operating fraternity that a Rule Book change was needed. Nowadays, locos are often put on the rear of trains because, in today's mostly multiple unit railway, places for locos to run around their trains are few and far between.

Traincrew Manager Malcolm Wall was a rather nervous individual, in his mid fifties, who had been a signalman for most of his career. While I fully understand the benefits of cross fertilisation, I am also of the opinion that it is quite helpful for a manager to understand the role of his employees. Malcolm, undoubtedly, struggled for the lack of this. He was, however, baled out by two excellent Traction Inspectors, both of whom later worked for me at Chiltern. Owen was my first Operations Director there and Allan is, at the time of writing, a seventy-year-old Senior Controller who knows all the tricks in the book, plus many that are not.

Owen Edgington had been a driver and driver instructor at Saltley in Birmingham, a 'Saltley Seagull'. When the 1982 ASLEF strike about flexible rostering was on, Owen who came from a staunchly Conservative family headed by his father who owned a butcher's shop, disagreed with his union. He, therefore, worked his booked job which was to drive an HST from New Street to Bristol and back. Further, he then took it on to Derby on overtime. He had the strength of character to face down all his striking colleagues when they came back to work. However, when he was promoted to St Pancras, the Chairman of Bedford ASLEF branch, Bill Davis, made it known to

Operations manager Les McDowell giving out instructions.

all and sundry that he was never going to have that 'scab' in his cab. Typically, Owen made it his business to seek Bill out on his first day. Bill's train came into the platform at Bedford ten minutes before train time. He got into the cab followed by Owen. The train left on time, with both of them still in. To this day, neither will reveal what was said.

Alan Newman had started at Nine Elms in 1962 and had, thus, had five years firing Bulleid Pacifics on the South West Main Line, much of the time with driver Bert Hooker. Then, like Owen, he got his driver's job at Waterloo and so had intimate knowledge of 'round the houses' jobs. He came to St Pancras after driving all kinds of trains on the SR and then training Cricklewood drivers on EMU's. Disappointingly, the custom of Traction Inspectors wearing bowler hats, as I had experienced at Crewe, had died out by this time.

Bill Bassett was a tall, heavily built, fifty-seven year old when I first met him. He had started as an engine cleaner at Camden in 1942 and, such was the rate of progression in London sheds at that time, was driving 'Lizzies' to Birmingham and Crewe by the time he was twenty-three. He would have been at Camden when Adam Blaikie, who we met at Bletchley, was there. He was the Area Relief Manager, a role that my predecessor found useful. I suppose it was, when during the long reconstruction phase, the only objective was to run a half decent service safely. When it came to finessing things a bit, like trying

Driver Bert Hooker and nineteen-year-old fireman Alan Newman at Surbiton in 1964. Courtesy Alan Newman.

Inspector Alan Newman taking a turn at firing Bulleid Merchant Navy Class 35028 on a Sunday Marylebone to Stratford-on-Avon excursion in 1986.

to improve some of the softer things, Bill was not in his element. Bull in a china shop comes more to mind.

Keith Robinson was the Area Passenger Manager. All the station staff reported to him but his real forte was helping all of us to think more commercially rather than operationally. In this, he was considerably helped by a recent ex-management trainee called Richard Hammerton. They worked well together as a team. Keith was a brilliant man but a very troubled one who suffered from severe depression and resigned a couple of years later. Tragically, he committed suicide shortly afterwards.

Chris Gibbard, the Area Personnel Manager, was a very serious young man who had recently arrived from his first job after management training, which had been as a carriage cleaning supervisor at Wimbledon Park Depot. As I had discovered at Heaton, managing a large number of working-class women was quite an education. For someone like Chris who, I think, had had a rather sheltered upbringing, it had been rather a shock. He was a good support for me.

The final member of my management team was the Area Parcels Manager, Mike Carroll. He was also in his second job, having just come from High Wycombe where he had been Station Manager. Later he worked for me as my very effective Head of Operations in Red Star. Some years after that, he was for a time Managing Director of First Great Western.

For the first time, I had no engineering responsibility whatsoever as the trains were all looked after at Cricklewood Depot by a very passionate Irishman called Micky Flynn. In his former role as a staff rep, I can imagine that Flynn would have driven his manager round the bend. However, now that he was a manager himself, there was none better. His determination was to deliver the best possible trains for the customer. If a few rules got bent and bureaucrats got upset, well that was just life.

After I had been in the job for a week or so I was summoned to see Malcolm Southgate, who was the LM Region General Manager and, at that time, was based just down the road in Euston House, the former LMS HQ. Malcolm was very much an 'operator' and he could not understand why his deputy, David Rayner, had appointed, of all people, an engineer to the Area Manager's job at St Pancras. In Malcolm's view (and he was not alone) engineers did strange, unfathomable things and certainly did not know anything about running a railway. The 'interview' went well and the GM agreed to come and have a day with me soon just to be sure that I was OK. I discovered that, despite all the argument about it, he had not personally experienced Driver Only Operation (DOO), so I took him in the cab of a couple of trains and explained it all to him. My explanation of why it was safer than having a guard was backed up by both drivers, rather to his surprise.

He was impressed when he witnessed a bit of slick operating masterminded by my Shift Manager. A freight train on the up slow was about to delay an up stopping passenger train behind it because,

I was instructed by the Inspector to drive 35028 which I did, from High Wycombe to Aynho.

No. 35028 *Clan Line* back at High Wycombe later that same day.

for some reason, it was going very slowly. The Shift Manager had the up stopping train, which could do 90mph between stations, put out fast line at Luton and back in at Harpenden Junction just south of Harpenden Station, thus overtaking the freight train. We were on the platform at Harpenden and witnessed the co-ordinated announcements telling passengers that their train would be on Platform 3 rather than Platform 1. Result: passengers knew what was happening in good time and the stopping train arrived on time and no other trains were delayed. This might all sound rather simple routine stuff. It was, but too often in those days no one bothered to make these sorts of things happen.

Finally his approval of Rayner's choice came when, on the platform at Moorgate, an old lady asked me how to get to Old Street Station. My immediate reply that she should join the Northern Line, City branch and it would be the second station rather surprised my GM who admitted that he would not have been able to help the lady. I thought that was pretty poor for someone who had once been Station Manager at King's Cross!

By the time I got to St Pancras, all the planned upgrading of the route had happened and the shiny new electric trains had been running fairly well for about four months. As often used to happen, BR had cut the scope of the modernisation when some elements became overspent. This meant that while most of the stations had been totally rebuilt, some like Luton, Harpenden, St Albans and Radlett, had been left with very scruffy car parks which could become a sea of mud in winter and were quite inadequately lit.

I soon learnt about the different types of people we had at different stations. Luton, for example, resembles nothing so much as a northern industrial town plonked down in the South. It had major industries that were in heavy decline, mainly hat making and cars and trucks.

This was no doubt part of the cause of crime and other social problems. I got virtually no complaints from Lutonians about any aspect of the service, but we did become acquainted with many of them through their 'forgetting' to buy tickets.

The very next station, Harpenden, however, was used by a clientele who were used to being treated with respect for the fact they had become successful enough to move out to a fairly posh and very pleasant outer suburban area. They, like everyone else who used the line, had had to put up with noisy, dirty building works and old, very unreliable, smelly and dirty trains together with frequent weekend closures for five years. Then, when they thought it was all over, the trade unions refused to operate the new trains for a year because they did not agree that a guard was not needed.

There was a very active Commuter Association in Harpenden who had made poor old Denis's life a misery. He and the other managers warned me to stay away from them, telling me that they were quite unreasonable, objectionable and thoroughly unpleasant. I took a different view. These were our customers and they had been through hell. It was my job to go to see them and find out what I could do to make their life easier, given that we were by then running a safe, efficient and pretty reliable train service. So I accepted the association's invitation to meet its members in a church hall near the station one evening. My managers were horrified that I insisted on going alone, but I thought that I could carry it off much better that way. I did not want to be seen to be hiding behind anything or anyone. Further, Chris Kinchen-Smith and I had been one evening, when we shared a flat in Tunbridge Wells some three years earlier, to a similar event at which the BR SouthEast Divisional Operating Manager, John Elliot, had faced a hall full of angry commuters on his own and had done very well.

Nevertheless, it was not without some trepidation that I met a couple of members of the association's committee in an adjacent pub on the appointed evening. After a tomato juice, I was led like a condemned man to the nearby hall which had seats for about 200 in tiered rows, which meant that they were 200 faces all glaring down on me. By the time we started a few minutes later, another 100 or so angry people had squeezed in and there were even numbers of faces peering through windows at the sides of the hall.

I started off by welcoming everyone and began to say how pleased I was to be there because I wanted to hear what they thought I needed to do better. Given the very hostile mood, it was inevitable that I would not get very far before being noisily and rudely interrupted. I have got quite a loud voice, if required, and managed to make some headway despite the interruptions. After a few minutes, an authoritative voice near the front broke in to tell the hecklers that he and others had come to hear what I had to say, not to listen to them. The voice added that it was to my credit that I had come alone to face them. From then on, things went well. I made a couple of promises that I would make various improvements they were asking for and told them when I would be back to report on progress. It all ended in a convivial session in the pub at which I was not allowed to buy any drinks! I did, of course, deliver what I had promised and, indeed, made many other changes at their request.

We were very fortunate in having commuter groups for almost every station and I spent quite a lot of time with them, usually in the evening. This was time very well spent because they were all passionate about their particular station and its train service and were very keen to share their aspirations, their wishes and their frustrations with us. If one of management's key tasks is to improve the quality of the product, and hence profitability, what better than to have articulate, interested customers tell you how to do it?

Not long after arriving at St Pancras, I asked Julian Drury (MD of Train Operating Company c2c at the time of writing), the Stationmaster at Bedford, to show me around his patch. This included the drivers' mess room at Bedford where we chatted to a few of them and I noticed that there was a table some way from the others where there were three drivers who did not interact with the others in any way. Enquiring about this later, I was told that they had worked during the ASLEF strike of 1955. Since then they had been ostracised by the rest of the drivers who had not spoken to them for almost thirty years.

One of the annual institutions in Bedford was the 'old boys' do' which took place at a club one autumn evening. Anyone who had been a driver, or one of their managers, was invited and the event comprised thirty or forty retired drivers and their wives along with some of the existing ones and a smattering of supervisors and inspectors, plus Mr Sibley, the last Shedmaster at Bedford, who had retired in 1965 when the steam shed was closed. As Area Manager, I was expected to go and did so for several years, including long after I had moved jobs.

Imagine the scene: rows of canteen tables with elderly drivers reminiscing, their wives looking as if they wished they weren't there. I enjoyed taking turns chatting to them and listening to all sorts of tales from the past. One ninety-four year old insisted on reciting every signal from Bedford to Toton as if he were sitting an exam for his route knowledge. The only thing was, they had all

Station Manager Julian Drury at Bedford. At the time of writing he is MD of C2C, the Fenchurch St to Southend TOC.

Part of Julian's responsibility was Bedford Carriage sidings, where the new EMUs were stabled and cleaned.

been removed twenty years earlier when the line had been resignalled! Others would tell me how, during the Blitz in 1940, they would book on and travel 'pass' to Luton and then, for example, walk the three miles to Chiltern Green where they relieved the crew of an '8F' 2-8-0 on a coal train. It would be nose to tail with many other coal trains from the East Midlands to London because, in those days, the easterly two tracks south of Luton were permissive freight lines. The delay would be because of bomb damage in London. Often they would be relieved eight hours later without having moved an inch. Yet another old driver told me of working over the North London Line in a 1940s' 'peasouper', as the dense fog of those days was called. It could be so bad that the driver could not see the semaphore signals until he was right up to the post. So he crept up, using his route knowledge to its best effect, and then stopped because he couldn't see the arm. The fireman would be despatched up the ladder to discover if the signal was 'off'. If it wasn't, he would put an empty bucket (always carried on a steam engine) on the counterbalance arm so that it would fall with a clatter when the signalman pulled the signal off.

I spent quite a lot of time with drivers, usually in the cab. You learn a great deal about what really happens by looking and listening. You can see how the driver is performing. Is he driving as he has been trained?

You can understand how different types of trains behave in different weather and load conditions. You can see what is going on at stations you pass through. You can see if the signalmen are on the ball.

Many of the drivers had really interesting stories. Harry English transferred at his request from Coulsdon North. He had been a driver there (about a mile from where I lived at the time as a small boy) since 1952. He would have known all the spider's web of lines into Victoria and London Bridge from South London and would have been expert at handling the Westinghouse air brake on the 'Marys', the 4-SUB, later Class '405'. It is probably true to say that he would never have driven a train at more than 60mph, yet at the age of sixty-two he thought he would try something new. His job with us, in the top link at St Pancras because of his seniority, was driving HSTs to Sheffield and back… it could hardly be more different.

Then there was Charlie Hoyle, an Anglo-Indian, who had come to England with his family at Independence in 1947. He used to tell me how his childhood memories were all about going with his family (father was a mail train driver, the top of his profession) to 'The Club' where they played cricket on manicured lawns, sipped cocktails fetched by Indian flunkies and generally had a privileged existence. I asked him if Indians were also members. 'Oh, no,' he exclaimed in shock. Indians would not be allowed in. Fascinating since, as a result of his telling me about his family tree, I had calculated that he was five-eighths Indian himself. Arriving in London in 1947, Charlie's dad, who had expected to walk into a train driver's job (as he could have done after privatisation), soon found that if you were older than twenty-three you could not enter the 'footplate line of promotion'. Thus the proud former mail train driver who had taken his family to the swanky club found himself for the rest of his career on the end of a broom in dirty, smelly, bomb damaged Cricklewood MPD. Seventeen-year-old Charlie, meanwhile, started on the bottom rung as an engine cleaner and, when I knew him, was in the top link like Harry English.

Fred Mayes was one of two Leading Railmen at Harlington, a few miles south of Bedford. Although he had lost his arm in a shunting accident in 1948, he produced this superb display every year.

Driver Charlie Hoyle, brought up in the privileged Anglo-Indian environment, came, aged 17, with his family to England in 1947. He started on the first rung of the promotional ladder as a cleaner at Cricklewood shed whilst his proud Mail Train driver father pushed a broom around for the rest of his days.

Then there was the big, heavily built Irish driver, also in his sixties. He had been a farm boy back home and volunteered in 1939 to join the British Army 'because I wanted a bloody good fight'. He said he enjoyed his war immensely and had a good go at lots of Jerries, after which shovelling prodigious amounts of coal into Garretts based at Cricklewood seemed a good option. He told me about the six suicides he had experienced over the years. Someone jumping into the path of your train is most drivers' nightmare. He said he just forgot about it, no problem. However, the next time, a few weeks later, it was a problem. He could not just shrug it off. He went completely to pieces and at the age of sixty-three never drove a train again.

Just after Christmas 1985, our new trains started to drop like flies. The problem was a particular type of snow, very fine and powdery (the 'wrong type of snow') which was blown up in clouds when it was really cold. Whereas big soft, damp snowflakes would not have been a problem, this very fine powder got into everything, including a big electrical coil under the floor which was called a choke, the purpose of which was to smooth out the electric current that went to the motors. Unfortunately the chokes, which were about the size of an old-fashioned dustbin, ran quite hot and melted the powdery snow. Now, as we know, electricity and water are not happy bedfellows and the chokes were failing all over the place.

We were supposed to have thirty-seven Class '317' four-car units every day. At the worst, we were down to just twenty. Consequence: much unhappiness among our rapidly growing number of passengers. I caused rather a stir by actually telling our passengers exactly what was going on. At the time this was seen as a very odd thing to do and, in itself, attracted press comment. I had a series of explanatory letters put out on every seat overnight as in those dark days, long before smart phones and social media, this was the best way to ensure that the message got across.

I did, of course, summon whatever replacement trains I could get hold of. This turned out to be two eight-car rakes of Mk 1 coaches together with a pair of 133 ton Class '45' 2,500hp diesel locos. Each of these just about made up for two '317's although, even on limited stop

Driver Terry Lawrence came to Bedford in 1984 when his depot, Wellingborough, closed. Because he had not been prepared to move, he was still a secondman at the age of forty-seven. Coal train to 90mph EMU was a bit of a shock!

Not quite what was intended! As a result of this experience, many years later I gave Steve Murphy, then MD of London Overground, a formal objective never to be on the front page of *The Evening Standard*. He succeeded where I had failed.

The LONDON STANDARD

Friday, February 7, 1986   20p   *Incorporating the Evening News*

600 TRAPPED IN TUNNEL

by Emma Lee-Potter

2-hour train ordeal of London commuters

SIX HUNDRED commuters were trapped on board a Midland Region train last night after it broke down in a tunnel.

The packed train ground to a halt in a tunnel between King's Cross Midland station and Kentish Town.

Attempts made to couple another train to it failed and it was only after two hours that railwaymen managed to attach a four-car train to the front and it limped into Kentish Town station.

Crammed

There the passengers were taken off and transferred to another train.

"The train was packed because there were so many cancellations last night due to the bad weather," he said.

"When the train left Kings Cross Midland station it broke down because it was on a steep gradient with a very heavy load and because of snow problems."

He added: "We apologise to passengers for what must have been a very uncomfortable journey. There was no question of them being in any danger."

The wife of one man on the train, Mrs Julia Watson, was waiting anxiously for news at her home

late I began to worry. I rang Luton station and all they could tell me was that something had held the train up in a tunnel.

"It was absolute chaos. My husband was half-dead with fatigue by the time he finally got home at 9pm—he's not a young man.

"Not only were the passengers trapped in the cold for so long but when they finally got the train moving it was still chaotic.

"The passengers were just herded off the train at Kentish Town and crammed into a small passageway leading to a bridge across to another platform.

services, they could not keep time. However, it was fun to ride in the cab of one with an experienced driver doing his very best. Hitting the end of the platform at Leagrave at 50mph where the driver 'dropped the lot' – i.e., made a full vacuum brake application – was quite

Since we could not offer anything like a normal service, I thought it was important to explain to passengers just what was happening and what we were doing about it. In those far off days the best way to get the message to most passengers was to put a letter on every seat.

≥ **British Rail**

Area Manager,
British Rail (London Midland)
St. Pancras Station
London NW1 2QP
Telephone 01-387 9400

TO ALL PASSENGERS

I would like to apologise sincerely for the delayed trains and crowded conditions which you have been subjected to in the last few days.

The principle problem is that snow, which is unusually fine and powdery because of the very low temperatures, has been finding its way into electrical equipment underneath the coaches. Unfortunately, this has seriously damaged a very specialised piece of equipment called a "choke" on many of my trains. Because it is unique to these trains, replacements are having to be specially made - which will take some time.

In the meanwhile instead of the usual 37 trains available each day for service, I have had 20 or so in the last few days, hence some cancellations and many shorter trains have been inevitable.

I am arranging to borrow as many replacement trains as I can from elsewhere although they may not be as comfortable.

It may become necessary to divert some Moorgate trains into St. Pancras. If this happens, London Transport have agreed that you can travel by the Circle Line from King's Cross/St. Pancras to Farringdon, Barbican or Moorgate provided you have a valid B.R. ticket.

After a steadily improving standard of service during 1984 my staff and I are especially disappointed to have let you - our customers - down.

I can only say that we are trying as hard as we possibly can to improve things. Many Railwaymen have willingly worked long hours and changed jobs - often in the bitterly cold night - to do their best for you next day.

[signature: Adrian Shooter]

Adrian Shooter
Area Manager, St. Pancras.

January, 1985.

exhilarating, especially when we stopped in exactly the right spot. Fortunately GEC, the supplier of the defective electrical equipment, responded very promptly to my 'encouragement' and within about a month everything was back to normal.

During 1985, the idea of reopening the route through Holborn Viaduct Low Level, the 'Snow Hill Lines', started to gain currency. As described in Chapter One, I had had the opportunity to walk this link some twenty years previously. At that time it was freight only and,

Area Manager
British Rail (London Midland)
St. Pancras Station
London NW1 2QP
Telephone 01-387 9400 Ext.

TO ALL PASSENGERS

I wrote to you on January 18th about the problems we are having with the "Chokes" on the Electric Trains.

Since then our design engineers have done a lot of work with the suppliers, G.E.C. Traction Ltd with a view to producing a new design of choke which will solve the problem once and for all. Unfortunately, I am told it is just not possible to produce this in time for this winter.

Meanwhile a tremendous effort has been made to get damaged chokes repaired. By February 8th, we had 34 trains in use (out of 37).

However, further very low temperatures and fine powdery snow over last weekend have set us back. Despite various precautions including reducing the maximum speed from 90 mph to 50 mph, 11 trains have failed so far, and there is the prospect of more.

I very much regret to have to say that the service will be inadequate. Trains will be delayed, they will be shorter and there will be some cancellations. We will however, working with the suppliers, get back to normal just as quickly as we can.

Adrian Shooter,
Area Manager, St. Pancras   11th February, 1985

This was followed up a little later with a second letter.

I'm sorry says BedPan boss

DELAYS and overcrowding on the BedPan line has prompted an apology from British Rail area manager Mr Adrian Shooter.

Mr Shooter, who lives in Biddenham and travels in by train every day from Bedford to his office in St Pancras, sent a letter to all passengers travelling on the line explaining the reasons for the trouble.

Over 10,000 letters were printed and left on train seats for commuters to read as they went to work.

Mr Shooter told the Beds Times: "It was my idea. It was obvious to me that we were not providing the service that we should. It seemed a reasonable way of solving the problem and I wanted to communicate to as many people as possible."

One of the many newspaper articles.

because of the way BR was organised in geographic regions, no one had any inclination to think how cross-regional schemes such as this might be useful. Accordingly, the route was closed in the early 1970s. Incredibly, the only reason that it was possible to reopen the route in the 1980s was that a junior clerk in the BR Property Board – who I have met – made an unauthorised intervention. His job was to conduct searches for developers to determine if sites they wanted to acquire were, in fact, clear. He had to deal with a request to put up a substantial building whose foundations would have obstructed the disused rail route. Without any authority to do so, he declined the application because he could see, when his superiors could not, that the route had great strategic importance. Pity there were not more like him!

Work on the new route started in June 1986 and I, with others, was involved in the specification for the new dual voltage trains, Class '319'. These trains have always been unsatisfactory because they had uncomfortable seats, and were very noisy because of wind noise and being sweaty in the summer. I and my commuter clubs lobbied strongly but unsuccessfully for better features, including air conditioning, which would have reduced the noise and the sweatiness. The accountants won. A useful lesson for the future. I have never let them get involved in train design since.

In due course I was invited to join the Euston House Junior Mess. This was an ancient institution on its last legs. You had to prebook and the idea was that you arrived at about 12.30, had drinks until 13.00 when you sat down to a very nicely cooked meal for which you were charged a paltry sum. I only went along two or three times, having much better things to do with my time, but it was obvious that some of the senior managers in the Regional HQ went there every day and were drinking from 12.30 until about 15.00, which left an hour or two to snooze in their offices before tottering home. It was not in the least surprising that Bob Reid closed all messes down the following year.

One manager who I did not see in the mess, despite his profession, was Dick Sanderson, who had been the Divisional Public Relations Manager before the London Division was abolished, and who helped me tremendously. He encouraged me to get to know my local newspaper and radio journalists and to have frequent and open communications with them. He fixed up initial meetings to get to know

And another.

Adrian puts his job on the line

ADRIAN Shooter is determined to keep on the right tracks in his new job.

For the freshly-appointed area manager of the electrified Bedpan line plans to keep closely in touch with commuters—by sitting next to them.

In fact, Mr Shooter is so keen to be the first to hear any grumbles about the line he now manages, he is about to launch a personal publicity campaign to forge new links with customers.

When he got the job he moved his family to Bedford so he would be able to keep a personal eye on his train service by using it every day to get to his office at St Pancras station.

He said he had no objection to anyone with complaints taking the matter up with him if they see him on the train.

"I don't think it's right to run a railway and not travel on it. If you use it yourself you pick up all sorts of things, little problems that need seeing to.

On Tuesday, February 5, he will be talking to the Harpenden Society about the renovation of the Harpenden railway station.

● The winter weather problems of the 90mph electric trains should be over in a couple of weeks' time.

Fine snow had got into the "choke"—a piece of electrical equipment under the coaches—causing quite a few to break down.

The problem is now being eliminated by engineers and older trains are being used to maintain the service, which uses 37 trains a day.

them and then left me to get on with it. His example has stood me in good stead for many years and enabled me to have very relaxed and productive relations with lots of journalists.

I soon found that local radio, then fairly new, was a very good way to talk to our customers. There were two local stations. One was BBC Radio Bedfordshire, which had just moved into a new, purpose built two storey building. It was lavish with a smartly uniformed 'Corps of Commissionaires' receptionist in his black paramilitary uniform, complete with medals.

The real hero of this very difficult time was Mick Flynn, seen here with his wife cooking for an invited group on his own ex-BR DMU. Mick had been a shop steward at Cricklewood and had made the life of more than one manager a misery. By 1984 he had been promoted to Chief Foreman at the depot which looked after our Class 317 EMUs. He worked absolute wonders to get the fleet back working after the severe problems. He was totally and selflessly devoted to getting the best deal for our passengers. When the depot was closed a few years later because the new Thameslink trains were allocated to Selhurst, I thought he was very badly treated. I was, therefore, delighted to have him join my engineering team at Rail Express Systems.

In total contrast, the commercial station was based in a seedy courtyard off Dunstable High Street. There, you had to ring a bell and, if the one employee on duty was on air, wait until he had put another piece of music on for a reply. You were then invited into the studio to watch and listen until it was time for your slot. Nothing was wasted and, it seemed to me, the content was that bit sharper and more up to date. The young journalist I usually saw was Sim Harris, who seemed quite interested in railways and, at the time of writing is editor of *Rail News*.

Another journalist, who I had first met ten years before at Bletchley, was Roger Ford of *Modern Railways*. He had done a series of 'days in the life' of various BR managers. Roger started his day by arriving at our house near Bedford early one evening. His article started:

'While parallels can be taken too far, there is more than a passing similarity between British Rail under Chairman Sir Robert Reid and China under Chairman Mao. Both men subjected rigid hierarchies to a cultural revolution; both men shared the philosophy that power and decisions should be devolved downwards to those who actually do the work. And in both cases change depends on small cadres of young enthusiasts for the new scheme of things.'

Reflecting on this more than thirty years later, I think Roger was right. This really was what was happening… and it was exciting.

First on the agenda, after supper, was a meeting just down the road in our local pub where the Bedford Commuter Association, chaired by Bob Lincoln, was holding one of its regular meetings. Topics that Roger reported included thermostats not working in Class 317 EMUs, the status of BR's proposals to reopen the 'Snow Hill' route connecting London's Northern rail network with the Southern, electrification to Kettering (which still has not happened at the time of writing), and likely stopping pattern changes in the next timetable. Discussion also

I thought that it was really important to meet all our local commuter groups so that I could understand what customers were thinking and how we could improve things for them. This is a meeting in a pub one evening with the Bedford Commuters' Association, who were very articulate and well informed. Courtesy Roger Ford.

focussed on the, then, draft spec for the new Class '319' trains for Thameslink. The association was disappointed that they sounded as if they would be configured for short distance journeys. I encouraged them to lobby for comfortable seats and air conditioning, neither of which were provided, to the regret and inconvenience of an entire generation of commuters.

The following morning I took Roger in the cab of the 07.06 HST to St Pancras, my normal train to work before entering the Shift Manager's office. There were five of these who, between them, worked twenty-four hours, seven days a week. They reported directly to me and they were 'Me' when I was not there. By this I mean that they were responsible, real time, for everything that went on when they were on duty. Obviously they worked closely with the functional managers who also reported directly to me. The system worked extremely well, especially since we had just entered the age where systems were such that they could 'see' just what was going on all over the area.

Roger was able to see how my first job, while having my first morning coffee, was to read the Area Log for the past twenty-four hours and took the opportunity to discuss current matters with the Shift Manager or one of the other managers who would also be there. Since our core competence had to be the safe and efficient operation of trains, it was always useful to have the two Traction Inspectors there as we could review incidents with them then and there.

An opportunity then arose to witness the Shift Manager come into his own. Two four-coach trains had been booked to couple together at 07.18 and then run to Bedford as an eight-car. One train had a minor electrical fault and had to be taken out of service. This delayed the departure by four minutes and, rather than prolong the delay, the Shift Manager decided to send just four cars to Bedford. This did not matter because there were only about three coaches full of passengers on this train normally (the Shift Manager had up-to-date passenger counts for all trains). However, what did matter is that the eight cars were then due to come back from Bedford to Moorgate, stopping at all stations to St Albans, then fast to London. It was usually standing room only so if it was half the usual size, sardines would have nothing on it.

The telex in the office at St Albans chattered out instructions from the Shift Manager: 'The 07.18 St Pancras to Bedford and 08.20 Bedford to Moorgate will be four coaches only today. All stations to tell passengers not to stand too far down the platform.' But wait; the first train booked to go to the depot after the peak has got time to run empty non-stop to Luton from where it can be started at 08.39, three minutes in front of the 08.20 from Bedford so that passengers from Luton, Harpenden and St Albans can get a seat. The telex lists all the consequential changes to stock working which will rebound until after 11.00 and gives instructions to stations, drivers, signalmen and supervisors.

Then it was upstairs to my office and a chance to go through the day's batch of customer letters. I always insisted on seeing all of them and, much to their surprise, would often telephone the writers to better understand how things had gone and, where appropriate, to explain any improvements we were making. Most of the written replies were done for me by Tim Casterton, who did a really good job, but I always signed them. Tim is now a civil servant and part time journalist and, no doubt, writes many letters for ministers. I have always felt that keeping as close as possible to our passengers helped all of us to do our job better and more profitably.

Throughout the day, Roger accompanied me as I went about my business as usual. First, it was a meeting with some people from the BR Property Board. My mission with them was to persuade them that they should start with finding out what would delight passengers when they are seeking new tenants. This was a foreign concept to them and they had great difficulty seeing that this might, also, be a route to greater profits. Not much has changed over the years as far as I can see!

Roger's day with me resulted in a six page article which gives a pretty good picture of the job of an Area Manager.

After a while, Malcolm Southgate was moved on from being LM Region General Manager to lead BR's activities with respect to the forthcoming Channel Tunnel. In a real 'turn up for the books', he then tried to recruit me to a senior operations role in his new organisation – me, who he doubted was up to the task of running the St Pancras area! I declined his kind offer since there were going to be no trains to run for several years and my attention span in a purely planning job would have been rather limited.

His place was taken by a slightly surreal character, Cyril Bleasdale, who had been the first InterCity Director. I rather suspect that Bob Reid had decided he needed someone in that important role who was more attuned to producing a rational, deliverable, profitable business plan. He certainly got that, in spades, with Dr John Prideaux, who took over from Cyril.

On the occasion of my first meeting with our eccentric new GM, I took him to West Hampstead signal box, which was the operational heart of my area. He was accompanied by his deputy, Ivor Warburton, who had taken to accompanying Cyril in order to extinguish any fires that he started before they grew out of control. I was aware that just before being moved on, Cyril had caused some tests to be undertaken to assess passenger comfort when trains were driven around curves at higher than the normal authorised speed. He had been assured both by rolling stock and track engineers that the speed limits were, firstly, for passenger comfort and were far below the speed at which there was any danger.

While in the signal box, one of my people showed him, with some pride, the automatic speed trap that was installed. It used the time taken to pass through a measured track circuit and gave a reading of the average speed over that section, and was a fairly new innovation. On seeing this, Cyril declared, in a voice loud enough for all to hear, that the signed speed limit was only advisory and that it did not matter if drivers exceeded them a bit to make up time. In the safety-critical and, essentially rules-bound environment of a signal box, this was heresy. I, therefore, felt I had no alternative but to say in a much louder voice: 'General Manager, on this area all my staff will obey the Rule Book to the letter. Anyone who does not will be disciplined.' At this, Ivor, who was standing behind Cyril facing in my direction, burst out laughing while the General Manager bore the closest look to contrition that Cyril ever did. My staff got the message.

Around the same time, David Maidment, my rather cerebral, but effective, boss moved on from being Chief Operating Manager and was replaced by Peter Rayner, who you might describe as a 'seat of the pants' operator. He had just come from being BR's account manager with the Post Office. Presently, he announced his intention to come and see me at St Pancras. We spent an hour or so in my office discussing, mainly, matters to do with drivers. He was adamantly against Driver Only Operation (DOO), not that he knew much about it. Later on he prevented its implementation on the West Coast Main Line, which will have cost millions at a time when almost all London suburban routes were DOO.

After about an hour, he said: 'Come on, my boy, we're going to lunch.' Since I had been warned that this would be of the liquid variety, at least as far as he was concerned, I told him that I wanted to go well away from the station because I did not want any of my staff seeing him or me (actually it would only be him) drinking contrary to the Rule Book. He was a bit grumpy about this but reluctantly acquiesced, although he did lose patience after I had marched him past four or five pubs. Eventually we partook of a tomato juice (me) and a couple of pints (him). He accepted my suggestion that it would be better not to come back to my office smelling of bitter. He did not, on principle, get involved in privatisation, but instead spent many years telling anyone who would listen how wrong it was and how dangerous everything would become.

One by product of reporting to the Regional Chief Operating Manager (COM) was that my budget was routed via his organisation. This sometimes resulted in the odd question about costs relating to drivers, but never about anything else. The fact that no one other than the Area Manager was going to do anything about customer service, for example, did not seem to matter to anyone before Chris Green arrived on the scene. One result of this odd situation was that I discovered that the COM had a budget of about £6 million a year earmarked for expenditure on things like booking offices, travel centres and other items that might be related to customer satisfaction. I also realised that no one in the COM's office at Crewe had the slightest interest in what this money was spent on and, accordingly, set out to ensure that as much as possible went to benefit my passengers. I should, at this point, make clear that I did not request any budget until my team had put together a rigorous investment submission to me. Only if I was satisfied that there was a sound investment case did I set out to obtain the cash, even though I did not have to jump through any hoops at all. Ridiculous. For two years I spent the entire LM Region budget on my stations. Probably there would have been better investments elsewhere, but no one was promoting them.

Examples of what we spent the money on include a better Travel Centre at Luton so that we could deal with more complex sales than were possible at a window with a long queue. One perennial problem for commuter railways with busy peak periods is the queue to buy tickets which can very quickly get far too long. We came up with a very effective solution which we applied at our ten busiest stations. It was simple and inexpensive, comprising a car park ticket machine which had to be only slightly adapted for our purpose. They were immediately popular and repaid all their cost within a year. We called them 'Queuebusters'.

The biggest project in this category was the 'Luton Flyer'. This came about because I became aware that a new airline called Ryanair had just had its application for slots at Heathrow turned down and was on the point of giving up because it had only been given some at Luton, which it thought was of no use. I sought out the principal and met Tony Ryan. 'Where the hell is Luton?' he asked me over a Guinness the following evening. 'Closer to London than Heathrow,' was my answer. By that I meant that at that time we had two trains per hour from St Pancras to Luton taking twenty-nine minutes. It was then a seven minute journey to the airport. Before Heathrow Express, the fastest public transport was the Piccadilly Line which took the best part of an hour from Central London to Heathrow.

The popularity of the new service very quickly attracted many new passengers which resulted in long queues at ticket offices in the rush hour. Richard Hammerton, one of our Management Trainees, came up with the idea of having pay and display ticket machines adapted for the top 10 fares. It worked brilliantly, was quick to implement and fairly cheap.

Another marketing initiative was the 'Luton Flyer', a bespoke bus that connected the half hourly fast trains from London with Luton Airport, which was just starting a major expansion. This convenient, through-ticketed service, laid the ground for the construction of Luton Airport Parkway station some years later.

Over a couple of years we developed a very smooth transfer, with specially converted buses meeting every train at Luton. The train stopped at the down fast platform just a few yards from the waiting bus. There were also through tickets available at St Pancras or from the airline. We put together, with the airport and several airlines, some fairly heavy duty promotional activity with many travel agencies.

One of my regular meetings with Personnel and Admin manager Chris Gibbard. Courtesy Roger Ford.

More than 500 of their staff sampled the new service in a few manic days. It all worked brilliantly well and over 80,000 passengers were carried in the first year. It led, eventually, to the building of Luton Airport Parkway station and, in 2016, the announcement that a light rail line to the airport would be built. The whole thing was put together and promoted locally. As for Ryanair, the rest is history.

There was a cautionary tale when some bright young things in the new InterCity Sector came up with a wizard wheeze. Wanting to encourage trial of InterCity travel, they arranged that a particular issue of *Modern Railways* would have a voucher that enabled the purchaser to have any InterCity journey totally free simply by exchanging the voucher for a ticket at a booking office. You might question whether that particular journal was likely to encourage new users but, be that as it may, it put severe temptation in front of a great many booking clerks. Some, like mine at St Pancras, succumbed. The scam was simple in that all a booking clerk had to do was go out and buy up every copy of *Modern Railways* that they could find. Then, when bona fide passengers came to their window and paid cash for a long distance ticket, the cash went into the clerk's pocket while a voucher went into the till. I sacked six booking clerks for doing this.

Many times since, I have encouraged marketing people to think about possible scams and, indeed, have sometimes had my auditor think about what scams might be devised and check that we had found a way of blocking them.

When I started at St Pancras, the Sector Director for London & SouthEast (L&SE), as it was then called, was David Kirby, who, many years earlier, had been a young firebrand who had made things happen in Sealink, BR's Shipping Division. My perception by 1986 was that he had run out of steam, as often seems to happen as time passes. The Chairman must have thought the same because at the beginning of 1986, David was kicked upstairs to be Vice Chairman of the BR Board where his contribution continued to be what you might call 'subtle'. At least that was what I observed.

His replacement as Director L&SE was anything but subtle. I had first come across Chris Green as a dynamic Divisional Operating Superintendent for the Southwestern Division of Southern. After that he became the Chief Operating Manager for the Scottish Region, in which capacity he had interviewed me for a job, shortly after which he got the top job as GM for Scotrail, which was 'Greenspeak' for the Scottish Region. There, he was encouraged by Bob Reid to make waves and he did not disappoint. He showed that if you ran a safe and punctual railway, had smart trains and stations and encouraged your staff to hold their heads up high, miraculously good things happen and you start to get lots more passengers.

Chris first came to see me at St Pancras on 28 February 1986 and was very much in listening mode. We got on well from that day on as he listened while I told him about the super railway that I had inherited and the many things that we were doing to make the lot of passengers better. He was very sold on what he called 'Total route modernisation': that is, you replace the trains, the signalling and the stations all at once to produce maximum effect.

In very short order, Chris's plans were in place and the evening before the public launch in June 1986, all the railway managers from around London were invited into the huge basement cinema in the J. Walter Thompson advertising agency in Berkeley Square. There, we saw a light and sound presentation quite unlike anything that stuffy old BR usually did. Finally, with a roll of drums and a puff of smoke, the new name was revealed: 'Network SouthEast'.

We were told how this was much more than just a branding exercise, it was a whole new way of doing things. We were going to put together all the London-based commuter lines and, for the first time, they would be managed as one coherent whole. We would seek out best practice and adopt it quickly. We would create a railway that everyone would be proud to work for.

Chris worked very closely with Ronnie McIntyre, the former Scotrail architect who he had brought with him. Ronnie's brief was to make the maximum visual change in the minimum time. Thousands of red lampposts at Network SouthEast's 600 stations were the result. They appeared in less than a month whereas reliveried trains took a little longer.

One other early tangible result of Chris's infectious enthusiasm was his ability to persuade the board to reverse its decision to close Marylebone station and some of the Chiltern lines. He reasoned that with railways in a new, resurgent posture there soon would not be enough capacity on the other lines. He was quite right, of course, but that was not the received wisdom then, since London rail commuters had declined in numbers for every one of the previous fourteen years. I think it is the track record that we were able to demonstrate that enabled Chris to argue that if you get the quality right, growth will follow.

I well remember the afternoon when John Oxley, one of Chris's senior managers, came to see me about some routine matter. John, usually a somewhat lugubrious, but very competent, individual, was positively radiant. 'I have just had the very best day in my railway career,' he enthused. He told how he had been instructed to go to the TUCC (Transport Users' Consultative Committee) enquiry set up to consider the BRB's proposal to close Marylebone, to catch the Chairman's eye and to state that the British Railways Board wished to withdraw its closure proposal.

One afternoon in September 1986, David Rayner, by now General Manager of the Eastern Region, called me and in his typically blunt way asked if I fancied going to Japan. I very soon regained my composure and said I would be delighted. David, who was clearly being lined up to become a future member of the BR Board, had been asked to select a couple of people and lead the group to find out what all this privatisation nonsense in Japan was all about. The subscript was that the board would then be in a better position to make sure it did not happen to them. As it happened, none of the three of us shared the board's distaste at the prospect. We were, however, very happy to go and look and learn. David, through connections he had made in the travel trade, managed to convince the powers that be that the best deal was to be had by buying a first class Round the World ticket for each of us. I never did quite get that, but who was I to complain?

The third member of our group was Peter White, a BR civil engineer. The three of us decided that, while we were away, it would make sense to call in to Hong Kong and see how the railways there compared with Japan, the rationale being that they were using 100% British equipment and management. It would be interesting to compare the result with that achieved in Japan.

We had two weeks in November 1986 in Japan as guests of Japanese National Railways (JNR) which was going to be privatised the following April. Our first impression of JNR was riding the Narita Express from the airport into Tokyo. This was very smart and much more impressive than anything we had in those days. Taking a taxi in Tokyo, however, we passed a couple of old-fashioned office blocks with sandbag emplacements outside, manned by what appeared to be armed soldiers. We soon discovered that these were JNR offices and that the armed 'soldiers' were actually Railway Police. Privatisation was not universally popular, it would seem!

Our two weeks comprised numerous presentations on how the changes were to be made, interspersed with site visits ranging from the very impressive Shinkansen Control Centre in Tokyo to a traincrew signing on point which was filthy and graffiti ridden. We also learnt that there was a considerable problem with driver drunkenness. One senior manager programmed to speak to us at 09.00 one morning was extremely apologetic when he turned up at about 09.20. It seemed that his home had been fire bombed the previous evening and, like most Japanese houses being made of wood and paper, had burnt to the ground in a few minutes, fortunately without loss of life. This was the work of trade union protesters against privatisation.

We learnt how the government had lost patience with JNR, which was undoubtedly inefficient and seemingly incapable of reforming itself. To say it was overstaffed was a major understatement. Having said all that, much of this malaise had been brought about by politicians' 'pork barrelling' and by the government using the railway as an instrument of social policy: encouraging unnecessary jobs as a means of reducing unemployment. As is almost always the case, this eventually had to come to an end.

The end was 1987 when more than 22,000 employees were put into what you might nowadays call a 'bad railway', a bit like a 'bad bank'. Basically they had nothing to do and the managers' job was to gradually find ways of dissipating them. The operational railway was split into six companies, three of which were expected to eventually be profitable, three of which were not. More than eighty branches were either shut down or, in a few cases, sold to become successful minor railways.

All this was somewhat easier than it might appear because Japan already had 180 truly private railway companies. These ranged in size from mile long freight lines to a dozen or so very substantial commuter lines which, together, carried nearly as many passengers as the whole of BR. Many of these were very impressive. Almost all electrified, they were immaculately clean (which could not be said of much of JNR) and full of interesting innovations. Many of them demonstrated the Japanese aptitude for copying other people's, often half baked, ideas and improving on them. One such was the idea that a commuter line could be made much more profitable if it had a constant supply of passengers rather than 'feast' in the rush hour and 'famine' the rest of the time. A train graph for many of these lines would be roughly the same density from, say, 05.30 until midnight. This was helped by, for example, building a department store over their city terminus, and sports and educational facilities at strategic points on the route. Of course, this idea was not new. Both the Metropolitan and Southern Railways had practised similar things in the first half of the twentieth century.

Eastern Region General Manager David Rayner, on our Japanese trip, along with one of our hosts who explained that it was the custom, even for senior managers, to wear uniform when they went in the driver's cab. Fortunately they did not have a uniform my size!

The high speed Shinkansen lines, state owned and part of JNR, were very impressive – fast, very safe and a significant engine of the Japanese economy. From them, we learned of

One of many lessons I bought back from Japan was that we needed a Convenience Store at St Pancras. Such things did not exist in the UK in 1986. I persuaded the BR property people to find some tenants who were prepared to take the risk. Here you see the very first of many Whistlestop convenience stores. I wish I had invested in it.

the measures needed to achieve consistency of performance, which is equally relevant to punctuality as it is to safety. They had not killed a single Shinkansen passenger since 1964, when the Tokyo to Osaka line had opened. Indeed, that record still stands in 2017. We produced our report which, as you will have noticed, did nothing to stem the flow of privatisation!

We returned via Hong Kong where we were entertained by both the Mass Transit Railway, which had been largely designed and managed by ex-London Transport people, and the Kowloon Canton Railway, which was similarly designed and managed by former BR people. Both had levels of performance and safety that were equal to the Japanese achievements and convinced me that we, back home, could aspire to much higher things… and should be able to achieve them. It was a very salutary lesson. This experience got me started a few years later on promoting an annual exchange programme

In those days, all the fast EMU services came right into St Pancras station.

Andy Baldwin, one of the Area Production Managers who kept everything moving.

involving, on one hand, the Central Japanese Railway Co., one of the now profitable parts of former JNR, and, on the other, the whole UK rail industry. Twenty-five years later, more than 200 UK managers have benefitted and I see the results all over the network.

One further spin-off from the visit was the fact that KCR was very interested in the DOO that we had. As a result, one of its operations managers, K.C. Ho, who became a good friend, came over for just three days to understand how it worked. He then implemented it over the next six months. They do not mess about in Hong Kong.

One afternoon in the autumn of 1987 I got an unexpected call from Brian Burdsall, who was the Director of Parcels, one of Bob Reid's five Sector Directors. He asked me to come and see him for a chat. I had not given any thought to working in the Parcels business, which struck me as rather boring, nearly as bad as freight in fact. However, Brian had other ideas and told me that John Nelson was about to replace David Rayner as GM York because David was going to join the BR Board. There was a pressing need to properly implement a new Point of Sale system, which would give Red Star a significant competitive edge and, apparently, I was the person to make this happen. I, therefore, started as National Business Manager (later changed to MD) for Red Star Parcels on Monday, 19 October 1987 at a salary of £25,830.

Another of the top performing team, PM Michael McCurdy, has just seen off a VIP, hence the garb.

On reflection, my experience of running a newly modernised passenger railway and finding out where some of the 'levers of power' were located was absolutely invaluable when, some years later, I had the opportunity to run one of the privatised Train Operating Companies. As it happens, I was wrong about Parcels being boring. I also learnt a lot about the commercial world there.

When Chris Green came to set up Network SouthEast in 1986 he initiated performance league tables. My instruction to my team was very simple. We were going to be at the top.

Driving myself home in 45.144, heading a parcels train, in my last week at St Pancras.

```
          NETWORK SOUTHEAST - PERFORMANCE MONITORING
          --------------------------------------------

                                                    4 WEEKS ENDING 12.
                                                    ------------------
PUNCTUALITY : ALL TRAINS RUN
----------------------------
                                Within 5 Mins         Right Time
                                (Target 90%)          (Target 75%
                                --------------        -----------
Midland Electrics                    97                   90
South Western Inners                 96                   88
North London Line                    96                   83
South Central Inners                 96                   82
South Eastern Inners                 96                   78
South Western Outers                 92                   78
Great Northern                       92                   73
South Central Outers                 92                   71
Watford-Euston/Liv St. DC            91                   79
Great Eastern                        91                   76
London Tilbury & Southend            91                   76
Euston Outer Suburban                91                   75
South Eastern Outers                 91                   74

TARGET-----------------------------------------------

Western                              89                   78
North East London                    89                   71
Chiltern Lines                       81                   67
                                    ------               ------
                                     93                   77
                                    ------               ------
```

Chapter Nine

Memphis Tennessee

My new office was on the second floor of Euston House and was next to Brian Burdsall's. I was asked if I would take, as my PA, Ann Smith, who had spent the last couple of weeks in a state of shock and confusion that had resulted from the fact that the Chairman had fired her boss, Harry Reed. Harry had been the ebullient and likeable MD of Freightliner, which was a Joint Venture (JV) between British Rail and the National Freight Corporation and had been created by Beeching to exploit the then new shipping container market. Harry had grown tired of the tedious restrictions placed on him which, he felt, were limiting the development of the business, and started talking to potential investors about a possible management buyout. The Chairman, as soon as he got word of this, acted swiftly and Harry was out. For the next two weeks, Ann just turned up to work but was treated like a leper as though, somehow, she was guilty by association. Later, she told me that she had absolutely no idea what Harry was up to. Brian, as Director Parcels, had the smallest of the five Business Sectors and was responsible for Red Star, the Post Office contract and the newspaper business which was actually made up of many contracts co-ordinated by the Newspaper Publishing Association (NPA). My two colleagues were Mike Tham, Post Office, and John Fitzgerald, Newspapers.

Their whole world was in the process of being turned upside down because Rupert Murdoch was fed up with the restrictive practices that were endemic in the printing industry. Before Murdoch made his changes, BR had carried the vast majority of daily and weekly newspapers throughout the country except for the immediate London area. There were even nightly trains to such close destinations as St Albans and Chesham. The scale of union restriction meant that it cost the newspaper proprietors about the same to get their product, on average, two miles from the presses in Fleet Street to the London termini as they paid BR to transport it throughout the country.

What enabled Murdoch, who trailblazed, to disrupt the status quo was the introduction of new technology that permitted journalists to input copy directly rather than go through the ancient, craft-based process whereby type was set up manually by printers. He set up a new publishing centre at Wapping for his *Times* and *Sunday Times* and dispensed with almost all his employees except for his journalists. Not surprisingly, this produced a sustained and vociferous reaction from the trade unions. Murdoch had clearly prepared very well for all this and, after many weeks of bussing employees into work amid pitched battles at his gates, he won. Almost all the other newspaper titles followed in his wake and, within a short time, were all operating in the same way.

The effect of all this was that BR very quickly lost all the substantial newspaper business, most of which emanated from London but which also had centres in Manchester and Glasgow, where the same transformation took place. Some magazines, printed in London, continued with rail for a while but this only amounted to about £6 million a year whereas the newspapers had been worth more than £40 million a year to BR.

As if this was not bad enough for BR, the change in the newspaper business very quickly plunged the Post Office business into the red. This was because the majority of the Parcels Sector's trains carried both newspapers and mails. If you took a train of, say, twelve vans and removed seven, you still had to run the remaining five vans at the same time because the Post Office network was a very complex, interlinked system with connections all over the place. Since most of the cost was with the locomotive and the traincrew, the immediate result was that a rather weak profit became a huge loss. In addition, the fact that the Post Office contract had been very badly managed by BR for years certainly did not help.

For these reasons, most of my Director's time was taken up with trying to sort out this mess and to find ways of escaping cost while negotiating a new contract with the Post Office to replace the five-year one which was about to expire. I was to get heavily involved in the Post Office contract and all the surrounding issues, in due course, but for the time being I had a major task ahead with Red Star.

Meanwhile, I had a very close shave because, on 18 November 1987, I went up the Northern Line escalator at King's Cross/St Pancras on my way home at about 19.00. This was a journey I had made many times before. Only when I got home did I discover that less than thirty minutes later the same escalator had been engulfed in flames and that thirty-one people had been killed and 100 seriously injured. For many years the Underground had been run as cheaply as possible, without proper policies for maintenance and renewal of its assets and with a marked lack of risk assessment. All this was to change significantly over the next few years.

Bob Reid's revolution was still very much work in progress in Red Star in 1987. The name and brand had been invented in 1963 as a far-sighted way of differentiating the long-established railway parcels business. From the outset in the nineteenth century, railways had sought to move goods of all sorts and, in doing so, had been a very significant enabler of the Industrial Revolution. For many years, almost every station had porters who would load parcels and packages onto passenger trains. They might include kippers from Grimsby, shoes from Leicester, hats from Luton or crabs from Cornwall. Anything that needed to be transported quickly was, for more than a century, sent by passenger train.

By 1963 the writing was on the wall for the much bigger 'sundries' business, which was mostly food and manufactured goods sent by rail in twelve-ton vans that were despatched to one of the hundreds of goods sheds sited near many stations. From here, deliveries were made to shop, factory or home by horse dray until the 1930s and then by motorised 'mechanical horses'. This business had the chair kicked from under it by the 1955 ASLEF strike, which greatly accelerated the inevitable transfer to the much more flexible and timely road delivery. Red Star was an attempt to salvage some of the higher value sundries traffic and to codify the extensive, but unmanaged, passenger train business.

I came to Euston House, which was built as the LMS HQ in 1929, to head a small team whose role was to foster the brand and to sell Red Star. Almost all the actual operation was still in the hands of the Regions, and there lay the problem. Each Region had a Regional Parcels Manager (RPM) who reported to the Regional General Manager and was supposed to ensure that Red Star operations were carried out in the best possible way. They were also supposed to ensure that the Post Office and NPA were delighted with the punctuality and efficiency of the many trains they paid for. In practice, the RPMs were disinclined to exert themselves to any extent, one being Les Binns... he of the green ink, whom we met in Newcastle. The result was that the whole operation was sloppy and inefficient. The one exception was Scotland, run by the very energetic and enthusiastic Bob Buick, who showed what could be achieved.

My first task was to implement a very significant and far-sighted project which rejoiced in the uninspiring name of 'Parcels Business Machine'. This was nothing less than a world first in that it had the potential to plan and then track the journey of every parcel from start to finish. Nowadays we expect this for the smallest package from Amazon, but in 1987 it was truly remarkable. Companies like Federal Express and Airborne in the US and TNT in the UK and Australia were working on such systems, but none were as comprehensive as the PBM. It was to have terminals in all 600 Red Star offices that would print a label for every parcel showing its entire journey, complete with any changes required. It had the capability of being updated at any point, and thus showing real-time status, and it could predict which parcels would arrive at any point and when. It also linked to the invoicing system. It was, for the time, quite brilliant and a fantastic sales tool.

Except that none of it worked!

There were terminals installed in most of the 600 offices and the mainframe (remember them?) was hooked up to them, but nothing was being used. The fact is that there was no heavyweight leadership and most of the RPMs were just too tired to get off their backsides and do anything. I spent a couple of weeks out and about and found several strong pockets of enthusiasm on the ground, coupled with huge frustration that this expensive system was just sitting there doing nothing. It also quickly became apparent that there were no standardised procedures of the type that you would expect with any such system. Different offices just did what they had always done.

Bob Buick required very little persuasion to uproot himself and his wife from Dunblane and move south to take over as my Project Champion. To rectify the procedures problem, we asked three very experienced and competent chief clerks from different offices to work together as a group and decide, for every situation, what was the best way of dealing with it. We recruited a young journalist who knew nothing about Red Star to be with them and to write up everything they decided in a simple, easily understood format. Six months later, and after a huge amount of encouragement, persuasion and cajoling, the new system was starting to work. We had the PBM terminals being used in the main stations. The new procedure manual was produced and being trained in, and the first bar-coded parcels were moving.

Meanwhile, the rest of the team comprised a marketing group led by the rather cautious Mike Bonser, a sales team headed by the larger than life Bob Constable, a south Londoner with a gravelly voice just like the comedian Arthur Smith, and a tiny operational section ably led by my former Area Parcels Manager at St Pancras, Mike Carroll.

Red Star had, under John Nelson's influence, started to project a very professional image through its above and below the line advertising, which was handled by the high-profile Saatchi and Saatchi advertising agency. Within a couple of weeks of arriving, Mike Bonser invited me to an 'advertising awayday' which turned out to be twenty-four hours in a very luxurious hotel. The Red Star advertising team of half a dozen or so young former management trainees swanned up in time for lunch on the first day, drank too much in the evening, apparently at the expense of their employer, and went home after a good lunch on the second day. They did not seem to me to be exerting themselves greatly in between. The working sessions mostly involved highly paid Saatchi people trying to invent new products which they could then charge us a lot of money to promote.

As may be apparent, I was rather less than impressed with the whole affair, especially when, in response to a question from me along the lines of 'How do you measure the value for money that you deliver for us?', the senior Saatchi guy got on his high horse and more or less told me that the agency was not used to being asked questions like that. It took the recession which came a couple of years later to put paid to that attitude which would be unthinkable these days.

After the event, I took Mike Bonser aside and said that I thought the level of expense was entirely inappropriate and represented a level of extravagance that was just not acceptable. The astonishing answer was: 'Oh, the agency pays for it!' The next one started at 09.00, had a proper agenda and despite some rather grumpy expressions was held in a Travelodge by a main road. I thought it was a great do and we did some useful business. Even Saatchi's, who had come to realise, after a couple of meetings, that I was serious about measuring their effectiveness, came up with some useful proposals. What annoyed me more than anything about this episode was that we were devising products for our customers without involving them in any way. It does not matter what industry you are in, you live or die by your customers. That is why, for the whole of the four years I was involved with Red Star, I made a point of seeing customers first hand for one or two days every week unless I was away.

In 1987/88, Red Star achieved sales of £55 million, which represented about twelve per cent of the UK domestic courier market. At that time, no one actually knew what the profit was on that turnover because of the diffuse way in which the business was operated. Various figures were confidently quoted, but none of then withstood even cursory challenge. What we did know was that our average price was about two and a half times the industry average so it was pretty obvious that if the business was to survive, it was going to have to be at the High Quality/High Price part of the market. We had the basis of succeeding with our PBM, but much more would be needed in order to improve our quality and to reduce our unit costs. The common perception had been that our handling and transport costs were low because our parcels got a free ride on passenger trains and were loaded and unloaded by porters who would be there anyway. Both these perceptions were starting to be seriously challenged because the Passenger Sectors were beginning to look very closely at every cost line and because new trains were starting to appear with no traditional brake van.

It was fairly obvious that we had better take a look into the future to try to discover what the world was going to look like then. The best way was to go and see what was happening in the US. Consequently, I agreed with my Director, Brian Burdsall, that I should go to the Air Courier Conference of America (ACCA) conference in Phoenix, Arizona, which took place in April 1988. Although I had been to the USA on holiday a few times, this was my first of many American conferences and I found it a really helpful and interesting experience. It was great to spend a few days with a bunch of relentlessly positive and constructive people who were very willing to share insights into their fast developing industry. It was almost like a re-run of the way that railways had enabled the Industrial Revolution. These guys were laying the foundations for today's e-commerce and 'just in time' regime which we take for granted now, but which was all new then. My first surprise, as I went for breakfast in the exhibition hall, was to be hailed in a loud Texan voice by a man in a Stetson: 'Hi, Adrian! How are you doing?' In my, relatively reserved, British way, my first reaction was to think to myself: 'How do you know me?' The truth, however, was that whenever you go to an American conference, your Christian name is shown in huge letters on your name badge and this allows Americans to plunge straight in and start a dialogue… which is great. After that, I used to get our people to arrange name badges similarly to help break the ice.

The conference taught me that there was no reason why we could not compete effectively if we put right all the things, described above, that were so obviously wrong and then drove the business hard. Later that summer, I got another opportunity to glimpse the future when I had a week with Federal Express at its HQ at Memphis, Tennessee. I knew a bit about FedEx because I had, for some time, been a student of the American management guru Tom Peters. Tom, who had worked for McKinsey, had observed that companies that were obsessive about customer service, provided they were well run, tended to be the most profitable. FedEx was one of his examples; Nordstrom, a high-end American department store, and Stew Leonard's, a Connecticut supermarket, were others. The common theme was that they all empowered their employees to provide quite exceptional customer service without counting the cost.

I had been a strong advocate of Peters' ideas at St Pancras and had shown my team several of his proselytising videos and then led discussions on them. The first concrete example of my team putting Peters' principles into action that I was aware of, concerned a woman who arrived two hours late at St Pancras because her train had broken down. Keith Robinson, my Passenger Manager, was out on the platform to meet the passengers and discovered that she intended to take a flight from Heathrow to Paris. (No Eurostar then!) Clearly she was going to miss her flight, so Keith just went ahead and booked her a later one at our expense. The ticket price was about three times the cost of her rail ticket and, in those days, we had no obligation to make any refund. Indeed, if Keith had not been there the response to her would just have been a shrug of the shoulders and, possibly, some commiseration. In the event, I congratulated Keith. Even better, the lady, who was amazed, wrote back about a month later to enclose a cheque for the full amount of the new airline ticket, having claimed on her insurance policy. Tom was right!

My entry into FedEx was unconventional in that, through a third party, I became aware of a very senior guy who had just retired from the company having been there from day one. By some administrative oversight, he still retained his security clearance and thus had unrestricted access to even the most sensitive areas. FedEx was founded by recently retired US Air Force pilot Fred Smith who, in a college dissertation, described a 'hub and spoke' system whereby all parts of the US were linked every night by freight aircraft which came together at one spot each night. The contents of each plane would be taken out, sorted and then reloaded for its destination. His paper was marked down as impractical, so Fred just went out and did it!

By 1988 the company had consolidated its position in the US and was able to offer a service whereby parcels picked up late afternoon could be delivered to most US addresses by 10.30 the following morning. Its main competition was Airborne Express and the much older and bigger United Parcels Service (UPS) which, at the time, was described as 'the sleeping giant'.

I was able to sit alongside a customer service agent in the FedEx call centre and listen in to her calls just as Tom Peters had. I, too, in the space of an hour or two heard several examples of outstanding service which went a long way to explaining the success of the company. I witnessed the three-hour stream of freighters, at that time mostly converted passenger aircraft, arriving at Memphis, and having their containerised contents stripped out in minutes and put onto the massive computerised sorting system. Parcels moved individually, at great speed, on a forest of conveyor belts. Bar-codes, which were then quite new, were used to automatically read the parcels destination, after which each parcel was routed to one of the containers for the correct plane. I chatted for a while to the immaculately dressed pilots in their mess room as they rested before the return flight. Most had trained in the military and had had a spell with a passenger airline before coming to FedEx, which was non-union and paid higher rates. All told me that they rated their employer very highly and FedEx was much more professional than their previous passenger companies. By 05.00 the last plane had left and the sorting conveyors were switched over to the lower rated ground parcels which were distributed by road.

I was able to talk to the FedEx development team who were devising a tracking system, similar in concept to our PBM, which they were planning to make available to customers. This was something we could do if we chose to. The lesson, for me, was that you had to have a sound basic product; excellent systems and processes; a very well trained and motivated workforce with whom you shared information and plans, and you trusted to make the right decisions; and you needed to provide outstanding customer service. If they, on occasion, made a mistake, you still encouraged them to take their own decisions and to do the right thing for their customers, but gave them some constructive guidance. This was pretty much what I had been trying to do for the past few years, but the FedEx experience reinforced my thoughts and showed me the success you could achieve if you were bold and really followed your convictions.

The other company that I learnt about in the US was United Parcels Service (UPS) which was founded in 1907 by a group of college graduates in Seattle. It had grown steadily until by 1988 it had 108,000 delivery trucks, every one washed every day, which delivered to every address in the USA. It remained 100 per cent employee-owned and had a very strong reputation for quality and reliability. It was, however, seen as very conservative and its main product was a two/three day nationwide road based delivery service.

These American experiences enabled me to formulate a plan for Red Star that I discussed with my boss, who gave the go-ahead. At its heart was the concept of creating Red Star as a free-standing entity employing its own operational people and directly managing its affairs. It seemed to me that this was a prerequisite for making the major changes that were needed. This change came about in January 1989 and now I had an operational arm, managed by Bob Buick, who had four Regional Managers and a total of forty, very carefully selected, Area Red Star Managers who were the key to local service.

Between them, they had some 2,200 staff who we inherited from the Railway Regions. So now we were able to set out our expectations and give the staff the training and encouragement to deliver the level of customer service that we needed. Of course, making this change was not without incident as I had to persuade the Regional General Managers to support the change, which meant their losing staff and some influence. In practice, however, none of them had taken much interest in Red Star and any resistance to the change was pretty half hearted. The trade unions, similarly, had not taken much interest and were reasonably helpful. This even continued to be the case when, at General Secretary Jimmy Knapp's suggestion, I addressed the entire executive committee of the RMT union. My message was simply that if Red Star was to survive in a very competitive world, it needed to lose more than 1,000 staff to get down to the figure of 1,200. In the same way as I had chosen to face the Harpenden commuters alone, I decided to go alone into the hornets' nest. In fact, after some political grandstanding, we had quite a sensible discussion in which they asked me to tell them how the competition was changing and asked me what we were doing to compete. We reached an agreement.

As part of this transformation we halved the number of parcel offices at stations to 300 and then invested in those. We had produced a Red Star design manual, similar in concept to the Network SouthEast one that Chris Green had created a couple of years previously. It defined the look and feel and the branding that would be used in parcel points, on delivery vans, on letter heading and on advertising. The idea was to create one consistent Red Star in just the same way as, for example, you would expect to see in any branch of Boots or McDonald's.

When I took over from him, one of the things John Nelson suggested that I would need to do was to decide what, if anything, Red Star was to do about international business. For very many years there had been a rather slow, but reliable, service run jointly by all the European railways. Parcels consigned to Europe would start off by assembling at Dover before crossing on one of the ferries to Calais. We did not advertise the service because the rates, which were fixed by international agreement, were very low. Nevertheless, we took a few million pounds a year. A second service had also been established whereby we arranged for outbound packages to be flown from Heathrow to Brussels, which was fast developing as a parcels hub. If you could get consignments there by about 23.00, they could be delivered in any European city by next morning. This was, in a sense, like the FedEx system except that it was wholesale, which is to say any small parcel company could use it. This worked for us reasonably well, except that the charges our agents made meant that we did not make many sales or any money out of them. We looked at alternatives and discovered that we could charter our own aircraft to Brussels and back for a much lower cost. Then the BR Solicitor, Simon Osborne, got to hear of it and pronounced it *'ultra vires'*, which is to say illegal because BR did not have powers to do such things.

I liked the fairly small BR Solicitors' department because they were very pragmatic and constructive, often telling you how you could, legally, get around such obstacles. In fact, Simon, before he had become the top dog, had helped me through the legal minefield that existed when wheel clamping of cars was first introduced. At places like St Albans, customers used to get very cross when others took 'their' parking space and did not even pay. We introduced, with Simon's help, a simple deterrent arrangement, a first for BR car parks. This time he told me, airily: 'You need to get the Secretary of State's permission to use the 1929 Railway Air Acts.' He then explained that in 1929 the four main line companies had jointly promoted four identical Bills which allowed them to co-operate in promoting air services that would supplement their rail services, which were beginning to face competition from airlines. In brief, they were given powers to operate passenger and freight services to and from anywhere in Great Britain and Europe provided they stayed west of Vienna. They were allowed to own and operate aircraft or to charter them. As a result of lobbying, they were not permitted to own 'aerodromes' or to make aircraft. They did, actually, set up a number of services, mostly operated by twin-engined de Havilland Rapides, at least one of which is still flying. When the railways were nationalised, the Railway Air Service became British European Airways (BEA) which, later, was combined with BOAC to become British Airways. One would have thought that the 1929 powers would have been extinguished in 1947, but Simon explained that the legal work had all been done in a rush and his predecessors were worried about removing something vital if they simply proposed extinguishing the rights. Therefore, they were retained and inherited by BR but with a codicil which specified that BR could not take advantage without the express permission of the Secretary of State for Transport.

Thus it was that I found myself, one day in November 1988, making a presentation to the new Railways Minister (the SoS having delegated it), Michael Portillo, who had taken over from an old boy called

David Mitchell who had held the post for six years. He was the father of Andrew Mitchell MP, who got into trouble for allegedly swearing at the Downing Street policemen many years later.

I was standing at the end of the table in the BR boardroom on the sixth floor in Euston House explaining what I wanted to do and giving assurances that I did not want to build aeroplanes or own aerodromes. Portillo was nearest me and his two civil servants (ministers are never allowed out on their own) were behind him. I was the only person who could see all their faces. Having been used to David Mitchell, who was not the sharpest knife in the drawer, they expected to respond to me on behalf of their minister, as they had been used to. Imagine their alarm and disbelief when the new minister, on his very first outing, replied immediately that he could see no reason why I should not get what I wanted and he would instruct his officials to arrange the necessary authority. I can still see their shocked expressions, not being used to a minister who could make his own decisions! Subsequently we chartered a plane to fly nightly from Birmingham to Brussels and back. This allowed us to give much faster service because of the excellent rail connectivity at Birmingham New Street, especially with all the overnight Post Office trains that we could use in those days.

I flew on one of the early flights from Brussels airport in our chartered Convair, which was a beaten-up turbo prop converted passenger plane dating from the late 1940s. It was sub-chartered from a Californian company and crewed by two cheerful young Americans. The plane was completely gutted, which made it very noisy, and was not pressurised. The cockpit was totally open to the rest of the fuselage except for a big net intended to stop the crew from being buried in parcels in the event of a rapid stop. I sat in a very basic 'jump seat' just in front of the net. The funniest thing about the whole hilarious exercise was when the co-pilot, who I had been laughing and joking with, stood up and addressed me very formally and notified me that we were flying under Federal Aviation Authority – i.e., American – regulations and that I must comply with them.

When I joined Red Star, all the deliveries to customers, which comprised a substantial and fast increasing percentage of all consignments, were made on our behalf by a company called City Link. It had been set up by Bob Thomas, an entrepreneur who had created a fairly sizeable franchise operation that covered the UK. Its quality of service was quite good but it was expensive and resistant to being measured in the way that we needed to assure the necessary cost-effectiveness and level of service. Also, our parcels were being delivered in a vehicle carrying the branding of a competitor. Worse, our sales team had countless tales of City Link salesmen stealing our customers. In addition, the salesmen had, over time, recruited more than 300 local firms, mostly taxi owners, to collect parcels from customers. None of their vehicles had proper Red Star branding, although a few did have amateur attempts which did nothing for our brand image. We, therefore, starting looking at alternatives, and Mike Carroll took on the project which was very successful. Over a period of about six months we moved to a situation where we had ninety local agents, essentially franchisees, all managed by the local Area Red Star Managers and all collecting and delivering with Red Star branded vans. Many of the agents were still local taxi companies which the managers, with some assistance, had selected. They had to work to standards set out clearly in their contract. This included having vans in a closely defined Red Star livery which we had applied to ensure consistency. As with UPS, the vans had to be washed every day.

The sales team, led by Bob Constable, was very professional and covered the whole of England, Wales and Scotland. It had been wrested from the Railway Regions some years before and was totally focussed on Red Star. There were sales targets by area and by product which formed the basis of the sales budget. Bob had arranged a whole programme of training courses and sales conferences which were intended to motivate the team and provide them with the skills they needed. I frequently went out on the road with salesmen because I wanted to understand, first hand, what customers were looking for. Depending on the circumstances, I sometimes went with the salesman as a 'trainee', sometimes as his manager and sometimes even as myself

Bob Buick ensured that the new Red Star livery was applied very quickly and consistently to all aspects of the business.

Red Star office at Kings Cross.

if the salesman felt it would be useful in clinching a deal. What was very interesting was that decision makers could range from secretaries to mailroom supervisors to warehouse managers to service managers to managing directors. There really did not seem to be any sort of pattern. Sometimes the decision maker was the recipient rather than the consignor (or shipper).

Marks and Spencer's was a case in point in that it required all its hundreds of suppliers to send samples to its HQ in Baker Street, London, every week. Hence, we would deliver up to 600 or so packages from Euston Red Star office every day. It was most interesting to meet many of these suppliers who, usually, were dependent on Marks for around eighty per cent of their business. It was a very dangerous position for them, as many told me. Another big customer was Gerald Ratner, the low cost jeweller, whose warehouse was in Birmingham. Every day his 400-odd stores would ring their order in (remember, no email yet) by 16.30 and our agent would pick up 400-plus boxes during the evening and take them to New Street for onward distribution overnight. Next morning, his managers would drive via their nearest Red Star Parcel Point to pick up their box in time for the shop opening at 09.00. We had many customers like this, but Gerald was the only one who lost

Some of our offices were in fine old buildings like this one at Newcastle on Tyne. Because they realised just how competitive the parcels business was, our staff here carried on working just yards from an RMT picket line during a strike in 1989. This attitude was typical and Red Star certainly did not disappear because of any lack of enthusiasm from its employees.

his business by telling the world in a very well reported speech that he purveyed 'total crap'!

Bob managed and motivated his team brilliantly but survived on insecurity, which sometimes took the form of trying to guess what my wishes were in a particular matter. After a while, I became aware of this and found it a little irritating that he wasted so much time asking all sorts of people what I thought about this or that. It would have been much quicker just to have asked me!

Perhaps encouraged by my enthusiasm for Tom Peters and his Outstanding Customer Service mantra, I had been watching closely what British Airways had been doing. Recently privatised, it had a reputation for being safe, solid but not especially customer focussed. A bit like BR, really. Colin Marshall, then Chief Executive of the airline, was determined to transform the way that the entire company thought about and treated customers and, therefore, embarked upon a massive training programme that involved every single employee no matter how deeply they were buried in the 'back room'. This was widely reported, and what made the headlines was that Colin attended almost every training session himself, albeit briefly. The effect of this was very noticeable. Many commentators reported on much more positive experiences with BA and I, too, noticed significant changes when I flew with them.

Why could not BR do something similar? The Sector Management set up by Bob Reid had paved the way for senior managers to concentrate on their business. Should not the next stage be to enlist the help of all employees? A small group of us thought so and took some advice from the training company that had worked with BA. As a result, we formulated a plan which we took to John Welsby, by then Chief Executive of BR. His reaction was fairly typical of the man, if a bit shocking at the time: 'Well, I suppose you can do it so long as you don't expect me to be involved.' Not quite the ringing endorsement we had hoped for, but he did say we could make a presentation to the full BR Board which we did soon afterwards. They seized the idea with enthusiasm and, in due course, the Leadership 500 and Leadership 5000 courses, modelled on BA's experience, were developed. Eventually these useful customer focussed courses were cascaded right down the organisation so that by the time privatisation came, pretty well everyone had been on them. One very important principle was that managers and, then, supervisors, had to go on the course before their employees, thus trying to eliminate the 'Oh, you can forget all that nonsense and get on with your job' syndrome that sometimes happens. Needless to say, Welsby did not follow Colin Marshall's example of speaking to every course, but senior managers did. This initiative had one unintended consequence in that my boss, Brian Burdsall, was appointed, in November 1988, to the new post of Director, Quality, to run the whole programme.

By mid 1989 Red Star was coming together very well as a coherent and high performing company. Bob Buick and his team now had measures for all aspects of performance and we knew that our on-time delivery, the most important measure, was in the region of ninety-nine per cent, which was higher than anything achieved by our competitors. The sales force, very competently managed by Bob Constable, revelled in being able to assure customers that they really could trust us to deliver. Furthermore, with the new agents who, like the rest of the team were very motivated, they had the ability to tailor collection and delivery arrangements to suit the customer. We were also, for many customers, able to offer very late pick-ups and still deliver by 09.00 the following morning by using the overnight trains still being run for the Post Office. We had a mission statement which, I really believe, was being used by many of our people. I, certainly, was aware of countless examples of our people going the extra mile to delight customers:

> 'Helping our customers to save time and make more money by tailoring fast, precise and consistent delivery of packages to/from and within the UK.'

With an excellent series of products, consistently delivered by a motivated team and, with a professional sales force very actively seeking out new opportunities, sales motored ahead to £150 million by 1989/90, double what they had been only two years earlier. Yet, when Charles Brown from the BR Policy Unit came to see me in 1991, I stunned him by saying that, in my opinion, the long-term profitable size of Red Star was only about £6 million a year. At work, Charles, who had a posh Edinburgh accent, always wore immaculately tailored grey suits and was very measured. Possibly outside work he dressed a little differently since he was part owner of a large transvestite shop right next door to his employer's HQ!

The reason for my prediction was that, although we had made our system work as effectively as possible, intrinsically our kind of network system, using the rail network as the long-haul carrier, was inefficient. My visit to Federal Express, and subsequent visits to UK road based copycats, showed clearly that to keep unit costs down you had to concentrate volumes and invest heavily in automation. Our network had relatively small volumes at any one place, except perhaps at Euston and Birmingham New Street, and relied on expensive manual handling on, off and between trains. It did not matter that the rail haul was free to us; the low productivity of manual handling incurred costs which, I could see, were going to swamp the business. In addition to the 1,200 people mentioned earlier, we relied on a great many platform staff on smaller stations to handle our parcels. As the 1980s proceeded, the passenger sectors, all heavily incentivised to cut costs, either did away with these posts or invited us to pay for them. This was just about manageable while we could charge customers two and a half times as much as our key competitor, TNT, but towards the end of the decade, the UK started to slip into a recession which made customers much more price-sensitive and willing to look at our competitors, several of whom had made considerable strides towards the level of quality that we had achieved. To make things more difficult, new trains that were starting to come in large numbers had no traditional guard's van and, hence, nowhere to put parcels. Finally, although hardly anyone had heard of email then, I had seen an early faltering example on the Universities Academic Network in 1979 and

Despite the free ride that we had on the trains, our handling costs eventually overwhelmed the business.

ten years later I had seen several multi-site companies using it within the company by leasing lines between sites. You could see that it was coming and that Red Star would lose all its considerable document business.

The consequence of all this was that we decided to adopt a strategy of 'enjoying it while we could', at the same time noting that the business would, in due course, need to enter a managed decline phase. In the event, after I moved on, privatisation intervened and there was a management buyout which was not well conceived and did not succeed. The National Freight Corporation then took over and, completely failing to understand the business, caused it to collapse very quickly.

When, in November 1988, Brian Burdsall left to become Director of Quality, Mike Tham, John Fitzgerald and I just carried on with our business, although after a few weeks we did wonder whether there were plans to replace him but did not hear anything from anyone. Then, about two months later in January 1989, I was told one day that I was required to go immediately to see David Kirby, who was then Vice Chairman of the British Rail Board, at his office on the sixth floor of Euston House. After knocking, I was told to come in and found David standing just inside the door. His first words were: 'Congratulations, you have got the job.' I stood for what seemed like ages, but was probably a couple of seconds thinking: 'What is he talking about? What job?' I had not had an interview and no one had spoken to me about it at all. As I composed myself, he continued: 'And the first thing you have got to do is get rid of that bloody silly Post Office contract.' That was it. End of audience and I had not even sat down.

As I went back to my office, the realisation dawned that I was now one of Bob Reid's five Sector Directors and that the Parcels Sector was now mine to manage. Between the five of us, we had the total income and expenditure for BR although my sector was, by far, the smallest. I now had substantial financial authority in the new role and could, for example, authorise up to £4 million of capital expenditure without referring it to anyone. I was delighted that Chris Green was the first to congratulate me and, as usual, was very encouraging and said that with such a small business, compared with the others, I would be able to be much closer to the customers and the staff.

My team: Bob Buick, Marketing Director Trevor Halvorsen, me and Bob Constable.

Getting rid of BR's oldest and biggest customer, who paid us £54 million a year, did not seem right. We had served the Post Office since 1838 and now ran an operation that was manifestly inefficient and simply must be capable of improvement. John Fitzgerald was demob happy and about to take early retirement so was not really bothered about my appointment. Mike Tham, on the other hand, was very disappointed, not because he had not got it, but because I had. Mike and I had known each other for about three years since he had taken over from Peter Rayner and had not got on particularly well. Nevertheless we had to work together and I started by telling him what Kirby had said about getting rid of the Post Office contract and how I had no intention of doing any such thing. At that time, we were just over a year into what both parties intended would be the last ever contract between the Railways and the Post Office. We were being paid £54 million a year but, for reasons explained at the beginning of this chapter, were losing money on that, to the tune of about £5 million a year.

The Travelling Post Offices which had existed since 1838 were rapidly becoming redundant.

Within a few days, Mike invited me to a periodic two-day meeting with his PO contacts which was held at a very expensive hotel at Bray, on the Thames near Reading. From BR there was me plus Mike and his deputy Charles Belcher. There were three from the PO also. To an extent this was a re-run of my first Red Star marketing meeting with Saatchi's, in that, again, I thought it quite inappropriate for managers, even senior ones, from a nationalised industry to be meeting in such expensive surroundings at taxpayers' expense. Additionally, I felt the meeting went very badly. Much of it comprised the PO guys complaining about poor punctuality of our trains leading to them failing their quality targets. We did not seem to have any convincing plans, or even any plans at all, to do anything about these problems. Worse, the PO guys then said that they wanted to introduce a load of further complications comprising additional swapping of rail vans from one train to another in the middle of the night at places like Crewe and Reading. Despite the fact that these could not fail to make punctuality even worse, Mike acquiesced.

At least Peter Rayner's informal method of taking the ground staff to the pub and encouraging them might have produced some temporary and local improvement. Now, it seemed we had not got a clue. This was the point at which I determined that we definitely were going to secure a new Post Office contract, that it would be fundamentally different from the existing one, that I was going to take the lead on strategy and that it was going to be delivered by Charles Belcher rather than Mike Tham. That latter took a little while to organise but it was achieved and Mike went off to assist Ivor Warburton who, by then, was Director of Operations at the Board.

I got Charles to brief me on what was really going on. It seemed that Bill Cockburn, who was the MD of Royal Mail Letters, was in the habit of visiting his local postmasters, of whom he had about eighty nationally, and then having dinner with a group of them each week. At those dinners he grew tired of his guys telling him that if only we ran our trains on time, they would meet all their delivery targets. Charles's view was that while there was quite a lot in what they were saying, it was certainly not the whole truth and the postmasters were not blameless. It seemed to me that I should go to see Bill Cockburn to introduce myself, pledge that we would improve our performance and seek his permission (which had been denied) to talk to his chaps about what a 'clean sheet' approach could look like. The appointed day, in April 1989, arrived and I went to see Bill in his office near Mount Pleasant. It was another of these very short meetings. Again, I did not get to sit down, although I did tell him that I was determined that we would improve our punctuality, and then I asked him if we could talk to his people about how we could do it for them a whole lot better.

'No,' was the uncompromising reply. 'You have shot your bolt.' I returned to Euston to report this to Charles and to tell him that I was not accepting Bill's 'No' and that we were going to find a way of changing it to a 'Yes'. The contract specified that ninety per cent of our trains, more than 200 of them every twenty-four hours, had to arrive within ten minutes of their planned time. In the first year, we had achieved just under eighty per cent. I made it clear that we would have to work out how we were going to achieve the ninety per cent within a year. I remember Charles looking a bit shocked at this, but he said he would see what could be done. Over the next few months he swung into action in a most impressive way, appointing, with my approval, a team of professionals including Paul Cloke from Crewe who headed the train planning and operations delivery activity. He was supported by thirteen locally based managers whose job, just like the Area Red Star Managers', was to ensure that everything went to plan on the ground.

A typical example of the problems they sorted out was Crewe station which, like Reading, York and Derby, was a hive of Post Office train activity every night. The plan, devised to give the customer what he wanted, required that numerous shunts took place so that a very large number of places had direct rail van services. This meant that every train that arrived at Crewe would have one or more vans removed and attached to another train while yet more vans would be put in their place. A meticulous analysis of these arrangements showed that six shunting locomotives, each with a driver and shunter, were required to do all this on time. What had been happening was that the local Area Manager, who reported to the LM General Manager, had noticed that a couple of the locos only had about an hour's work. He, therefore, decided that four would be fine. This, of course, immediately meant that it was absolutely impossible to deliver the timetable. The Regional

Parcels Managers should have been on top of this, but they were just as ineffective here as they had been for Red Star. A year's worth of hard work and attention to detail by Charles's team caused the punctuality to rise ten points to just over the contractual ninety per cent.

Exactly a year, to the day, after my first meeting with Bill Cockburn, I saw him again. This meeting was equally brief but much more satisfactory in that he said to me: 'You really want our business, don't you?' 'Yes,' I said. 'It shows,' he replied. With that, he gave me permission to get my guys talking to his about what they would really like in a new contract. In brief, the Post Office, which itself was subject to much criticism for erratic deliveries, wanted to totally reconstruct its network to achieve a guaranteed First Class delivery almost everywhere by 09.00. For distances up to about 200 miles it could do this by running a network of trucks directly between its local offices, while for more than 800 miles, air was the only option. The PO's problem was this 200 to 800 mile band, for example Exeter to Newcastle or Tonbridge to Carlisle. It had hired Peter Rickard, who had conceived the TNT parcel logistical model, which copied what FedEx had done with planes in the US. By having an automated sorting hub at Atherstone, more or less in the middle of the country, it enabled a 10.30 delivery universally using trucks for the trunk haul. We soon realised why the PO was lobbying for First Class mail to be delivered by 10.30 rather than by 09.00 in that it, too, could have done it all by road. Naturally we lobbied for the retention of a 09.00 delivery for First Class! Later on, when the PO had to admit defeat on the timing question, it terminated Peter's contract quite abruptly one Friday lunchtime. At 09.00 the following Monday he was in my office wondering what I wanted him to do. 'Exactly the same as last week, Peter. We need to know what we have to beat.'

Charles and I had many conversations and, eventually, a plan emerged. We were simply going to recreate Memphis, Tennessee, and substitute trains for air freighters. That bit was easy. More tricky was working out how on earth you could do it. Because of the way the railway network in this country developed, with all the main – i.e., fastest – lines radiating from London, it was pretty obvious that 'Memphis' had to be there. All we needed to find was a place that had good, fast connections to main lines in all directions. After lots of poring over maps, it quickly became obvious that somewhere in the Willesden area was the answer. One of the by-products of focussing activity away from London termini would be that, we calculated, the PO could do without about 900 staff whose only job was to move mail in vans across London. Rod Gray was Charles's development guy and I took him to America to show him the sort of place I had in mind. This time it was UPS's air hub at Louisville, Kentucky, a somewhat smaller version of Memphis. Rod got the concept straightaway and put in a huge amount of detailed work to create an offer which excited the Post Office. This led, in 1993 after I had moved elsewhere, to the signing of a massive new, very profitable contract which came fully into effect in 1996 and was worth more than £600 million to BR and its successor EWS. Meanwhile, Charles worked assiduously to create what was, in effect, the first Train Operating Company with its own locos, rolling stock and staff, mostly drivers. All this, together with a strong corporate image, helped to focus everyone's mind on delighting the customer. He had his own Locomotive Engineer, David Barney, then Kevin Loney, who concentrated the loco fleet on Crewe Diesel Depot, site of many of my early adventures twenty-odd years earlier. The fleet was standardised on Class '47/7s' which had long-range fuel tanks, and control was centralised at Rail House, Crewe. Drivers were transferred over by 1994.

Part of the plan was to use dual-voltage EMUs which would be able to get from Willesden to anywhere on the Southern, via the North London Line, direct onto the West Coast Main Line and, also, onto the ECML and Anglia routes. Our plan, which we got approved by the BR Investment Committee, was to rebuild Class '307' 25Kv EMUs which were, then, being replaced on the Liverpool Street lines. They were basically BR Mk 1 cars and hence very easy to convert. The Post Office, however, once it bought into the whole concept, decided that only

Another casualty of the changing world was the Post Office Underground Railway, which had opened in 1927.

This simple trolley, based on one used by the Dutch Post Office, was the key to loading and unloading letters efficiently.

brand new trains would be good enough for its operations. The Class '325' dual-voltage 100mph units were the result although, just to hedge its bets, the PO had them specified such that they could be converted to Class '319' passenger EMUs if needs must. As a postscript to this, in 2006 after the end of the PO contract, when most of the '325s' were in store, I approached the PO to see if I could acquire them for a franchise bid we were doing. Unfortunately, no deal!

Although we settled for retaining the fleet of Class '47/7s', we had tried to make the case for new General Motors diesel locos. As a part of this process, I visited the GM factories in La Grange, Illinois, and London, Ontario, and was very impressed by the level of standardisation which, of course, means costs can be much lower. I was particularly struck by the fact that a new loco just completed, and ready for a customer many thousands of miles away, would simply be taken to an adjoining freight yard and would be worked, in service, by several crews belonging to other railways before eventually arriving at its new home. You could not do that if it was not very standard.

As part of this trip, I rode in a new GM loco at the head of an Amtrak train from Buffalo, NY to Albany NY, where the engine was replaced by an electro-diesel in order to work through to Grand Central. At Albany, I asked the Road Foreman of Locomotives – read Traction Inspector – if I could continue in the cab of the elderly 'FL 9' electro-diesel GM loco. He replied that he could not accompany me, but he would ask the engineer. So we went into the crew locker room at Albany and met Ronald L. Berben, Chairman of the local branch of the Brotherhood of Locomotive Engineers. Ron was very happy to take me in the cab of his 1,750hp loco which, he explained, should have been in multiple with another the same. 'Shortage of power,' he said.

Our acceleration was sedate, on account of the load of twelve old-fashioned heavyweight coaches, as we headed towards New York alongside the beautiful Hudson River. Ron and I were exchanging experiences when he suddenly stood up and said: 'Get in there.' Pausing for a moment, I soon realised that he was inviting me to drive his locomotive. The first few miles were pretty straightforward, although there were a great many unsignalled grade crossings and, it being a Saturday morning, a lot of fishermen using them. I got plenty of practice on the horn, soon to be followed by having to stop at three stations. This was a little challenging as our pre-war cars had triple valves, rather than distributors, which meant that if you tried to lap the brake 'off', perhaps because you thought you were going to stop too soon, you lost the lot – i.e., had no brakes at all until you recreated full brake pressure. You could easily run into something in the time it took to do this. UIC air brakes, as used at home, can be graduated on and off without this risk. Fortunately I knew all this from SUBs, which also had triple valves, on the Southern. When we got to Croton Harmon, about thirty miles from Grand Central, the conductor rail for the Metro North EMUs started and I expected Ron to switch over to third rail. When, after a few minutes, he had not, I asked about it since I knew that the only reason the 'FL 9s' had been specified as electro-diesels was that there was a New York City ordinance that banned steam and diesel locos from using Grand Central and its approaches that are all underground. It became obvious that diesel operation was the norm at that time.

Our plan to acquire new GM diesels, which was only anticipating what Ed Burkhardt did a few years later, was not accepted by the BR Board, almost certainly because it knew that the Treasury would veto it despite having a very sound business case which postulated, just as Ed did, that we could operate with a lot fewer locos which, in turn, would be very much cheaper than '47s' to maintain. Therefore we developed a Plan B which involved a programme of improvements to our fifty locos and, also, fitting them with some quite groundbreaking technology which was being developed by BR Research. A very bright guy called Kevin Preston, who made a business of it after privatisation, had devised a series of measuring and predictive techniques which could be used to anticipate equipment failures. We identified six which were crucial to greater reliability, including coolant level, brake block wear and battery condition. The system was set up so that if any loco exceeded a pre-set threshold, a message would be sent to Crewe Control, hopefully in time to prevent a failure rather than after it! This sort of thing is commonplace now, but in 1991 with analogue phones it was absolutely cutting edge.

One venture which was not a success – in fact, you could say it was a resounding failure – was Track 29. The idea, which was to use spare space on PO trains to carry pallet loads, was sound in principle. The trains certainly served useful, potentially high volume, routes but we never managed to bring in enough business to cover its overheads, despite the product working well and being competitively priced. It was closed down after less than two years but continued to haunt me for many years since I often had cause to drive past a Track 29 liveried truck parked in Aylesbury.

As one of the Sector Directors, various opportunities came my way, some more pleasurable than others. The then Labour Shadow Transport Minister, John Prescott, made a habit of visiting each of us occasionally and I had the pleasure of 'Two Jags', as the press called him, for a couple of hours one afternoon. When he arrived, he had the rather surly, dismissive attitude of an old-fashioned trade union boss. However, he soon warmed up and we had a very lively discussion across the table in my office. It was unusual in that I was able to study, at close quarters, his well-known habit of mangling the English language. While discussing the business, and many other things, I was able to study him. It was plainly obvious that he was very bright, with a quick brain, and that he wanted to fire out comments like a machine gun. That was fine, except that his speech delivery apparatus was quite unable to keep up. His impatience would not allow him to slow down, so his voice box simply discarded chunks of sentences leaving the listener to work out what was missing. Great fun!

I was delighted to be invited, along with thirty or forty others, to an event that was at once pleasurable but also very sad. It was the retirement dinner on Thursday 29 March 1990 of the best Chairman BR ever had. He had been passed over and had to endure the indignity of seeing the government implore Peter Parker to stay on for two years because it could not find a replacement. He had been told, in no uncertain terms, so he told me, that if he did not perform he would be fired. Yet Bob Reid was quite outstanding. He had worked his way up since 1946, he had been there and done it, yet he had a vision and a ruthlessness which enabled him to deliver, as several senior people he fired may have attested. On the other hand, he could be very kind and considerate. A man of few words, but the very best.

In 1988 I was invited to join BR's 'Research and Technical Committee', which was a sub-committee of the BR Board. It was chaired at that time by David Rayner, the guy who had appointed me at St Pancras four years earlier, and who was now a board member. There were several eminent external men on the committee from whom I learnt a lot. There was Prof Sir David Davies, Vice-Chancellor of Loughborough University, who then became Chief Scientist at the MoD. He had been one of the 'bright young men' brought into BR Research in the 1960s. I particularly got on very well, for the entire eight years that I was a member, with Prof Sir Hugh Ford, who I first came across as President of the IMechE in the 1970s. Hugh had started on the Great Western Railway as an apprentice in 1929 and had so excelled academically that he was granted leave of absence to attend the City and Guilds College, now Imperial College, in London. He never returned to the GWR and, instead, worked for Brunner Mond, which became ICI, where he was one of the team who, during the war, invented polythene which was a vital insulating component of radar, then being developed. Afterwards, he combined an academic career with consultancy in the steel industry where he was internationally recognised and was still advising Tata Steel when he was ninety-five. I asked him, in 1995, to help me find a chairman for my Management Buyout Company. He did this very successfully. Listening to the way these guys, and others, questioned those who were seeking our approval for new engineering projects and suggested new lines of enquiry was a real education for me.

One project that we championed was 'Control Centre of the Future' which, if Railtrack had not immediately rubbished it in 1994, would have greatly improved operational planning and control more than twenty years before it actually happened. Another project we championed had a much happier outcome. At the time, it was called the B2000 bogie and was a very clever piece of work which, having an aluminium frame and inboard bearings, lopped several tons off the weight of bogies for fast trains. We put money into its development and it is now used extensively by Bombardier under EMUs and DMUs.

One of the 'pleasures' of being a Sector Director was the monthly budget review run by our boss, Chief Executive John Welsby. I thought it was unfair because, while we were not allowed to bring our Finance Directors with us, he always had his, a very nice chap from Derby, David Allan. One always had the impression that John was out to catch you out. I do not regard this as a constructive way to run a company and have never inflicted this particular form of torture on my own direct reports, or indeed suffered it from anyone else myself. Chris Green (Network SouthEast) and I were usually fine in that we knew our businesses and understood what the numbers were telling us. John Prideaux (InterCity) and Colin Driver (Freight) were always complete masters of their briefs, which left poor old Sydney Newey (Provincial), who must have wished, every time, that the floor would open and swallow him. It was 'lambs to the slaughter' and not fun to watch.

After I left the Parcels Sector in early 1992 to help start the early preparations for privatisation, I was able to reflect that we had come a very long way in four years. Red Star was totally transformed, although for reasons set out earlier, it did not survive. It did, however, prepare me and many others for the competitive world that was just around the corner.

Eventually, I managed to start a conversation with Bill Cockburn, MD of Royal Mail. We then got on very well and continued that relationship when, later, he was running WH Smith and I was at Chiltern.

On the other hand, that 'bloody silly Post Office contract' had not been got rid of. It was well on the way to becoming a long running highly profitable contract, parts of which exist to this day. Additionally, major passenger stations were no longer places where passengers had to run the gauntlet between rafts of PO trucks being hauled by electric tractors, with little regard for passenger convenience.

My first twenty-one years in 'The Railway' had been hugely enjoyable and, as it turned out, the next period was to be even better!

Charles Belcher, who I appointed to secure and then deliver the Post Office Contract. Without Charles, mail by rail would now be but a distant memory.

Index

Advanced Passenger Train. 55, 157, 158, 172

Belcher, Charles. 230-233, 239
Beeching, Richard Dr. 22
Blaikie, Adam. 101, 107, 123
Blake, David. 159, 178
Bletchley TMD. 100, 120, 150, 162
Bryant, Alfie. 115, 116
Buick, Bob. 216, 223, 229

Carroll, Mike. 185, 216, 223
Class 40. 74, 77, 83, 93
Class 45. 30, 31, 67, 212
Class 47. 31, 34, 35, 45, 52, 94, 97, 146, 235
Class 50. 67, 77, 84-86, 89, 90, 92, 93
Class 52. 65, 117
Class 55. 129, 133, 141, 146
Class 67. 67
Class 85. 103
Class 86. 47, 65, 97, 99
Class 165. 67, 72, 167, 168
Class 168. 67, 168
Class 310. 100, 101, 108, 112
Class 455. 168-171
Class 508. 159, 162, 165, 168-170
Clements Freddie. 87, 88, 95, 114, 141, 142, 144, 155
Clothier, Alan. 127, 128, 140
Cockburn, Bill. 231, 232, 238
Constable, Bob. 216, 223, 226, 229
Crewe Works. 30, 32, 64

Derby Loco Works. 32, 43, 62, 63, 73, 76
DP2. 77
Drury, Julian. 189

Edgington, Owen. 173, 183
Ellison, Bob. 126, 127, 132
Fell, Col 75, 76
Flynn, Mick. 185, 186, 198
Ford, Roger. 122, 198, 200, 201

Gilpin, Bill. 125, 142
Green, Chris. 205, 206, 212, 220, 237

Hammerton, Richard. 203
Hardy, Dick. 87, 88, 114, 156, 176
High Speed Train. 48, 55, 93, 125, 134, 138, 140, 172
Hodgson, Bill. 144, 150, 154
Hughes, Cec. 76
Huskisson, Geoffrey 99, 115-117, 119, 141

Jarvis, Ron. 81

Kirby, David. 205, 228

Lowe, Jack. 88, 91

Maguire, Maurice. 141, 156, 159
Maidment, David. 179, 202
Marson, John. 96, 101, 120
Marylebone. 99, 100, 112, 113, 150
McDowell, Les. 182, 183

Meredith, Peter. 73, 74
Miller, TCB. 47, 140

Newman, Alan. 184, 185
Pardoe, Frank. 97, 101, 142
Parker, Peter. 20, 121, 137, 138, 176, 177, 236
Playford, Rev HB. 15
Powell, Ken. 173, 174

Red Star Parcels. 56, 177, 185, 211-217, 222-228, 232, 238
Reed, Harry. 213
Rayner, David. 179, 186, 187, 206-208, 211, 237
Reid, Bob. 100, 177, 178, 199, 201, 205, 211, 214, 226, 228, 236
Ribbons, Dick. 78, 91, 92, 95, 96
Rollin, David. 83
Rose, Cedric. 60, 88, 176
Rushton, Gordon. 59

Shooter, Jean. 7-9, 11-14
Shooter, Prof R. 8, 11-14, 17
Shooter, Rev A E. 7, 9

Thompson, John. 141
Turk, Andrew. 20, 26, 27

Vine, Jim. 159

Walker, Denis. 181, 188
Wallace, Prof Tom. 9, 10
Wallis, Barnes. 28
Warburton, Ivor. 201, 230